What People Are Saying About ChristWire

"Since 2008, ChristWire.org has emerged as the leading Internet site for ultraconservative Christian news, commentary, and weather reportage." —*The New York Times*

"We're not sure if this is a satire or not, but from the looks of things, no one really knows." —The Huffington Post

"In the world of ChristWire, the Glenn Beck rally made Martin Luther King Jr. proud, Hurricane Earl is headed toward the Gay East Coast to reap God's vengeance, and the recent increase in pet-on-pet rape is a pernicious consequence of same-sex marriage."
—*New York Magazine*

"One of the Internet's best kept secrets . . . Hats off to ChristWire." —*The Atlantic*

"I am the anti-ChristWire." —Howard Stern

"Your satire has to be pretty spot-on if even the King of All Media, Howard Stern, gets taken in." —*Business Insider*

"The Net's fattest troll [winner of Best Comedy Blog in Best of the Web 2011]." —*LA Weekly*

"ChristWire's genius (or evil) lies in its hyperbolic, worst-case-scenario, Christian coverage of everything from wife-beating to ferreting out whether or not your husband is gay." —Jezebel.com

"The site's greatest strength and biggest curse? It's so good—and people on the Internet today are so insane—that no one gets it."
—*The Village Voice*

"What happens when you take reasoning out of the religious? Christ-Wire, our biggest rival for making you laugh and shit your pants in fear at the same time."
—Cracked.com

"Terrifying evidence of how nuts right-wing America is."
—*In These Times*

"The bad news about a free and open Internet? Sometimes you get had by brilliant satirists."
—Rachel Maddow

"According to ChristWire, there are over 2 million couples in America who are secretly struggling with homosexuality in their marrages, and they're offering a means of possibly detecting this issue in one's husband."
—Ryan Seacrest

"PRICELESS! Okay, it's satire *but* . . . the sad part is that *many* will take it as gospel. As Jesus would say, I love this guy!"
—Billy Burke (from *Twilight*)

"CHRIST ON A WIRE."
—John Hodgman

"You know you're living in screwy times when you're not sure if even the most bats**t insane rantings are real or satire—which is, of course, exactly the point of ChristWire, some of the most insightful parody of anti-gay attitudes that we've seen in ages."
—JoemyGod

The Christwire Handbook

STAYING SAVED IN A WICKED WORLD

JACK GOULD, TYSON BOWERS III,

AND THE CHRISTWIRE FLOCK

ILLUSTRATIONS BY T.M. MALONE

CITADEL PRESS
KENSINGTON PUBLISHING CORP.
WWW.KENSINGTONBOOKS.COM

CITADEL PRESS BOOKS are published by

Kensington Publishing Corp.
119 West 40th Street
New York, NY 10018

All Kensington titles, imprints, and distributed lines are available at special quantity discounts for bulk purchases for sales promotions, premiums, fund-raising, educational, or institutional use. Special book excerpts or customized printings can also be created to fit specific needs. For details, write or phone the office of the Kensington special sales manager: Kensington Publishing Corp., 119 West 40th Street, New York, NY 10018, attn: Special Sales Department; phone 1-800-221-2647.

CITADEL PRESS and the Citadel logo are Reg. U.S. Pat. & TM Off.

First printing: January 2012

10 9 8 7 6 5 4 3 2 1

Printed in the United States of America

CIP data is available.

ISBN-13: 978-0-8065-3510-4
ISBN-10: 0-8065-3510-5

To Claire, Jazze, Millenium, The Comedian, and the rest of the heathens who bombard our community with hate-filled speech: your words of confusion let us know our job is far from done.

"Science is man's poor attempt at understanding God."

—Tyson Bowers III

CONTENTS

FOREWORD

My beautiful and righteous friends, our world is facing one of the most heinous challenges mankind has ever known. Will we survive to see moral wisdom once again return to this earth? Will we even survive to see tomorrow? Radical liberals have joined forces with hardcore lesbians, college students are experimenting with sodomy and socialism, pot smokers have infiltrated our workforces, music bands are promoting ghetto gunplay in our safest suburbs, and now sheltered teens are turning to Facebook for intense graphic sexual education. But wait, it gets much worse. Are you even aware that right now atheist Asian totalitarian states are conspiring to financially enslave our families? Did you know that perverts from south of the border are plying our women with whispered fantasies of loose clothing and even looser ethics? Are you turning the other way as our political leaders are dancing up close with the most perverted of the homosexual element? Sadly, militant violence has become a normal part of our everyday lives thanks to all this lunacy.

Lost in this cultural storm, the confused children of America are desperately looking for something meaningful. They crave God! Can they see it? Or are those blistery winds stirred up by the anarchists and atheists blinding them? Let us open up our moral umbrellas and shield our youths from their terrorist raindrops of left-wing tyranny! Let us go face-to-face with these deadbeats of spiritual decay! Deep in your hearts you know who they are! It's time we all admit the truth.

Yes, it is your neighbors and friends, maybe even your very own families, who are destroying America. Is it wrong to point the finger at those who have ruined everything glorious about our world? Of course not! They need to be intensely ashamed for promoting Socialism and hate on our very own soil. I dare you to point your beautiful, righteous fingers at these companions of carnal corruption and say, "You are the reason I cry for the fate of humanity!"

Yet there is hope! I implore you to seek the wisdom contained within this good book and hold it tight against your bosom. Pastor Jack Gould, one of this nation's leading youth ministers and a man with a golden touch when it comes to children, has inspired a cultural revolution on the Internet with the invention of Christwire.org. Under his guidance, some of the greatest thinkers and faith leaders in the United States today have come together on that website to delight in the glory of American global preeminence and Jesus's love. They are a veritable guerrilla force hiding in the jungle, poised to overthrow that gruesome dictatorship of sex, drugs, and radical liberalism! My dear companions Tyson, Amber, Reverend Clyde, Pat, and the rest, they are our storm troopers of sanity, sharpshooting down those sentries of the Hollywood media elite with words so precise, they will leave you breathless. Using the suffocating simplicity of compassion, they crush the debaucherous in page after page of glorious graphics and pristine prose. Their work is unequivocal and truly humbling. Yes, you will be humbled by this delightful work of faith!

My beautiful and righteous friends, if I were to say that the book you now hold in your hands is the most significant work of the new millennium, would I be wrong? I dare you to prove otherwise.

With love and the guiding light of Jesus,

Stephenson Billings
Investigative Journalist

STEPHENSON BILLINGS is an investigative journalist, motivational children's party entertainer, and antique soda bottle collector all in one special, blessed package.

MISSION

Dear friends, we are living in cruel days. Evil hours. Yes, these are certainly dark times and it's time for the moral majority to once again step forward to bring freedom and liberty to the world.

Our culture was built on the guiding principles of conservatism and Christianity, from which all morality is born. As such American heritage was meant to be passed on from generation to generation, ensuring that our principles ... our values ... were never compromised.

But alas, the Left Wing Conspiracy and Liberal Agenda are spreading like a plague not only through our fine society, but through lesser cultures as well. Their sinful antics and attempts to pass off their wanton carnal desires into mainstream culture are destroying society and mankind.

That's where we come in. Together, in this community, you and your Moral Leaders will combat the evil liberals of this world and once again ensure that a bit of freedom and righteousness once again permeates every country, and let those who don't abide by our teachings know the eternal pit of hellfire shall be awaiting!

Sincerely,

Jack Gould
Youth Pastor/Motivational Speaker
Langley CC

The
Chris✝wire
Handbook

CHAPTER 1

Values and Lifestyle

EPHESIANS 5:23–24

"For a husband is the head of his wife as Christ is the head of His body, the church; He gave His life to be her Savior. As the church submits to Christ, so you wives must submit to your husbands in everything."

INTRODUCTION

A deep, dark age of lascivious carnality and gross decadence has fallen upon Earth's golden champion: America. Gone are the days of morality, when mothers would proudly tuck their children into bed and every man proudly worked hard to provide his family with food, a home, and private health insurance.

Today's world is a scary place, one that not even the divining pen of Aldous Huxley would dare write. This is no longer a world of the brave or the free: it is one of mistrust, of Socialist aggression and oppression of the righteous.

The voices of our moral forefathers are haunting us, ringing in the distance through strangled whispers. The cold grip of Satan has emerged from the shadows of homosexuality, Socialism, and foreign invaders.

With his menacing hands, the great devil of Sodom has blinded society to the lessons of history, blurring the vision of objective reality with the sulfuric fumes of fecal sins, the poisonous theories of wealth redistribution, and the unthinkable implications of betraying America's historically declared Godly heritage.

The lessons of our forefathers—those of the proud patriots who fought the redcoats who dared tax our young America without representation, and those of our Greatest Generation, who liberated the world from a global threat named Blitzkrieging Nazi, are being suffocated. They are being perverted by a liberal disease that makes the most unkempt Vegas brothel bedsheet seem purer than a bleached dove in comparison. Make no mistake, the liberal propaganda machine is of strong velocity and has made us a society of crash test dummies without restraint.

A big, dark barrier has manifested within the heart of Washington, D.C., and he is blocking the world from its fate of salvation as dictated by our sage and noble Christian President George W. Bush, a man of gut-faith instinct and unparalleled presidential prowess.

Our steadfast adherence to Christian principles is the very reason God has chosen the U.S. to lead humanity, be it by blessing us with bombs of peaceful freedom that can end global wars, or being the printing house for the fabric of unity—The Dollar—that mended a broken Europe and quelled the most seething of Asiatic fury.

Good friends, beware! There is a growing liberal agenda that is so sinister and precise in its meticulous machinations, that it has secretly crippled modern America and therefore, the whole core of humanity. Together we all stand before an encroaching firewall of chaos and anarchy, pushing us to a dismal future of social welfare, suffocating sharia terror, and atheist orgies of damnation and destruction.

You and your family, friends, and loved ones are caught in the fray, no better than fresh sheep to the slaughter upon the altars of elitist greed and exploitation. We are being sacrificed before a new pantheon of demigods who believe they rule mankind, not unlike Roman caesars and Egyptian pharaohs of ancient lore.

Take heed, dear reader, as the false gods of old have been replaced by Chinese business executives, whom the Democrats are allowing to buy into the Western world's debt and to take jobs from hardworking Americans. We are being ruled by Muslim oil bandits, before whom former Illinois Senator Barack Hussein Obama will bow upon knee and whose hands he will kiss. How is it that after even the most holy of Inquisitions and Crusades, that a sable Moor is able to freely masquerade as the Hope and Savior of humanity, in the White House of democracy?

How can we be safe in a world where the leader of the Free World bows before the throne of Saudi oil greed?

The very values and mores that have ensured our freedoms for many generations are now being sold out in the most nefarious socio-political scheme in the history of mankind.

The left wing media will rabidly deny these truths. Their "journalists" will run to the printing presses of *The Times* and *The Atlantic Wire* and any other dirty street corner, all to yell loudly and repeatedly say anyone who is against them is against progress and equality. These jesters will lampoon those who defend freedom with comedians who masquerade as newscasters and then unleash former Civil Rights "heroes" who masterfully play the race card to discredit the truth of any Godly Republican and observant Christian.

Such unethical antics have tainted reality and silenced the most venerable voices of freedom. We must realize that at the roots, there is no pronounced difference between a demagogue and a democrat; both are diseased rodents who gnaw away at the foundations of framed stability. The deceptive media tactics of the left have hardened the hearts of our youthful generation, sullying their minds with Trotsky-toking ideals so perverted and salacious that even Stalin's tortured soul screams with ecstatic ecstasy from his torture chambers of hell's deepest bowels.

Resonating within those very deep bowels is one other jubilant voice: It is that of Satan. The great beast of Revelation prophecy loves a cheerful sinner, so it is no surprise that he is greatly enthralled by the increasingly leftist nature of our falling society.

As we make efforts to understand the bizarre fate that has befallen not only our great country, but every lesser people upon Earth, we must understand the battle plans of the enemy. We must review, analyze, and find the weakness of the core elements and tools being used to undermine American authority and domination of Republican policy in global affairs. Without the unadulterated governance of America, we see the consequence: an indecisive world of communism, uncertainty, and tribal defiance.

It is as if Senator Joseph McCarthy's sterling leadership and pruning of dangers never took place, and the frigid spirit of Siberian Soviet bloodlust churns through the minds and heart of every government on this planet.

One of the most spirited deceptions that spooks us today is this: America was not established as a Christian nation. This blatant lie was one born in the mustiest parlors of liberal think tanks and Ivy League schools, where the concept of reality is skewed by rowdy parties containing the wildest sexual urgency, sloshed martinis, and the most illegal of smoked drugs that overlap a professor's lecture and business meetings.

There is no Line of Decency in the school of liberalism and we need only to scrutinize the morals of the most prominent Democrats—the John Edwardses and Billy Willy Clintons of politics—to know how these people regard public responsibility, family, and unwavering faithfulness to righteousness in the presence of Lady Adultery's puckered face.

The mind of the modern liberal Democrat is inseminated with entitlement, soaked in aggrandizement, and splattered with weak resolve of ethics. These are the people who kneel before the sprawled loins of Satan himself, oft times without knowing, and tightly close their eyes as they spew out their festering rhetoric more quickly than they can take in the most destructive seeds of thoughts in our nation's history.

Democrats like to typecast people. They are trying to paint a false reality where those who stand for decency and stability in America play the role of the bad guys. New-age patriots of the Tea Party are being lauded as rednecks and uneducated sots. The turbines of the most hardcore left-wing propaganda engines cannot churn enough headlines against the endearing snow-vixen Sarah Palin and heartily repentant like the late Richard Nixon, Dr. George Rekers, and Edison Misla Aldarondo.

These great people are among the new Moral Majority. They are with the rest of us who are trying to save America and therefore the rest of humanity from a terrible fate where our culture, our very society, drowns in the putrid tar pits of a festering homosexual agenda, deceptively domineering foreign aggression, the technological innovations of morally bereft atheist scientists, and the most dangerous of all, the American Liberal Elite.

Each of these interest groups have an agenda of their own, a will they want to force upon each and every one of us. The Constitution of America is based upon the Bible, thus the concept of free will is a freedom to be enjoyed by every American. The enemies of morality want to strip away this free will until we lie shivering and vulnerable, naked and prostrate before them, as they forcefully thrust their wild, selfish desire into the normal life of every decent man, woman, and child.

There is a dangerous agenda to weaken America from the inside, so it can be destroyed from without.

Our enemies realize that their agendas must be crafted to weaken America from the inside, so our once-majestic glory will rot with narcotizing corruption and decadence, while it is picked apart by hovering foreign vultures from without.

Abraham Lincoln, a Christian and Republican, is eternally respected because he gave his life to free the chocolate people of our society from the burning ovens of oppression and he gave his life in trying to keep a bickering country unified. This man, so loving and complete in his Protestant wisdom, knew one absolute truth:

"America will never be destroyed from the outside. If we falter, and lose our freedoms, it will be because we destroyed ourselves."

At the heart of America is the nuclear family. And as any doctor knows, without a warm, beating heart, the body shall decay. The American family is constantly bombarded with images of adultery and false pop idols, flashed before them in subliminal Communist

Cold War fashion. Even today's grocery stores are stocked with anti-American family magazines, prompting housewives to leave their husbands, move to New York, and go on fantasy shopping sprees with their new "bi-curious" best girlfriends.

With the common housewife being ripped from the warmth of the kitchen, the children are now being highly affected. A lack of home-cooked meals has made children turn to violent videos games, Internet porn, and ghetto black rap music. No more are children fed nutritional lunches, tucked in at night, or provided with a closet full of neatly pressed clothes.

Due to the stress and disconnect of the modern American home, the once brave and dictative male has been brought to his knees. No more can a man run a tight ship with the snap of his fingers. Now he is forced to have emotional conversations and treat his wife as a partner instead of an extension to his home.

The heartbeat of America is now in asystole, our friends. We suffocate under the clotting fats of perversion and a salted gluttony of unholy pleasures. Perhaps the most troubling aspect of the diseased family is the new "American Lifestyle" being peddled by the Liberal Elite. It is a death trap, a ruse that is even more dangerous and addictive than the cloudiest nicotine lobby of Big Tobacco's corporate offices.

From such corrupt upbringing at home, we see our sons have fallen into a state of weak morality and impotent spiritual fortitude. Our daughters are defiling their holy temples, becoming whores for Don Satan himself with the spiciest marination of combustible sins. From the most innocent of kindergarten playgrounds to the hallowed halls of collegiate academia, we see the same story playing out again and again.

CHILDREN—THE FUTURE OR DEMISE OF AMERICA?

The year was 1952. Young teenage boys were proper in that time; their thoughts swimming with baseball statistics and meeting up for frothy malts with their best buds after school. Girls wore dresses and remained silent, their minds preoccupied with visions of confectionery delight and makeup-blending techniques. To this very day, if you wake up early enough to catch a glimpse of our elders from that time, you will see the men neat and sharp—dressed in sky-blue pants and proudly opening the door for their wives, who are fully made-up with their hair neatly set in the requisite old-lady-grayed, tight-curls style.

Contrast these facts with today, where we find our schools to be war zones. Around every corner, a young hoodlum from every flavor of race is wearing baggy pants, where you can see their boxers sticking out. They have their pants on the ground and you would think they'd be ashamed, but you never know how many of them are trying to entice a fellow gay or girl, or earning street cred in bizarre baggy-pants rituals.

There are dangerous games these new breed of teenage children play, all behind the backs of their parents. One that hit the mainstream is the "choking game". Many of you beautiful readers have heard of this dangerous "game". When stories of the ritual hit national news, it jolted the hearts of parents into giving quick, corrective action. Children would choke each other on school buses, seeing who could stay conscious the longest. The origins of this game remain a mystery, and the destruction it caused to brain cells was more dangerously destructive than a bottle of dirty Mexican tequila filled with the hallucinogenic magic mint "marijuana weed" that infests the Californian coast.

This game was a product of the coital Clinton era, when our children were forced to hear erotic talk of "cigar phalluses" and an American president who cheated on his country with the steamiest lies about musty bedroom shenanigans and broken oaths. The liberal media will howl and furiously stamp their muck-raking feet, claiming that Clinton's lying under oath and abuse of his interns was not a causal factor in Generation X's general failure at thriving.

We see this is not the case. Even though our Generation X children have now grown up enough to be considered technical adults, we find in their wake they have left behind an even more disillusioned generation. They have passed down to their little brothers and sisters the stories of their "Loss of Innocence."

Generation X, they were our little doughboys and bakergirls braving an America that was more caustic than the hazy mustard-gas fields on the Western front. The Clinton world was cold and dark. The children were lonely and afraid, not even able to ask the president himself for guidance, lest they wanted to be puffing in shamed, red-faced ecstasy upon the cap end of a light-bodied Cuban. The times were soaking wet with depravity and the kids needed the money. They turned to illicit hard drugs and these bizarre school-bus games and barely passed high school to go into our nation's colleges.

The younger cohorts, the children of the naughty aughts, are just as lost. There was a brief return to morality under the proud leadership of President George W. Bush, where no child was left behind and interns in D.C. didn't have to worry about the president scoping their behinds. It was a good time to be a youth: decency was brought back to public schools and the president was a vessel for God's will in America.

'50s.

'60s: Rebellious and interracial.

'70s: Lost-caused druggies.

In 2008, however, the adults betrayed their children. Maybe it was a combination of all the Kennedy-loving adulterers or neo-beatnik sodomite radicals of Generation X; maybe it was because everyone fell for Obama's race card. Whatever the case, loving and tested parents like brave Senator John McCain and the adorable visionary Sarah Palin were husked out of contention. Instead, we elected a cobbling man of inexperienced morals and questionable origins: Barack Hussein Obama.

Again, we find our children have turned to the wild side to make sense of all of the confusion. Why are our businesses failing, and why can't little Johnny get a 2012 Pontiac Grand Am for his graduation? Why are Chinese businessmen staking out D.C. and killing American enterprise, all while Obama has drafted ObamaCare policies that will send our guiding grandparents on Bataan death marches and is allowing the most innocent of children to be tossed into atheist fire pits of abortion?

What a depressing time to be a child and it should be no shock to find the kids have turned to two bizarre games, in a confused cry for help and attention.

"THE PHONE GAME"

Gripping reports of sexting have intensified parental concern. Every parent is now worried when their children's fingers gloss over their cellular phones' keys, wondering if their blurring, wizardly hands are working up a spell of naked pictures transferred to strangers all around the world.

The problem with modern technology is that when a new development gets us into a good scare, something twice as terrifying is developed by the most binary basement dwellers known to mankind. It should be no real surprise to find a team of calculating Californians have used their computer-savvy HTML skills to develop a new app called Shuudi. Its purpose: sinister; its aim: to give your child more ways to instantly share high-resolution photos of their most naughtiest of places.

Sexting is no longer the pedophilic game that threatens our children. With any other type of sexual deviance, the urge to go further and deeper always comes about. Look at what happened to the sex-addict lead singer of INXS. His urge for masturbatory pleasure was so great that he ended up hanging himself in an attempt to mix the adrenaline and endorphin rush of a near-death experience and topped off with the demonic pleasure of a self-induced penis explosion.

To understand this program, one must know the new threats of today are the use of cellular phones and all the little devil treats called "apps" that can be downloaded directly to a child's phone with no parental firewall. Each app brings your child one step closer to the gates of hell. While checking their latest pokes from Facebook friends or seeing the new gossip on Twitter might seem harmless, it is the information that kids aren't sharing with their parents that leads to the alarming rustle from a furiously brandished red flag.

Shuudi lets our little texting tantrum-throwing tycoons create digital polls for their friends to vote on. Sounds harmless, but when you look at what they are voting on, the app turns into a dark tool of unadulterated perversion. From images of bare-breasted women to men asking fellow female users to vote on their exposed flesh sugar canes, the polls are filled with vulgar (NC13) rated comments by random delinquents.

College boys have been known to use photos of their ex-girlfriends and upload them into a poll asking their frat buddies to vote on which girl they would rather perform mouth-sex acts on. The unaware victims of these types of sex quizzes have their faces plastered to hundreds of viewers in a sick and twisted revenge game by their Ritalin-abusing ex-boyfriends.

Alcoholic little college boys aren't the only ones abusing this technology. Girls have been known to have pillow-fight parties just to capture images of their milksacs and post them for their male schoolmates to visually ogle and vote on which girl has a firmer set of gland bags.

We asked a group of college freshmen what they most commonly use this Shuudi app for. The highest response was "To see images of our classmates naked."

This is far worse than sexting or even Google. Sexting only involves sharing among two or three people per preteen steamy photo. This program of whorish proportions has the ability to share a single image to its whole user base at the click of a button.

BLOOD-HUFFING GAME

In the most ancient, startling texts of European history, we find references to creatures so dark, so vile, they would bite the necks of their unsuspecting neighbors. Plague arose from the ashes of purulence and damnation; the scent of rotting flesh was so wrenching, it turned the belly of God as if he had stumbled across a slithering den of gyrating brown pipers in the slimiest venoms of poisonous sexuality. It took the most brazenly taut and glistening of epic men to combat the seething sea dragon that emerged from the cold, choppy seas of fiery violence.

Today, the stories of old become like new behind every darkened door of our nation's schools and under the smelly seats of the rumbling school buses. There is a new game being played by the children and it is deadly: the name, The Blood-Huffing Game.

What happens is that children first take turns biting the necks of one another, then let blood into cups blessed under the most crescent moons of *Twilight* lore. Inundated and inhabited by the spirits of Tolkien darkness, these kids then chant "spiritus Satanae te suscitat" as they spittle through mouths filled with the most delectable of elven lunchtime cookie crumbs.

Do not make light of this game, for children are raiding the offices of their nurses for syringes. There is a nasty new product called an e-cigarette and it is unregulated, giving teens a free tool to use in this Mayan blood oath.

The e-cigarettes are pumped full of the most erotic cocktails of blood mixed with sugary concoctions of brewed energy drinks, only to be sprinkled with solutes of drug residue that grossly excites docking ports with Viagral glee.

Kids feel that with each puff of smoke, the blood of their acolyte friends fills their lungs with dark dust and transfers any ghoulish spirits from the blood directly into their bodies. They believe this transfer of blood smoke makes them become one with each other and infusing their band of knockoff spirit shamans closer.

Whether it's texting tantalizing tasteless nudity or smoking vampire blood, American youth are on a path of becoming Satan's new errand boys.

Where did it all go wrong, parents? Kids today cannot enter a school without stepping through a metal detector and having their security ensured by several armed police officers on duty. Such police actions have not been necessary in America, since the time the will of the people was thwarted by Lyndon B. Johnson, a man who hated democracy and free will within our school systems.

It is no surprise that all went wrong in our schools in 1952. The data does not lie and you will see in 1953, there was a sharp rise in teenage pregnancy, smoking, and cross-race relations.

Dark and deadly hardly describes the horrors that lie in wait for your child in public school. These children are smoking the blood of each other while dazzling the eyes of their friends with sultry, under-age poses. The teachers are molesters, women violators being tared on the scales of sweet justice based on the weight of their midlines and busts.

In 1952, the Supreme Court removed God from public schools. Read those words and your brain shall know the truth: without the Ten Commandments in their lives, our children are no better than the forsaken children of Israel who danced beneath a golden calf and a mountain's thundering wake, all behind the loving back of Father Moses.

Satan dances on the grave of children's morality. And the prom dress is his sexual straitjacket for young females. Binding them to his tasteless agenda of unimaginable deeds.

DIRTY PROM DRESS REVEALS SATAN'S PLAN TO GET YOUR DAUGHTER PREGNANT

High school senior prom is a very immoral ceremony in which boys seduce girls into having premarital sex. They will ply your daughter with alcohol and then do grinding dances to devil's music, all so they may put their serpent scepters into your precious girl's no-no zone.

I'm here to tell you today, parents, that you must not let your daughter go to prom this spring. Over 86 percent of teenaged pregnancy happens at senior prom and stats do not discriminate. Any girl can become pregnant.

When your daughter naturally cries and tells you it's not fair that you forbid her to go to prom, ask her how she would like to be dying a slow, bloody death of herpe AIDS and pregnancy while the rest of her moral friends are off enjoying their studies at college the next year.

High School girl dressed up in prom-dress-whorish fashions!

At this point some liberal parents out there will try to convince you that senior prom is not all about sex and that your daughter won't get pregnant or catch AIDS.

You just tell them to be quiet because 86 percent of teenage pregnancies happen at prom and if that stat isn't reason enough to scare you into keeping your girl home this year, look at the new sinful dresses.

Look at the placement of the pink slits in the dress's skirt area and try to tell me that's not innuendo and foreshadowing of what a boy expects your daughter will be showing off later that night.

My friends, Satan's favorite food is your daughter's virginity, so please don't let some boy sow his sinful seeds in her fertile holy place. The gardens of evil and sinchilds that spring from it will only lead her to a life of disease, welfare-mom prostitution, and death. Keep your daughter from prom and make God proud.

Satan's influence doesn't just stop at the door of a prom orgy, but also speaks sweet nothings into their whispering eyes after high school graduation.

VAJAZZLING, THE NEWEST THREAT TO YOUR COLLEGE SON

College used to be a place where a young mind was groomed for excellence; now it is the breeding ground for late-night sexual pillow fights, homosexual experimenting, dangerously addictive magic-mint-induced "study groups," and protesting in anti-American gay parades.

Even worse than any of these things is this new vaginal modification craze called "vajazzling" that is being reported in almost every liberal-arts campus nationwide. If you've sent your son to school for edification, rest assured he has paid witness to a female's diamond-encrusted sintreats. Our studies into this new phenomenon shed more light into the mind of the new modern femme fatale feminist and the new-age fraternity softies yelling "Sassafrass, sassafrass!" as they fall under the daughter of Eve's spell.

College girls are now "vajazzling" their privates with jewels in efforts to tempt our solid young men into fornicating with them and having babies.

Females are distracting young men from their studies, hindering their academic progress and dreams of becoming the doctors, lawyers, and corporate executives of the next generation.

Hordes of prowling college girls on campuses nationwide have vajazzled private regions, hunting down smart, fit young men. Is your son prepared to resist this threat?

In these hard times, male college students are more focused than ever on their studies and building lifelong associates, and references, by joining fraternities and other extracurricular organizations.

This trend has caused females to resort to patently whorish methods in order to distract young men from their hearts' true desire in college: study and become successful.

In the 1950s and before, things were much better on campuses nationwide. At that point in time, women were still more inclined to stay at home and raise a family, as nature intended.

Colleges were the place where men of a proper background and upbringing would go, to further edify their academic savvy in a course of study to gain perspective, leading to professional status.

This process was hindered during the 1960s, when a resurgence of liberal thought caused a massive flurry of atypical students to plague the university classrooms. Women could not only focus on study, however; short skirts, drunken sorority parties, and constantly being in heat led them to victimize their male counterparts, with sexual temptation.

You see, parents, females instinctively desire to seek out a quality mate and tempt him to have children with her. We cannot fully fault college girls for being victims of their feeble, near-sighted minds. It is innate to the XX gene set.

Even now, college females are relentless in their efforts to tempt, subdue, and trap a mate. There is only so much a study-weary, home-sick, and naive young man can do against such odds.

So that leads to today, when college female students are now "vajazzling" their private areas. They are adorning their erogenous suprapubic area with jewels, and then trying to tempt men to follow the sparkles right to a place where only the married belong. You get my drift.

This behavior is nothing short of whore antics. I wish I could say I was surprised, but as should be known, it is rare to find a woman who does not have a cheating, slutty, and whorish side to herself. This dangerous vajazzling trend is just another part of the downfall of America.

Studies show that 60 percent of college graduates are now women, only 40 percent men. This is due to the fact that young men are being forced to drop out to take care of babies, while women get government assistance and can continue their degree course after having their babies.

Parents, please warn your sons about these whores. And if you have a college daughter, at least talk to her and tell her to keep her antics to herself, not using her vajazzled groin to attack young men at fraternity socials or at late-night study hall meetings.

THE LIBERAL AGENDA IS KIDNAPPING OUR CHILDREN

The steamy dorm brothels are not the only place Satan shrouds youth in sinful debauchery. With the help of the liberal agenda, Satan has extended his vile phallus into your children's schools, comic books, TV shows, music, videos games, and movies. The praising of prostitute-like pop stars and fanny-chasing homosexuals has become the new norm for the post-Obama entertainment world.

TELEVISION

An innocuous little show popped up on America's TV screens late last year. Its name is *Glee* and it's full of vibrant teens dealing with the gentle challenges of high school life. These are fresh-faced kids, hardworking and motivated, who can break into song at the drop of a sweaty football. But is there more to this sugary pop of a series?

An in-depth analysis of *Glee* will certainly raise the eyebrows of parents across America. It contains a surprising number of mature scenarios—from premarital sex to drug use, from adultery to abortion, from premature ejaculation to explicit homosexual experimentation. *Glee* goes out of its way to appear wholesome at first glance. The first fifteen minutes of every episode is quite polite and that's part of its success. It is colorful and cheerful with a scent of innocence. The message it seems to send is that teens should stay in school and aim for college. Yet beyond that (once the adults in the room tune out), it descends into a much darker place.

The Parents Television Council warns that *Glee* contains, "gratuitous sex, explicit dialogue, violent content, and obscene language. It is completely unsuitable for children." This is reason enough for parents to tune their teens out of *Glee*.

Instead of a real-world high school, we have a fantasy land of happy, shirtless teens hanging out in the showers or dancing on million-dollar stages. Why must the producers of this show have so many shots of the football team in the locker room? They're constantly dropping their shorts and jumping into a steamy shower, showing off tight biceps or lathering themselves all over with a fresh bar of soap. Is this some crafty attempt to appeal to the homosexual segment of the show's audience? Is it really appropriate for today's male teens to let this sort of softcore utopia influence them?

Additionally, the show has far too many musical numbers. From R & B hits to showtunes to classic rock 'n' roll, the boys and girls of *Glee* really can put on a performance. But it's not convincing on that million-dollar stage. They come across as trying too hard with their exaggerated facial expressions and hip posturing, the soaring voice ranges. They've clearly been coached. The singing is just too finely polished. The dance numbers are too excruciatingly choreographed. No high school kids can put on these sorts of shows at the spur of a moment. These things require years of gut-wrenching training.

Ultimately, these ad hoc songfests give children a very false impression about talent and success. They are led to believe if they just spin around and shout, they're creating world-class music. They are led to believe we live in a world where anybody and everybody can succeed as long as they have heart. But this is far from true. Some people are born with the vocal cords for music, others have the bodies for football, and others have the brains for math. That is reality. But this show is a drug of false expectations that will inevitably harm our children. It convinces impressionable teens to avoid serious career training in favor of having "fun" in the "arts." Also, the music numbers just drag down the plot of the show.

On a related note, *Glee*'s actors constantly make the argument that excelling at athletics does not contribute anything to the college application process. They posit the theory that a singing club will make you more likely to get into Ohio State or Princeton. This is false and it's reckless for the creators of this show to promote such disinformation. Athletics have been a proven stepping stone for academic and business success for over a century. The number of athletes who have gone on to full scholarships at the very best universities in this country are legion and legendary. Nothing even close could be said of a minor high school singing club. If children take this belief to heart, it could wind up seriously hurting their chances of college survival as well as their health (sports are essential for keeping fit, strong, and attractive!).

Glee Moral Rating: H (Heathens) for
Sinful dancing, explicit homosexual content, anti-college matriculation, sporadically long musical numbers, liberalism, racism

Another threat that has emerged from the teen "drama" genre is a show from MTV (malicious television) called _Skins_, a show that features amateur actors who promote flinting homosexuality, binge drinking, and drug-infused lifestyles. With the new teenage girl already being the equivalent to an Easy Bake Oven, there is no need to drizzle them with more of Satan's strudel cream.

The show is so pornographic that Taco Bell pulled their ad and the PTA says, "Viacom has knowingly produced material that may well be in violation of several anti-child pornography laws." And one of the show's stars has been quoted saying, "It's what teens are doing. It's the way teenagers believe, I think, especially you know in certain situations when you come from home lives where your parents don't really support you or really listen to you. That's what most of these kids are going through. And so, um, the drugs and the sex, they're vices, and that's what teenagers have." Sorry, sweetheart. America is a melting pot of vanilla ice cream and a few bad ingredients, but we don't need your devilish sugar and spices added.

Skins targets children as young as twelve years of age, with its sin candy of drug-addict, lesbian garbage. This form of child abuse has gone too far and is tearing our children away from childhood.

Skins Moral Rating: P (Pornographic) for
Child pornography, lesbians, homosexual mouth sex acts, fish-cave worshipping, lesbian clam dabbling

COMICS AND CARTOONS

My friends, there is a threat being marketed to your children by a crafty cabal of dark liberal media companies. These strange people hide their agenda behind the word "comics" so you think your children are simply getting a dose of fun and happiness when they buy a comic book.

The truth is the sin-marinated pages of each comic will lead your child straight to the barbecue pits of Satan!

As you know, comic books have been used by the atheists and liberals alike to spread propaganda for the Homogay Agenda, Soviet Communism, evolution, and even NAZIsm.

There is nothing funny about how studies show comics cause over 20 percent of young boys who read them to turn to drugs, male gay prostitution, and then death. I won't even make you fathers out there cry about the findings of what happens if you let your daughters read comics.

Here is just a small sample of the innuendo these atheistic wonders paint in each of these comic books. Keep in mind these are not close to the worst.

BATMAN AND ROBIN

Batman and Robin are a pantyhose-wearing boy/man team who both champion the Homogay Agenda for DC comics. We have only started to review these characters' origins in detail, but it's obvious these comic books probably account for at least .5 percent of the 2-3 percent of gays in America.

Batman and Robin entice young boys to think getting into the car with a stately old man with candy is a good idea. They'll have a life of cool gadgets, beating up villains, and being rich, all if they play "fun" games with their old-man benefactor. You know the truth is they'll get twiddled then end up getting traded around in Eastern Russia's black markets. We spit with disgust on this filth!

THE SPIDER-MAN

The Spider-Man is just about one of the most anti-moral comic characters ever created. President Joe Quesada and his little immoral writing hordes at Marvel use Spider-Man to spread evolutionist propaganda and destroy the sanctity of marriage.

If that's not bad enough, Marvel shows that Spider-Man also supports Barack Obama, meaning this character is trying to make your kids think killing babies is okay and it's nice to give money to America-hating terrorists.

Research shows this damaging character was created initially by a man named Stan Lee, then due to fervent prayers and enforcement of morality on comics via the Comics Code Authority, this evolved man-spider lost popularity. That is until a new writer named Brian Bendis recently used his skilled, if not spirited, hands to once again tempt children to read this dangerous propaganda.

Our heart fears for our children because in addition to all these crimes against morality, Spider-Man is also no stranger to promoting the Homogay Agenda.

SUPERMAN

When you think Superman, you may think that he stands for America. You think back to the Christopher Reeve *Superman* movie and perhaps an old World War II History Channel documentary where you saw footage of Superman slapping Japanazis; you get a little tear of Americana pride in your eye.

Well, each time you or your kid buy a *Superman* comic or support these products, God sheds a little tear of sorrow because Superman has pulled the wool over your eyes.

That scarlet letter *S* on his chest may as well stand for Supersin, because deep down Superman's origin and intent is to lead you to the eternal flames of hell.

Did you know that Superman is meant to convince you Jesus did not exist? Much like the sinful writing duo behind the *South Park* cartoon, Superman was created by two Jewish young men.

Siegel and Shuster created Superman during World War 2, borrowing the story of America's Christ and overlaying it upon their comic-book messiah. Superman has all these unbelievable, fantastically far-fetched-for-a-man powers and was sent by his father, Jor-El (remember, El means God in ancient Hebrew) to Earth to be a "light" for the people. His name is Kal-El, translated to "the swift voice of God."

Sound familiar?

Superman is not Jesus and each Superman comic is just a little slice right out of Satan's diary. Now if his origins were not dark enough and warned about in Revelations, the modern handlers of Superman use him to promote, you guessed it, the Homogay Agenda. What is it with these comics and trying to make our kids embrace homolove (or gay tendency)?

Like pornography these "comics" are drugs for the mind. They will addict your child to weird thoughts and then fry their brain up with the high heats of hell.

Comics are not alone when it comes to filling children's minds with visions of Vegas erotica: it has a dangerous half brother that is streaming pixilated perversions of animation directly into your child's retina. The cartoon genre has been created as a colorful sin guide for your children to reenact in real life. Every day, kiddie shows are becoming more and more violent and explicit with fiendish plots to take over our youth's minds.

One of the main culprits of this new form of mental raping is *South Park*. *South Park* is a dangerous children's show created by two Jewish mishegas who hate family values. Time and again this show has been responsible for tragic new stories where normal children have been tempted to do evil things, kissing girls at school, drugs, prostitution, and even murdering a person's parents and putting their body parts into chili at a carnival.

Parents, you must not let your kids watch this filth, as this creation by Matt Parker and Trey Stone is another cartoon that will lead your precious children into a life of drugs, whoredom, and death.

South Park Moral Rating: S (Sinister) for
Pixels of pornography, cussing, Jewish propaganda humor, ghosts, false Catholicism, bribing, beauty pageants, Hell not depicted as scary/brutal enough

MOVIES

When children aren't being violently back-bothered by the television, their minds are being dissected by the big screen. Modern movies blend the lines between fantasy and reality with stellar computer animations that act out the nastiest of scripts.

Do you know your movie-going children are being exposed to homosexual erotica, possessed toys that can talk, transsexual cross-dressing, pixie-dust black magic, teen idol demon worshipping, and bestial bedroom antics?

One of the biggest tween sin cupcake crazes is *Twilight*, an immoral book and movie series that teaches your teenage daughters how to worship vampires and do blood ceremonies at slumber parties. This film reel shows premarital relationships between girls and effeminately costumed vampire coeds who sparkle under the sunlight and howl in orgasmic sin like a menstruating midnight moonwolf.

We found that the last *Twilight* movie led to a 26 percent increase in teenage violence and a whopping 56 percent increase in teenage drug use. We won't even scare mothers with the numbers for teen pregnancy.

As reported by the *Des Moines Register*:

A 13-year-old boy at the Des Moines school was referred to juvenile corrections after allegedly biting 11 students between Feb. 10 and March 13, a Des Moines police report said.

According to the report, the boy bit a 13-year-old female student on the right hand at a track meet on March 13. Vice Principal Connie Sloan investigated the incident and found that the boy had bitten 10 other students.

When police contacted the boy's father, he said that his son didn't mean to hurt anyone and that he was biting other students because of the movie *Twilight*.

At this point panic and fear fill your heart. Is your child, sibling, or loved one influenced by this Satanic film? Is your child a new-age vampire or werewolf, the very type of beast we saw arise during the Bubonic plague, which wiped out one-third of Christian Europe in a blinding explosion of blood, tears, and fiery sweats, only relieved by

Team Jacob and Team Edward girls fighting over Satanic Hollywood demons.

mouths filled with bricks and pillars of fire that left Europe asunder, drowning under the blackest smoke of human damnation?

Is all of that what you want to happen to your child, just so they can be a Johnny Bridgejumper and see a demonic film like the rest of their friends?

Associated with this movie is a marketing campaign, whereby college girls and younger align themselves with "Team Jacob" or "Team Edward." In high school and college campuses, children are relentlessly peer-pressured to choose if they would rather have sexual relations with an overly sensitive vampire or a steroid-addicted werewolf.

Terror rips at the heart of good parents, as they will find their son or daughter has likely been exposed to this film. If you know a child who shows any of these terrifyingly telling signs of vampiric or wolf possession, immediately run to their rooms and confiscate any demonic paraphernalia. Rip it apart and burn it. Your teenage child may become vicious and rebellious and might even run to their Twitter account and say, "@ihatetheworld my parents are horrible #FML." Just remind them that blood rituals are now the most common cause of AIDS in their age demographic. And for the smart-lipped liberal college-aged child, just remind them their tuition money "may go missing" if they keep defying your parental authority and not stop their twiddling *Twilight* habits.

Twilight Moral Rating: D (Demonic) for
Prancing homosexual vampires, sexual content, sex with animals, Satan worship

As if bi-curious vampires and roid-raging horndogs weren't bad enough, the filmmakers from Hollywood press the envelope by pushing black magic and pedophilic teachers playing magical wands with their prepubescent students onto the silver screen.

Complicit to the new-age epidemic of female teachers attacking our pure teenage sons with unwelcome sexual advances, *Harry Potter* is a book-gone-Hollywild that pushes the ideology of homosexual encounters with a magical homosexual teacher named Dumbledore, who is modeled after the sodomy-driven wizard Gandolf the Gay in the equally dangerous *Lord of the Rings* movies.

The movie's aim is to normalize the homosexual agenda for youths by making the phrase "playing with magic wands" seem normal. Harry Potter had no idea that when Dumbledore said, "Let's play magic wands," it should have sent up red flags and that by wands, Dumbledore was using technical euphemism for playing Satan scepters with each other and Harry doing some "magic tricks" with his wand. This is why gays love Harry Potter, because it makes it easier for them to trick children into their dazzling lifestyles.

Not only are young boys targeted with this movie's gluttony of filth. The young female, Hermione, is used to press modern female sauciness and independent thinking onto impressionable future homemakers. Hermione is also teaching girls how to use their Satan parts to take control of a man's rational thinking. Sass and prostitute sashaying is not something we should be teaching our young women. It's bad enough the modern housewife is already falling into the cracks of sin via feminist shows like *Sex in the City*—why should we allow movies that turn American princesses into future Jezebels?

These things are all audaciously awful for the mind, so how exhausting to know of studies that show after seeing Harry Potter, the risk of a girl catching teen pregnancy increased from 2 percent to a shocking 63 percent. The risk of experimenting with drugs and alcohol a whopping 18 percent. *Harry Potter* movies make it seem like it's normal to be friends with gays and not have them try to dally you, like that is something to expect when in reality, for every one gay, four children get dillied. It is a sad and true fact and these movies try to obscure these realities from children, encouraging them to partake in a dark lifestyle of blood rituals, vampires, and wizardly wormholing, which leads to premarital relations, pregnancy, desperate heroin drug overloads, disease, and then death.

J. K. Tolkien is now a billionaire gay because of this movie. He laughs all the way to the bank with your dollars and Satan laughs all the way to bailed-out banks of hell with the blood diamonds of your children's souls.

These are only two of myriad movies in the archived lexicon of sin that haunt the souls of your children. Satan is a great ticket master and loves to give out free passes to hell's eternal theater of flames and suffering. Let's keep our children out of Beelzebub's box office and remember his deep, searing voice rumbles at the end of every call to Moviefone.

Harry Potter Moral Rating:
P (Pedophilia) for
Child pornography, unicorns, boy-man love erotica, sassy female character, black magic

VIDEO GAMES

Speaking of black magic and wizardly homosexuality, did you know that your children may be engaging in digital sin via their keyboards and mouse pads? A brand-new online free-to-play game has shown its snarling face in hopes of entangling your children into drunken revelry or magic fairies and polytheist ogres.

World of Warcraft is a dirty virus, the likes of which has not been seen since the Black Death ravaged the lands of thirteenth-century Europe. Parents, you have no time to waste if you're to save your children from this plague!

This graphical twenty-four-bit threat will pin them down and ruin their lives in every form and fashion! As you should expect, this gaming disease is another creation inspired by the Godless wonders known as the Japanese and its purpose is sinister!

It is a dangerous game that will infect your child's mind with all sorts of vile spirits and be their gateway into a life of alcoholism, violence, gay orgies, drugs, and laziness, as the product indicates on the game's packaging.

Recent studies show that over 73 percent of youth under the age twenty-nine who play this game immediately lose their jobs, relationships, and senses of sexual identity. It's common to see *WoW* players wide-eyed, confused as they lurk about in Cheetos-stained shirts in between their gaming sessions.

The infatuation with "leveling up" and buying new "magic weapons" for their characters on this game is so strong that followers of this gay-inducing *WoW* have been known to lock themselves in their rooms for weeks on end, playing sometimes until the point of death.

Neuroscience shows that the mind of a *WoW* player truly becomes a burnt wasteland, as the addictions to this perversion activate the same dopamine pleasure center as a lifetime of drinking alcohol.

The fried, scrambled minds of a *Warcraft* player are naturally addicted to this game. And like a true crack drug fiend, they will stop at no ends to level up and continue their endless quest to nowhere! They are driven by the forces of Satan to do crazy, depraved things, even if it involves becoming a devilwhore.

Consider the following heartbreaking story of a young woman, Olivia—or as she is known by her polygraph friends "xxElfLiviaxx," a level-eighty-seven undead night elf priest who is decked out in tier-twenty-seven season-four gear—sold her body to receive what's called an epic mount. An epic mount allows characters to "evolve" to the point to where they can cast evil spells on their enemies from the sky. Allegedly, one young woman's desire to have this epic mount was so high that she purportedly offered premarital infidelities to ANY person who would give her the mount!

Olivia reports she was mounted, twice. The second mounting led to a sin-child whose father is a kamikaze North Korean *Starcraft* world champion.

Such a tragic fate is hardly what one would want to befall a loved one. This *WoW* game has now addicted twenty million people world-wide, from the shiniest shores of America to the deepest dark jungles of Africa.

What's even worse is that expansions are released to this game, in efforts at niche demographic marketing for cultures that expressed no interest in this vile video simulation program. From homos to housewives, this whore machine shows no signs in the distant horizon of slowing down.

MUSIC

When God created mankind, within us he instilled the ability to create good music, as can be found in our nation's Bible (Psalm 150:1-6). Being a debaucherous demon, our enemy has done all he can to corrupt this gift, placing the boom-boom of sin into our hearts to ensure his sultry siren song always lures humanity to a fate of false treasures and eternal suffering.

For years now, Satan has snapped his fingers and bopped his head to the same ol' meter and cadence. From dance floors that hosted the Charleston to the aromatically pungent fields of Woodstock, the spirit of evil has consistently used music to drift into the mind and bodies of good, normal people.

Secular music is no stranger to threatening the lives of our youth; decade after decade, offensive musical bands and composers have corrupted souls with hellacious crescendos and rhythmic drums that encourage the most pronounced of pelvic gyrations.

We need to look no further than the dangerous crack-factory continent of Africa to know that the drum's origin takes place in the most bizarre tribal rituals, ones where the mumblings and incantations are so drenched in macabre evil they are utterly unpronounceable by the American-speaking tongue.

During the sixties, the advent of the flanger and no-no box of a screeching rock guitar solo fellated the minds of the impressionable women in such perverse ways, that 4.3 million babies were born nearly every year of the tumultuous time. From the pre-Communist classical scales of Tchaikovsky to the Socialist solos of John Lennon, we've seen millions of youths crippled by maestro Satan's violin-accompanied sin octaves.

Back in the early days the devil used backmasking as his favorite tool to turn harmless music into a weapon of mass demoralization. Backmasking was when a hell-bent sound or message was recorded backwards on to a track that was meant to be played forward during God-denying Ouija-board orgies. This form of musical fornication was popular in the seventies with glam bands like Queen, The Beatles, Rod Stewart, and Ziggy Stardust to just name a few. Rumors have even been sparked that the anti-Christian Thomas Edison himself secretly added sadistic God-hating messages in his recordings. The message was "I have never seen the slightest proof of the religious theories of heaven and hell, of future life for individuals, or of a personal God. If there is really any soul, I have found no evidence of it in my investigations."

Gone are the days of phonographs and record players as today's youth are well-connected in the communication age, using their Friendster, Twitter, and Soviet Napster accounts to instantly download shared formatted music to each other's cassette players and even CD-playing technology.

No longer can one raid the closets of children for milk crates brimming with rebellious devil's music. Satan has his ear pressed closely to the chest of today's youth: he has a keen ear tuned into what musical style and antics cause their heartbeat and pulse to go tachycardic with sin. We must never forget the enemy has posed himself as the "hip cat daddy" of today's generation. He will employ any trick and gimmick necessary to make his musical artists seem more talented and entertaining than people whose voices are truly inspired by Christian morality and the need to inspire today's youth with music that espouses conservative values.

Modern music floats all around you, seemingly silent in its invisible destruction. The audio devices of children can instantly snatch this music from these hidden airwaves, "downloading" the most offensive sounds and lyrics in the biggest subversion to parental authority known by modern history.

A cursory scroll through the FM radio band waves will bring one truth to your ears: musicians of the modern age lack a certain quality. In cultures across the world, this quality is often referred to as "talent" and even though older band teams may have been patently evil, at least their singing voices were from a natural source.

These new-age artists are nothing more than parading eye candy who don sequined clothing to dress up their talentless goose steps and choreographed exposures of oily legs, all to a sexualized soundtrack. The liberal music-promoting whore machine knows and understands that there is an overwhelming culture of sexualization being pushed upon our youths. Thus, they simply find the most voluptuously vile of Vegas-caliber showgirls—the Delicious, Tasti, Luscious Lamar, and Stiletto Stellas of the world—and then slap more family-friendly names on them: Britney, Miley, Justin, and Jennifer.

We cannot stress enough how music is bringing the destruction of the American culture. And now with modern technology, liberal record labels can produce a wide variety of venomous treats for your children's ears. From pop rock to bum bandit steamy disco techno, Satan has his full grip on the music industry.

Insatiable in appetite, the wallets of corporate music producers have funded a cunning "Auto-Tune" technology that allows any talentless hooker or minstrel to sing with masterful precision and perfect pitch. Such a stealing and misappropriation of God's given gifts is no better than when America found the blood-red Communist Chinese proudly exclaiming, "We've the nuke!" after Juggalo Bill Clinton sang them all of our blessed nuclear secrets.

Auto-Tuning is now being used by every major musical artist to produce perfectly pitched musical pornography for the ears of the youthful masses.

In this process, new and dangerous music gang-shooting acts such as Eminem, Doctor Dray, Snoopy Dogg and even a boy named Justin Bieber's off-key singing is "auto-corrected" through a phase decoder to sync pulsing wave harmonics in nodal modalities. This is all Satanic speak for this technology can take a horrible singing voice and make it hit the very notes that even the angels themselves could never harmonize.

We even find this deceptive method used in soft melodies of pop music sung by teen idols like Katy Perry and Cher. Female pop artists use this new form of hypnosis with the combination of their mysterious milksacs and devil whorish clothing to entice young men into demon whacking themselves and to produce devil DNA.

The incidence of violent hipped-hopped music streaming into your child's ears has hit a critical value. These digital tones of blatant hate and sexual sin are encouraging our young porcelain-skinned youth to becoming crack-dealing street walkers or a breast-exposing ploozies.

Satan's two favorite foods are Communism and modern music, so please stay off his dinner table, my friends, and make him starve.

WOMEN—THE DEATH OF A HOUSEWIFE

The Bible gives man charge of his house and family! Church has made that point abundantly clear and America's Declaration of Independence details our subservience to God, who inspired the greatest of men to write the words of the Bible and Constitution.

Human history will show that the most prosperous, successful times are seen when women are tending to the family while men toil with the rough elements and society, father bringing home for his family loving discipline and prosperity from good work ethic and morals.

Something, however, is amiss in America. Like a virus, the mysterious phenomenon of the "defiant female" even spreads to the world at large. A routine look about the Internet will show children have turned extremely vile, creating nasty communities named "Reddit" and "5chan", where the most brutal examples of liberal lechery and gross imagery exist.

We are talking about out-of-place women here, friends. And one of the key components to understanding why humanity is in such dismal form and shape is to understand where God has chosen to incubate all life. Why has the modern woman forsaken her role to nurture?

To understand all of this, we must first review the backstory. The details of female H. sapiens' history start in the first chapters of the Bible. During the initial passages that detail creation of life and the binding physical science of Earth, we see how God sculpted females from the deoxyribonucleic acid within the firm, God-puffed chest-cavity of the first man, Adam.

This passage serves as a reminder. Even though women would be fated to give birth to girls and boys, it must not be forgotten that it was from the rib of man that all women take origin. By this logic, men have authority over women. Women were created from the rib of Adam. God is a man, Jesus is a man. Women are to be equals in love and respect, but always submit to a husband or father's authority.

For a period of time, all was well with original creation. Eve obeyed

God and Adam, walking about and not eating of the forbidden fruit of evil knowledge. Adam was happy with his new companion. Husband and wife stood as equals, side by side as they named the animals of creation and marveled at each other's starkly amazing personalities.

Unfortunately, there comes a time when the scent of marriage wafts into the sniffing nose of Satan. The marriage aroma makes his tongue salivate and his belly rumble with an unprecedented hunger for adultery. Being that he didn't have the wiles of Facebook or iPhones to tempt the weak female with secret messages in those days, Satan simply called Eve into the hidden gardens of Eden to talk her into the lustiest of Judasian marriage betrayals. Boytoy Satan taught Eve the most raunchy uses of her secret place, a location she never knew existed.

Every married man understands it does not take much to seduce and fool a wife: women can be very naive and fickle. It was only a matter of time before Satan broke down the moral defenses of the first woman, Eve, as he taught her to touch his "Satan scepter" and convinced her to eat of "forbidden fruit" in the Garden of Eden.

We see the passivity of Adam in marriage left room for Eve's infidelity. Adam was too trusting and we see that after Eve was convinced to eat the apple of Genesis, she cheated on Adam with Satan and the Bible just leaves that part to implication since it is pretty obvious.

If Adam had gone to Eve and just said "No" when she brought the apple, we would not have sin. Even something as horrible as marriage betrayal would not have taken place. It's all due to Eve. Adam thought he could trust her, and she led him to sin as well. Now we all suffer. So, yes, a man needs to keep a woman in place. Adam failed to do that and look where it got us: ObamaCare welfare babies, invading Chinese bankers, PMS wife nagging, and having to hear women complain about only nine months of carrying our children, as if it's harder than protecting a family for a lifetime.

As a woman, Eve had a naughty and mysteriously rebellious side to her. Satan knew how to tickle her fancy to make her dark, defiant nature more prominent. Eve defied her role as companion to Adam and daughter of God, by binging on the saltiest carnal concoctions of sweaty purulence and apple-baked sins that Satan could muster.

Eve was a latent whore and this is the fate that awaits all of her daughters, if they don't have a man with a strong hand in their lives. The strong hand of man can provide the most gentle of tapping discipline and love: without it, we find evil arises. Adultery, feminism, deadbeat mothers and abortion-toking teens. These are all the products of Original Sin and Female Rebellion against nature.

All of this has greatly upset God. After Original Sin, God recoded the bodies of women to be vessels for the offspring of their children. With such flagrant disregard for conservative values, God knew that one man could never be trusted with eternal life in carbon-based temptation: a man has to live on through the lives of his sons and grandchildren.

The price of betrayal for Eve was to be a birthplace—a fate served to all women. It is one that is with nobility; for now, all children are housed and nurtured by their mothers. God did this so women could become more in-line and appreciative of their natural roles. Satan even works to destroy this lesson from God, and as we will find, his biggest supporters are the most dangerous and rebellious of all women: feminists.

The deformity of the independent daughter of Eve has forever closed her devil flesh wrap to her birth-given duty to be an obedient homemaker and attentive mother. Not having the woman tend the kitchen and make sure her family is fed is a fatal disease that has plagued America throughout the 1900s until now. Of course there was a short span of wholesome family nutrition during the Reagan years, as he put the American woman back into her place with a gentle slap of good old-fashioned male muscle.

FEMINISM IS DESTROYING SOCIETY

For far too long, men, and the moral fabric of Western society, have been on the receiving end of a very long societal shaft. The metal of this shaft was first welded by none other than the successors of Susan B. Anthony. It has continually been shined up and adorned with spikes in the smeltering rooms of every anti-man rally.

You see, friend, the fact is this. There should be relatively equal rights between man and woman. Not many will argue against such an adage. But when you give woman an inch, she will take a mile. She will take so many miles, however, that she'll naturally get lost and out of her place.

And that's where we are today. A society with women far out of place and men left behind, trodden down and out of sight. The women who have been using the phrasing "equal rights" as a green light to gain ground on men have now caused effects that are destroying society itself.

Some of you may argue that women have fallen far out of step with their God-given roles of cooking a proper dinner and tucking Junior into bed. It seems historical trends do tend to agree.

Back in the 1950s, women cooked dinner for their families. They would take time to wear starched aprons, buy fresh food from the market, and make sure a well-balanced dinner was awaiting their family by 5 P.M. as nature intended.

During those times, families were fit and appreciated nutrition. Girls were comfortable with their bodies; there was no reason to have a McDonald's on every corner. Obesity wasn't an issue because women were performing their natural duties.

Contrast such things with the travesty of today's society. On every playground you see hordes of kids, Cheeto-stained hands, clamoring about with no mother in sight. The food court of every mall is filled, people snarfing down their daily Taco Bell for dinner. Meanwhile in homes across our society, kitchens are empty.

We wish we could say this was the worst of our problems, but it's not the case. Today we have issues such as high divorce rates, broken families, and school violence. Jack Thompson wants to blame it on video games. Grace says it's our lack of good role models.

I'll tell you the real answer. It's the rampant irresponsibility of the women who want to put career, and their desire to top men, above properly raising a kid and nurturing their families.

TV is not the solution to raising your kids. It is not meant as a babysitter. TV dinners and takeout aren't instructing your children on how to eat healthy. Your grandmother-in-law would be ashamed.

Much as the women of today were improperly raised in the sixties and seventies, children are being taught that TV life is real, men are naturally pigs, and fast food makes a healthy diet. The cycle is in the process of repeating itself, hence all the problems with today's "youth" being reported in the media. Over-aggressive feminism that encourages bad parenting and desolation of family is the root of societal downfall.

So I speak to every career woman and instigator goose-stepper without family when I say this. Stop destroying society. Every once in a while, making a nice, warm dinner and tucking the kids in can go a very long way.

In day-to-day life, we find men make better doctors, lawyers, and sources of hard labor. Affirmative-action laws obscure this fact with mismanaged job placements and skewing of demographic data. Women make better secretaries, attendants, and other assisting jobs. It makes sense, as women are made to be attentive and nursing (as the woman's main life function is to have children). Feminists who read this will mew and hiss with scathing anger, denying these facts, and when doing so, please take time to look in the mirror. You will see God has designed your bodies to have babies and then nurse them.

THE WOMAN'S ROLE

We need to get our women back into prenatal, culinary shape again. Below is a list that all female readers need to take seriously, if there is any hope for our families to become whole again.

- Women have no opinion greater than their husbands'. Just remember women are there to enforce their husbands' choices. Remember, a quiet wife is a married wife.
- A fed husband will always stay in love with his wife. Making sure your husband has a proper dinner each night will ensure that his attention is not drawn to another, younger, prettier, and skinnier female.
- A child's room can get messy. Make sure that their rooms are constantly kept up. A mother's love for her children can be measured by the crispness of the folds in their sheets.
- Keep female emotions to yourself. A man already has so much going on in his mind, the last thing he needs to stack on is to hear about your unimportant feelings.
- Stop asking "Do I look fat in this dress?" The answer is yes. A man is not there to give you fashion tips.
- Taking up a career means you're putting your family in second place. If you have enough time to work a nine to five, then that means you aren't putting a full day's worth of work into your household. Stop thinking of yourself: instead, keep yourself busy with learning new recipes or new ways to make your husband satisfied.
- Fitness is a must. Your goal is to make your husband look good to his friends and no one wants to be seen with a plumped-up, C-section horse. If your appearance fails, your husband fails in social interactions and it could affect promotion advancements at work.

America the Beautiful has become America the Disfigured, because neo-femi women are birthing an ugly culture of meth-faced youths and heinous marriage habits. Some women are so demented that they have been caught fondling the mammalian ludicrosities of other females in the nastiest of ways.

With the storehouses of eggs gone bad, we find the last line of defense for modern families being God's original creation: man.

Is modern man up to the challenge of salvaging the nuclear family and tending to all creation? Remember, at the center of America is the nuclear family. There is a battle going on, one not on the physical plane but on the supernatural. The forces of evil actively seek to destroy the core of America; for when America falls, so does humanity. We saw it during World War II. Even before that, the world was dark and under terrorizing redcoat rule of extended pinkies and twiddlywink monarchy waving in defiance to democratic capitalism, all before God himself had enough and reached down to create America with the help of a truly great man, George Washington.

The freeing morality of Puritan ethic and our Christian forefathers have been instilled in this country: Are the lessons still resonating in the mind of modern men, the bold frontiersman in this new age?

MEN—NO MORE GRIT

The male role in America has become flaccid. Beaten with female equality, men no longer dominate their homes with morality. Instead, they have been castrated in households worldwide and have let their home, once their empire, crumble into a liberal breeding ground of female dominance.

Men now sit and have chats with other men, while drinking homo-creamed-flavored lattes, about the newest yoga positions or about how American Eagle has a two-for-one sale on designer taupe-colored man purses. You now even see men setting their DVRs to Bravo, so he and his prude, Botox-injected, cheating, non-cooking wife don't miss an episode of some flamboyantly infused show on contemporary home decorating.

The modern man is weak, too weak to make his kids go outside and grab a branch for him to swat them with. Too weak to give his wife a gentle backhand to the face or bend her over his knee, when she has stepped out of line or made some type of uneducated-female comment. Too weak to take back his workplace, where a woman was once a secretary and not a boss.

Why have we allowed the male to become so light and fresh, like a pitch from a vaginal-cleaning-product commercial. Maybe that is why they now wear designed skinny jeans to the office.

After recently speaking with a few middle school students, we have been able to see how young children view their father figures. Unfortunately, we're unable to get a good grip on how a African American father is portrayed, as 96 percent of the sin-skinned students had no idea where their fathers were.

Most of the children that we interviewed said pretty much the same thing. Their fathers were just some guy who leaves the house at 8 A.M. and comes home at 6 P.M. to sit in front of the TV until bedtime, which is right after some late-night show on the Oxygen channel. Some children even expressed that they felt that their mothers were more athletically dominant then their fathers.

This is not a good sign. We are seeing that men don't even have an active role in their children's upbringing and without that our children are destined to grow up with some type of antisocial, hippie disorder or even worse, gay.

If you wish to be a constant doormat for your less intelligent, double-X-chromosome wife, then keep being weak willed and spineless. Keep using body washes, so your male parts don't smell of their God-given odor. Keep applying silly products to your hair, so it looks like you just got out of bed. Keep letting your kids disrespect you in their new-aged hipped-hopped sassy tones.

Man needs to become the masturbatory fantasy of women again. Take back their God-given role as twelve-o'clock-shadowed men.

Lady Liberty is confused and out of place, sticking her thumb up the rear of the very gender who gave her freedom. It is time to re-teach the male population about who they are and how they are meant to act.

Testicular torsion is deadly, so it is no surprise to find our men are having their manhood strangled by the twisted, emasculating culture of modern America.

Women are usurping the roles of men in many fields, usually at the behest of nasty affirmative-action laws. Why is one hundred and ten-pound-dripping-wet Sally Firefighter filling the boots of New York's finest, the grizzled men who stood proud with heroic Mayor Rudy Giuliani in the wake of 9/11?

Are modern men to believe that the little glittery girl at the mall, with Juicy adorning her hind end and a Prada bag vasectemizing the poor, pink-vested male Chihuahua dangling from her scrawny arms, is tough enough to work in the most poisonous black-lung mines or hard-hat areas? Where is room for pride when media are pushing the notion that whatever a man is meant to do, the woman next to him can do it better?

For over 6,000 years, man has survived and been fruitful without the need for scientific devil drugs to artificially stiffen the love muscle of a man with Viagral excitement. Suddenly, now, one cannot turn on the television or computer without ads everywhere for such products. The spirit of mankind has been beheaded; his will to endure and take charge is fleeting and dysfunctional. There is no need for euphemism to say the fortitude of mankind has been clogged by a culture that swats away the once-proud holders of homunculi and bearers of priapismastic endurance.

Man's true nature is like a hearty stew, brimming with bold chunks of meat and a sturdy broth of warming comfort the whole family can enjoy. The aroma of man's original sauté cuts with the ferocity of pure testosterone, sweaty enough to burn the most glazed of eyes and spicy enough to clear the mucky, exacerbated sinuses of an eighty-year-old chain smoker.

How is it that a creature of such fortitude, fearfully and wonderfully made by the skilled hands of God, has come to such a broken point: it is because Sous-Chef Satan has thrown one nasty ingredient to the balance of life. Some foreign tongues call it "la leche mala," while others accurately say banshee sweat or Jezebel juice, but most commonly, the scientific name of this human extract is estrogen.

Estrogen is man's mortal enemy and has been used to weaken the male spirit. Now liberals will balk at this wisdom, politicizing genetics to make claims that all human life actually starts out as female. This is just a small slice of the crisped pie of lies served by typical Congressional Democrats like the fallen Charlie Rangel and Nancy Pelosi, the master chefs of deceptive gluttony and gut-wrenching greed.

Moderns-day ma: $85 haircut, scarf, tight jeans, and miserable.

The Democrats will stop at no end to please their gay-supporting, minority-agenda constituents by funding faux-science studies.

Scientists have been hired to claim that within every person, there is a wild-card gene called SRY (Sex-determining Region Y). Funding that could be given to our brave oil-liberating troops in Iraq is instead used to plant a nuclear Hiroshima-sized, secret, subliminal lie into the minds of upcoming men. The Bible makes it abundantly clear that man came before women, yet wild evolutionary scientists blur the lines of standard gender roles by claiming this mysterious SRY region can allow hard callused XY females and Kleenex-soft XX males.

Modern culture and media are buying into this false science. Walk through a mall and you will see peculiar young men, dressed in skin-tight jeans and holding hands, all whilst peering upon the suspiciously Arab makeup kiosk.

Man needs to stop allowing the evil secretions of the modern world to back him into a corner of hopscotch and jump rope. I say we stand up to our postpartum-depressed women and make them realize their role is to be gatherers, while we hunters have a God-given right to be rulers of our own cave. Liberal Hillary Clinton says it takes a village to raise a child. What she didn't realize is that it takes a strong man to tame a woman.

LET'S BECOME MEN AGAIN

No longer should men be made to sit and watch movies about postmenopausal women traveling the world in search of a young underwear model to fornicate with. No more should man be dragged to some three-day black-magic, fantasy-filled theme park, where everyone is smiling and splashing, frolicking under the sprinkling golden streams of gaydom.

A man's home is his holy sanctuary, as is his body, and therefore it is a man's responsibility to ensure God's law reigns supreme over his home, children, and marriage.

Children and women need guidance. The Bible makes this fact abundantly clear, and since the 1950s, when true, loving discipline started to lose ground, we have all bore witness to the cultural decay that results.

Without proper fatherly authority, children are becoming the world's next street thugs or heroin-infected, slut queens. Kids are running wildly into urban crack-driven neighborhoods and not looking both ways before crossing the streets right into hell. It is the man's job to properly groom and primp children into holy, conservative, Christian citizens.

We need to break Satan's poopimpish hold on our daughters and place God's chastity belt back onto their secret gardens. Daughters need to be more interested in cooking and cleaning and not be exposed to books that encourage them to enroll in liberal arts programs at some non-accredited two-year college.

As recent studies have shown, girls who had sissy fathers, had a 48 percent chance of becoming pregnant by boys of a different race. 36 percent were at risk of becoming devil dancers at a fully nude strip club.

Satan licks his lips at such statistics, as he knows the farther away from dad, the easier it is for him to control their already feeble minds. By controlling their minds he can control their moist camel humps and turn them into his personal concubines.

These statistical numbers have been on the rise ever since the nineteenth Amendment was fraudulently created, giving women the right to vote. When we gave women the right to vote, we also gave them the right to disrespect all male authority.

Teaching your daughter to fear the sting of a man's scorn is most likely the best life lesson you could ever give her. By fearing this, it has been shown that they will become less snappy and more respectful to the male gender, which also prepares them to be better, obedient homemakers.

Let's not leave out the young sons of America and how they need a strong man in their lives. It is bad enough they are brainwashed into thinking that a fancy-pants homosexual is now considered an actual male. But, boys are also being taught to be in touch with their "inner female" so that they can lower their natural intelligence to be able to communicate better with the growing population of feminist women teeter-tottering between lesbianism and normal motherhood on playgrounds across the nation.

You now see boys taking homo-ec classes and doing limp-wristed aerobatics on the cheer team, while the girls are being allowed to play football. This role reversal is the first step of turning our young men into crybaby liberals.

If your wife has enrolled your son into anything that might be seen as a possible threat of making him grow ovaries, rip him out of there and put him in some type of extreme martial art or gun collectors' club.

Also don't be afraid to toughen up your boy with some abnormal house chores. One good example is to have him scrub the driveway with nothing but a toothbrush and when he is done, yell at him for not doing a good job and make him do it over again. This will make him never question your judgment and authority in fear of being made to do more backbreaking chores.

Not only do our children need discipline but, sometimes in marriage, the grave and solemn responsibility to politely tell the wife to be quiet and stay in her place falls upon every husband.

Wives need gentle "proddings" when they step out of line, much like children. Just as you would swiftly rap a child's hand should he try to stick a fork in an electrical outlet, the same may need to be done to a wife's cheek should she challenge authority in a damaging way. "NO," you should tell her should she do something that is harmful to her or the family, but she may be too fickle or naive to immediately see.

As Abraham Lincoln once said "You cannot build character and courage by taking away a man's initiative and independence." He was saying, "Men, take the damn steering wheel and tell your wife to shut up."

THE MAN'S ROLE

A man should measure his alpha-male birthright to the likes of Sir Sean Connery. Mr. Connery is a man with sterling swagger and knows how to handle his lady in a classy, well-mannered fashion. The list below will help the male population regain their rightful household empire and allow them to command and conquer with a hand trained to deliver the most gentle of loving God-taps.

- A man should outline his favorite meals and add them to a calendar. This is so his wife does not anger him with the mistake of making meatloaf two nights in a row. This will also help your wife's inherently distracted, wandering mind learn how to keep a timely schedule.
- After a long day at the office, make sure not to go home with large amounts of stress. Stress can bring unhealthy energy into the household and sometimes leads men to snap easily when the wife makes an uneducated comment, as the Bible warns women will do. Instead, make sure to take an hour or two each day to go out and enjoy some time with your friends. If you find yourself spending more than three hours or so and are concerned about missing dinner, simply text her and say, "Forgiveness is a virtue." Don't worry, your wife will be there to whip you up something fresh no matter what time you decide to return home.
- Make sure to always let your wife know about any celebrities or female coworkers you find attractive. Keeping your wife on constant alert will make sure she does her best to always look in tip-top presentable shape when you decide to take her out in public.

- Being the king also means being the enforcer. Punishments aren't just for your children; they're also meant to be lovingly given to your wife if she becomes out of line with any nonsense talk that you might hear from one of those babbling, cud-spitting cows from *The View* (excluding our Christian, conservative vixen, Elisabeth Hasselbeck).

- If you are a father of beautiful Christian children and do not want them to die young, you must make sure that they are not influenced by new-age hippie, Prius-driving, vegans. Don't let secular parents out there try to tell you that it is okay to let your little princess dress up like a *Twilight* vampire hooker or that it is okay to buy Johnny Jr. a *World of Warcraft* game board. Your job is to protect your children from all liberal and homosexual evils in the world at all costs.

MEN, GET OUT OF THE KITCHEN

Much like the hidden threat of Charlie communism our brave veterans faced only decades ago, the man of today must battle a new secret villain: mystic homosexuality.

Today, we find more men than ever marching through the mucky quagmire of homosexuality. While all people are born of normal mind and body, history reveals that somewhere along the trail of decency lie explosive landmines of emasculation. When trodden upon by the steps of mankind, these insults to Mother Nature can cause a lifetime of damaging shrapnel to be embedded in the minds of men from the most wholesome specimens of stock and breeding.

Uncle Sam laments, wagging his head in shame as gays now proudly gallivant across the battlefield, telling of their full embroilment in the steeping pots of steamy San Francisco tea-bag tetherballing. The twisted ballad of these battling boys named Sue is played over the sounds of raucous applause, femanating from the voting boxes of Liberal Democrats who care not that we've created a society that stands against nature and the will of God.

Friends, we are talking about the destruction of the vessel of life itself. Genesis reveals that within man, God breathed his enduring fortitude and crafted the ability to create life. With such a great responsibility, the Sons of God, the Men of Morality, are tasked to be diligent leaders with unique propensity for leadership.

Instead, we witness man after man lost in the deep, dark mud puddles within the thick jungles of alternate lifestyles and Thai-boy temptations.

From our most dashingly brash businessmen to the most tight vested of professing Republican politicians, we have seen the most Roman of Bruté betrayals and bathhouse plunger pounding. No longer can we trust the market value of our business leaders or the harmonically loud orations from our gold-tongued politicians to be guarantors of morality: it seems any person can be infected by this terrifyingly wild Culture of Feminization.

An all-seeing look into the bathroom stalls of our nation's children reveals a fate where schoolboys are afraid to pee while standing up and struggle with chafing from silk-lined panties. Gone are the lessons from our rugged fathers with blistered hands, who taught us to be proud and shake when finished. These new-age young boys are growing up not knowing the difference between right and wrong!

The once-proud streams of morning manhood are now the gentle raindrops of a tinkling sissy, sitting with hands folded on lap.

Good friends, brewing within the deepest bowels and bladders of masculinity is the most brutal of yeast infections. Look within the office of any gynecologist, and you will see that even waiting husbands dare read the words of poison from *Women's Weekly*, *The Advocate*, and *Vogue* with the most zestful zeal of dirty, shameful interest.

Has this culture of Women in the Office, Men in the Kitchen, given us a nightmare of social cross-dressing so rotten in texture and presentation that not even Chef Gordon Ramsay could make out if he's yelling down a weak man, a bisexually dapper Dan, or a tucking Stan?

It is the controversial issue of Sodom and Gomorrah over again. Our ancestors, when the Earth was even younger than today, battled against the darkest of iniquities that caused the angered nose of God to blow the hottest steams and make the paltry biceps of fandango-footed, anal-ferreting men flail in the drowning pools of burning decadence (Psalm 18:8). From such lows, true man did arise!

When Nixon's manly Moral Majority took charge of this great democratic nation, they had the courage to face down the masses of homosexual enablers and liberal Civil Rights crusaders who wanted to turn everything upside down. Lusty and looming hordes of tough, leathery women and men of eccentric ethics assassinated decency with floodgates of petty scandals and a battle cry of bisexuality for all!

Again, society reached a low. The eyes of God squinted while watching in dismay; the battle lines were redrawn. Men and women of values and decency, conservative in their modesty and realization of the family necessity in American globalization, were again at war with the legions of licking lesbianism and hemorrhaging masculinity.

Good warrior of the faith and creator of life, you must stand your ground! We care not where the battle is fought, but the end must always be a victory for family values and gender roles that ring clarion in the ears of our precious sons and daughters. Our future, our creation, the lifeblood of morality and future protectors of humanity: the offspring of a proper man and a normal woman, a creation that cannot be made by those who dock in sin with the same gender.

Do not let the manhood of life be twisted by the churning mixers of liberal culture. No, friends, do not let the fate of comet-stricken Sodom and burning Gomorrah be the judgment of our people! Our enemies are resolute and sassy, the men carefree in their little daydreaming office secretary duties and touchy-feely nursing jobs. The women of liberalism! tough and of a strong chin. If they say, and believe you me they will, that bisexuality is good and we must loosen our exit muscles and welcome a sexual fist like every other nation has, we reply that we shall deny bisexuality, homosexuality, transgenic transgenderality, and any other-ality that is not of God! We will say that this is the United States of America, One nation under God! Our pledge is eternal and our money is true when it says In God We Trust! If they shall not like it, then they can get out of our blessed country!

You shall not nail mankind upon a bed of lavender-scented thousand two hundred-thread-count Egyptian-cotton sheets.

CHAPTER 2

The Homogay Agenda

LEVITICUS 18:22
"Do not lie with a man as one lies with a woman; that is detestable."

INTRODUCTION

America's true sleeper cell has planted itself into the American marriage. Satan himself has masterminded a plot to destroy the covenant between man, woman, and God. His weapon of choice: Homosexuals.

Men Beware, the Gays Are Out to Get You!
by Dan Nordgren
—FROM *The Christian Daily Star*

Dear friends, today I bring you a great warning and personal testimony about the true nature of the Homogay Agenda. It's truly frightening.

As you know, the gays have been actively campaigning for decades now to destroy the American nuclear family. With every little victory they get, the more we see the rising divorce rate, economic failure, and deadly disease spread through our fine country. Those scientific facts and statistical data you already understand and see day to day.

What we don't always run into, however, is personal confrontation with the gay agenda. Today, I unfortunately had the displeasure of having to endure a gay hit-on. It was sick and my lunch still does not sit well in my stomach.

Before going to a food-court Chick-fil-A with several friends, I went to the men's room to take care of business. As I walked up to use the porcelain standing device, a guy in what could be described as dapper clothing also came into the men's room, going to the standing stall next to me.

What happened next is shocking and purely sick. He peeked. I thought my peripheral vision was playing tricks at first, but he was clearly peeking and then upon my ears I heard a whistle, the type that a construction crew in New York would give to a passing woman.

"Wheew, wheew, I like what I see here," said the gay. I have never been so disgusted in my life.

Being a good man of the faith, instead of belting him in his face I turned the other cheek. I told him about how he was wrong for being gay and saying such things, and he claimed he was just having fun and that being gay is okay. I reminded him of the story of Sodom and Gomorrah, and he just laughed and went skipping away. He didn't even wash his hands first.

The moral of the story is that even when you least expect it, the gays are everywhere and now more bold than ever before. No man is safe. The gays find all guys attractive and will hit on you, so this warning especially goes out to you college guys.

Do not do things like leave your drinks lying around. Gays may try to drug you and then do all sorts of bad things to you while you're passed out. Their boldness now only grows since Barack Obama supports them getting married and such.

Homosexuals are probably the greatest threat to America. Causing incurable diseases, viciously exposing our children to homo exotica, plotting the demise to the sanctity of marriage, and rapidly importing sin-colored babies from overgrown jungle countries.

Homo gays are SIN-sational deceivers, whether it's using Christmas to entice Johnny into a man-boy love relationship or funneling tax-payer dollars to place butt-plug-removal machines at every street corner in San Francisco, the Homogay Agenda is fierce and out to get you.

Satan's cabana boys now have their fecal-flavored hands in a plot to gape a hole in the American household, by planting themselves into heterosexual marriages, so they can increase the divorce rate in America and make normal sex-having couples look unfaithful.

IS MY HUSBAND GAY?

Right now in America there are over 2 million couples secretly struggling with homosexuality in their marriages. Are you one of them? Are you having intimacy issues? Are you suspicious about your husband's late-night activities? Or are you oblivious to a problem that could be putting your health and the livelihood of your family at risk? Don't tell yourself that you're simply being paranoid without taking a closer look!

Homosexuality can pop up at any time during a long-term relationship. Your spouse may have been experimenting with the "gay" lifestyle even before you met. Maybe he's just using you as unwitting cover as he seeks playmates in the homosexual world. For these types, the shame of being "outed" is so great that they will go to extremes to hide their lustful activities, even tricking women to marry them to appear normal in society. Sometimes it's the nervous family who has rushed a young man into marriage out of a fear that his secret will be exposed. For others, homosexuality can appear later in life when men crave some escape from the monotony of careers and home life. Same-sex experimentation is also connected to drug or alcohol abuse. Crystal meth and other narcotics are proven to lower inhibitions and to drive people to take incredible risks to feed their habits.

For the wife unsure about her husband's proclivities, the most important thing is to first confirm your suspicions. Drawing on the expertise of spiritual and medical professionals, Christwire has put together a list of fifteen commonly accepted characteristics of men struggling with homosexuality within a marriage:

1. Secretive late-night use of cell phones and computers.
Porn addiction is closely associated with homosexuality, and a secretive nature implies he's trying to hide something from you. Be on the lookout for a man who doesn't want to web surf or answer phone calls in your presence. Texting is another favorite trick used by adulterers. For the sake of trust, a married couple should share everything, including phone logs, email accounts, chat friends, and website histories.

2. Looking at other men in a flirtatious way.
When you're out in public, does he spend too much time looking at other men? Is he fond of winking at people? Does he get visibly upset when someone does not return a compliment about his physical appearance?

3. Feigning attention in church and prayer groups.
Have you noticed a lack of interest in spiritual issues? Does it ever seem as if he's just using church as an excuse to spend time around young men? Does he volunteer to mentor in all-male groups?

4. Overly fastidious about his appearance and the home.

Natural men have a certain amount of grit about them. They sweat and they smell. Homosexuals often abhor this sort of thing and will also be incredibly particular about the cleanliness of the home. Does your man tweeze his eyebrows, trim his pubic hairs, or use face moisturizers? Is he picky about brand-name shampoos? Does he spend more time getting ready for a night out than you do?

5. Gym membership but no interest in sports.

Gay men use the gym as a place to socialize and to have secret liaisons in the bathrooms. They like to work out their bodies without the competition of sports play. Afterward, they use the showers and steam rooms to engage in sexual activity beyond the prying eyes of women. If your man returns from the gym too exhausted to talk or have sex, that is a worrisome sign.

6. Clothes that are too tight and too "trendy."

Gay men don't need words to communicate their availability for sex "hook-ups." They silently broadcast the news by showing off their lean, hard bodies in designer clothing labels. If your husband owns skinny jeans and looks at his buttocks in the mirror or if he wears an inordinate number of small-sized T-shirts, it is probably worthwhile to pay more attention to his private activities.

7. Strange sexual demands.

Fetishism is a sign that a man is seeking a harder thrill beyond the normal intimacy of heterosexual relations. The woman may not appeal to the deep desires that are coming to the surface as the marriage drags on. If there is a sudden interest in sodomy, sadomasochism, lubricants, role-play, sex toys, or other non-traditional intercourse methods, this is clearly an indication of deep emotional abnormalities.

8. More interest in the men than the women in pornographic films.

Pornography is a dangerous element in any marriage, but there are many Christians who feel watching it does add something to their sexual lives. If you have gone down this road and find that your man perks up at the sight of the men in these sorts of videos, you should be concerned. If he selects films because of specific male actors, this is an obvious sign that he is suffering from a crisis of ego and desire.

9. Travels frequently to big cities or Asia.

Some husbands will spend a great deal of money traveling far from home to hide their deplorable same-sex actions. Big cities offer indulgence of every kind. From gay bars and clubs to prostitutes and sex bathhouses, a man seeking encounters can find them easily if he's so inclined. Is there ever really a good excuse for a husband to visit Thailand or San Francisco without his wife?

10. Too many friendly young male friends.

Someone who makes an extra effort to surround themselves with younger men should raise concerns in any community. If this is the case with your husband, ask yourself if he prefers their company to that of women. Do they touch each other or embrace in long hugs? Do they exchange expensive, personal gifts like scarves or cologne?

11. Sassy, sarcastic, and ironic behavior around his friends.

A man who is secretly engaged in homosexual activity with others may exhibit feminine qualities when they get together in a group. In a sense, he has "let his hair down" and this will be seen in excessive back talk and speaking with one's hands.

12. Love of pop culture.

It's quite common for young men to enjoy the science-fiction end of popular culture, but when your husband becomes overly obsessed with romantic and feminine shows, that is cause for alarm. Gossip websites, *Glee*, and *The Golden Girls* are three well-documented icons of the gay movement that genuine heterosexual men avoid.

13. Extroverted about his bare chest in public.

Does he go shirtless in the backyard or at picnics when other men are around? Does he wear a Speedo at the beach? Does it seem like he's purposely standing right in the middle of a crowd to show off his chest and arm muscles, peppering people with questions about how strong he looks? He may be craving physical affirmation from other men and desperately looking for hints of shared desires in those around him.

14. Sudden heavy drinking.

Sometimes people dealing with an unbearable emotional issue like homosexuality will turn to alcohol to hide their distress. Does your man disappear on drinking binges for long hours without answering his cell phone? Is there a strange odor about him when he returns, some strange mix of cigarettes and gel? Does he cry frequently?

15. Ladies, have you dated men in the past who turned out to be gay?

This is an important question to ask yourself when your marriage starts to have problems. Statistics have shown that women who have encountered gay men romantically in the past are the most likely to repeat this mistake in future relationships. If you answered yes, you should ask yourself whether you're honestly looking for a man or just a shopping companion. Is sharing gossip more important to you than raising children? Ultimately, it's a question of getting your priorities straight!

Not only do the gays have their sin-soaked hands up the rears of our American household, these reverse poo pushers' influence can now be seen on the playgrounds and kitchen tables.

During the mid-ninetees, the Homogay Agenda took a radical, modern approach in their endless quest to seem like normal people. These homosexual loin lusters unleashed a three-pronged dildo attack against American decency, so things like "gay sex" and "clam-dabbling" could seem like normal words spewed over dinner tables across this great nation.

Long gone are the good days when gays lurked only in the dark shadows, knowing that stepping out into the light would get them branded with a sizzling *S* for Sodomites! Now, these little scarlet-stained crusaders hide behind Civil Rights laws and politically correct speech!

They try to pretend like their cause is as worthy as that of the blacks, who suffer their woes due to a socio-genetic condition! The roots of homosexuality are not a part of science; it is not a part of God's plan. If so, would not a child appear in the belly of every homo-man who let Dabblin' Dan stick his steelrod up his sewer hole? Would not two fishmonger lesbians haul out a baby from their foul play!

It is not the case, my friends. The only way we get proper children is when a man marries a woman and then gives her the seed of life to incubate and it is birthed from the woman's baby hole. A child is born and that is the way of nature.

But gays don't want us to believe reality. They are using politics, media, and technology to press on us a bizarre lifestyle. These raging Rainbow Warriors want us to think it is natural for them to marry. From their anal-scented mouth turrets they fire words like "equality" and "same-sex rights" when the Bible tells our Christian nation the homos are doomed and cannot marry. For every gay "union" that's allowed, God winds down his counter for fiery destruction and Armageddon.

Gays are the modern Machiavelli, the fearful princesses of pissflaps who try to rule us with backyard terror. When they have us all scared, they then woo our families with sitcoms about boyish dandies spilling their sugary coffee in the office.

This modern Homogay Agenda is a powerfully confusing movement, the likes of which the world has never seen. It has crafty captains at its helm, from the loopholing Ivy-Elite scholars to the smooth-voiced Ellen DeGeneres, who softens the blow of lesbianism with a memorable smile and gentle humor for housewives nationwide. The Ship of Homosexuality is deeply anchored in the heart of America; for at the heart of America is a world of television and Internet.

And who uses the television and Internet more than our children, the protectors of our American future and trustees for our wealth of conservative values in this cruel, wicked world?

Being of a smart and new generation, the neo-gays are devilishly clever and brilliant. Their agenda hides behind minced oaths and out-sourced allies; but if we look deep enough, we can see the sleight of hand they are trying to pull at the poker table of national politics.

Their ace in the hole is gay adoption. Even though they account for only 2 percent of the population, these card-dealing sharks want to indoctrinate our children in thoughts sugarplummed with anal sins. They will take little Johnny into secret gay clubs like The Back Spade and little Cindy to The Quiver Lip Queen, where they will learn all sorts of alternate lifestyle advice from their "two mommies" or "whistling daddies."

Ninety-eight percent of America is not homosexual and does not want diagrams of gay sexual techniques in the health sections of our children's science books. As if the theory of evolution were not a big enough lie to swallow. Now, the gays want to top it with a heaping pile of homo-sapien-mating-with-a-monkey theories.

It may seem strange, but the chocolate speedway merchants understand that if society believes in evolution—that mankind is the product of bedroom relations between a man and a female lemur monkey—then it won't seem so shocking when they are having orgies at every park and street corner in your hometown.

These frisky felines and scat daddies are bigots. They don't care that the majority of America says No to Homo. Gays understand that even by the standards of nature and evolution, they cannot evolve because a child will never come from two scrambling eggs or swash-buckling flesh swords.

These sex-crazed homos know the true hope for their agenda is gay adoption. If they can be allowed to adopt children, their agenda can indoctrinate and brainwash America's future to think being gay is okay. These children will grow up and then vote homosexual propositions into World Law.

Homosexuals are like the veiled wolves of scary lore. They try to hide their agenda under a sheep's wool, making it seem cozy, warm, and soft on the outside, when underneath it is rabid and snapping, looking to slit, rend, and cleave flesh of the innocent, and that of our precious children.

Gay adoption must not be allowed to take place, unless we want all of our children in the belly of the beast.

THE DANGERS OF GAY ADOPTIONS

People of lower intelligence believe we should allow a dynamic gay duo to adopt our foster-home children. These same people believe we should give criminals a second chance and allow them to walk the streets freely. It is a sad day when America's more concerned about giving child predators the right to raise a baby in a broken home than they are with the abuse and social confusion that the baby will endure during its upbringing.

Before it was made legal for gay couples to steal American babies from future straight foster parents, these devil prancers would illegally smuggle kids from other third-world countries.

Just like their fabulous drugs, gays would use their money from their monthly gay welfare checks to pay the black market to import children. Since children of non-American rule are so easily stolen, the gay couple could choose the style of baby they wanted. From a sin-colored, nappy-haired Afro baby, to a porcelain-skinned, blue eyed little German.

These adopted heathens are like trading cards to the sin-docking fathers or fish-cave-licking mothers. Gays would show off their new imported accessories to their other same-coupled friends to see whose child came from the more poverty-stricken country. Just like the diamond is the more precious gem, the dark-colored children were more expensive and having a painted baby made you look richer and gave you more street cred in the fanny fruit world.

We weren't worried about the gays corrupting non-liberty-loving children, but now with the courts openly allowing our American-born children to be snatched up by these drug-using sexually disturbed addicts, our youth are faced with many new challenges.

DRUG USE

According to studies 89.4 percent of male homosexuals are avid users of hardcore drugs like ecstasy, heroin, the pot, or acid, or have a heavy prescription addiction. Homosexual lesbian females have been shown to have a slightly lower risk, but just because it is the lesser of two evils doesn't make it acceptable.

Children who see their parents partake in the use of devil nectar have a 76 percent greater chance of being drug users themselves. If you notice, the usage of drugs in teenagers is on the rise and this can be directly associated with the approval of gay adoption.

Just like drugs these outrageous statistics confuse the mind, so we should not be too perplexed to find the correlation between drug use and increased incidence of lesbian pregnancies.

HIGH PREGNANCY RATES

Startling new studies reveal that children raised by gay and quad ovary couples are up to seven times more likely to get pregnant than children raised in heterosexual households.

According to a study by the *Canadian Journal of Human Sexuality*, a statistical survey of thirty thousand students showed that gay-fathered boys were more likely to get girls pregnant. Daughters who had pearl fishers for parents have a 10.6 percent or 7.3 percent more likely chance to get pregnant than a normally raised girl who had partaken in premarital sins, respectively.

One of the main reasons why female teens raised by sodomites get pregnant more often is the guilt they face due to the sexual and bizarre actions they have seen their parents engage in. These actions by the homo parents create a craving for teens to develop feelings of abnormalcy and force their kids to act out in a sexual manner.

HIGHER RISK OF GETTING DISEASES

Gays are known to be stuffed with incurable viruses given to them by God for defying him, so of course these same sicknesses are being exposed to children being raised by a these walking zombies.

The scientific definition of Gay Bowel Syndrome is outlined in the Bible. In the New Testament, gays were warned that their merry lifestyles would result in leaky sewers, mouth sores, crippling blood pathogens, and lesions of despair.

Derivative from this, we find gay mouth disease occurs when backside sins enter the mouth, then the gingiva become impacted with fecal matter. This results in the typical black gums and foul breath that is common for gays in their community. Dentists say every year, there are over twenty-three thousand deaths due to gay mouth disease and it is contagious.

Just like the increase in teen drug use, we see a gangrenous growth in syphilis and chlamydia in children. Maybe this is due to the fact that both diseases have skyrocketed with a 500 percent increase in the past three years within the gay community cream bubble.

With these numbers being so grand, it is predicted that the average child who is raised in a house of sin has a 47 percent chance of catching one of these illnesses, just by being near their queer authority figures. That is twenty times higher than the likelihood for those having unprotected heterosexual sex.

With all the horrible things that can go wrong with a child being raised in an unholy homosexual home, why would we want our children being gay adopted, or should we say gay abducted?

To the couples who are unable to adopt a child, they find themselves in a downward spiral of prepubescent obsession.

The gays are great hunters and if they can't get their bouncing baby via the already corrupted government, the prowling street walker will stalk its prey in an unsuspecting American neighborhood or unguarded public-school playground.

When a feral gay has set his eyes on his prey, he is filled with uncontrollable anal tinglings of lust and malice.

CHILDREN ARE THE PREY OF THE GAY

Gays are always on the hunt, preying upon our innocent children and thinking of new and creative ways to drag them back into their lairs. Some of their newer tactics would even make Himmler and Goebbels *ah* in envy.

Right before our eyes and without warning, the Homogay Agenda has sprung forth with many tactics to lure your children into the back doors of hell. A untrained eye might not be able to spot these dangers, but with proper homosexual-awareness training any parent should be able to see one of these sugarplummed devil traps from miles away.

GAY ICE CREAM TRUCKS

As summer winds down and parents relax their guard, the homosexual agenda unveils its latest plot to covertly slide their fornicated lifestyles into our children: gay ice cream trucks.

When children hear the siren calls of an ice cream truck, they can only imagine the cold, juicy Popsicle that will cool them down on a warm late summer's evening.

What they don't know is that the new pied piper of summer coolness is a gay man, and the only thing he wants to deliver to their life is abduction, disease, and shame.

Granted that they have no qualms with violating the sanctity of marriage, it should not shock one's heart to see living proof that homosexuals have no issues with violating the innocence of youth.

An obsessive bone smuggler might use these tactics to entice kids to run up and buy some tasty vanilla icy treats. In reality the ice cream is laced with sleep drugs and the back of the truck is a world-class torture chamber filled with such items that would make a terrorist jealous.

Children never think to see danger and would never expect that the neighborhood ice cream man presents a veiled threat that will ruin their lives. How frightening for parents to know the gays are always out on the prowl for our children!

PENIS-SHAPED TOYS

Our colon-sin-pounding enemies are out targeting our children with gay toys. The gays have been getting more and more blunt with their agenda on making our youngsters light-footer Peter Pan fairies. Their newest homo creation is to make toys shaped like a large adult gay vibrating defilator.

These toys are a prime example of how the homos are trying to get our children used to gay things. They are hoping that kids will be so used to toys like this that they can run up on them and pull out a "toy" and ask young Billy to come over and play. Children will think "If all the kids are playing with the newest and coolest toy, and mister homo queer is playing with it, then it must be okay for me to go to his house and let him shove it in my naughty spot after he drugs me and it won't be a bad thing."

These gays are very sick people! If they like their gay anus love so much, then let us take one of those squirt toys, fill it up with holy water, shoot it up their dirty tunnel, and cleanse them out with steaming hot morality!

COMPUTERS

Ever wonder why Apple's first logo was an apple colored in with a rainbow? It was to show that they are secretly controlled by the Homogay Agenda.

If you look closely you will notice that the apple has a bite taken out of it. That is a symbolism of when Adam took a bite out of the forbidden fruit. This was their way of showing that they wanted the users to taste the rotten fruit of homosexuality.

I guess Apple doesn't believe in Adam and Eve, but Adam and STEVE Jobs.

Gays are marketing these machines toward our children, so they can flash subliminal Homogay Agenda propaganda on our children's iTones, iCellphones, and iComputers.

Any parents who buy Apple products for their sons or daughters are saying "Please have homo sin-hole sex with my child" or "I want my daughter to be a fish-sin-slit worshiper."

If we don't stop this microchip whore machine, one day you will see a commercial from Apple with a homogay man asking "Where is the nearest elementary school?" and a voice will say "Oh, sweetie, there is an app for that!" It will be called the homo's pocket GPS for raping America's children.

NURSERY RHYMES

There is no nook or cranny that can be safe from this new form of homo terrorism. The gays have been caught pushing their sick and twisted fantasies into the minds of developing children by using nursery rhymes as lyrical brainwash.

We found three songs that have the most harmful titles to children and we ask you to investigate any music sheets that your child may be bringing home from school.

"I LOVE LITTLE PUSSY"

This is a song that was created to teach little girls that being a fish-hole lover is acceptable. We found that girls are put into a circle while they sing this horrific song over and over again until it is solidified into their brains, so that when they go off to college, they will be victims of partaking in a lesbian dorm pillow fight.

"IN SPRING I LOOK GAY"

You shouldn't look gay any time of the year! All this song does is teach boys that it is okay to dress like Freddie Mercury in spring time, while skipping hand in hand with another fellow. Why did they stop at spring? Why not "In Summer I Look (enter a gay disease of your choice here) Ridden"?

"RIDE A COCK HORSE"

The title alone is a sin against God. Why should the word "cock" even be displayed to young children? They had to change the word "nigger" to "slave" in the *Huckleberry Finn* book and I bet Afro-Saxons would rather have their coal-colored children learning about that instead of learning how to pet a man's flesh cupcake.

The titles are vulgar and are a perfect example of how the gay's brain works when it comes to small children.

As you can see, our sick friends have no moral conscience and will go to great measures to harm our little ones.

To fully understand the mind of a perverted wild animal of sexual stalking, we must journey deep into the habitat in which they live.

SWEAT, SODOMY, AND RADICAL SOCIALISM: A SHOCKING LOOK INSIDE AMERICA'S MOST DANGEROUS GAY BARS

Recently, national debate brought attention to the construction of Islamic mosques on American soil and the risk these cells of fundamentalist activity pose to the safety of this country. Yet there is another threat entrenched in our very communities that has gotten far less attention. Like Muslim centers, these institutions serve as recruitment centers and training grounds. They prey on our most naive young men. They ply with promises and threats, stimulants and fantasies. Sadly, the danger these dank halls of hedonism pose to the future of our nation is far more heinous than any cloistered Arab sweat lodge.

Yes, it is the gay bar of which we speak. Gay bars were once something of an urban legend, an odd rumor that someone who knew someone may have sighted in the shadow of a big-city train station. They were down ghetto side streets and had wide, swinging doors. No elaborate signs announced their locations for they were painfully shameful places, intentionally hidden from the concerned eyes of normal society. All that has changed in recent years. Now an itchy rash of these businesses is spreading to our towns and rural communities They're on our Main Streets, next door to diners and hardware stores, appearing as legitimate as any McDonald's. They are blistery places, announcing themselves with shrieks of disco music and brightly laminated flyers. Don't let the cheery visage fool you, however, for they transform into something decidedly sinister once the sun goes down.

Simply put, America's gay bars serve to falsely legitimize a notorious lifestyle choice. To say these places are un-American misses the point. They are much worse. They enable obscene physical violation, addictive drug abuse, and the heights of political subversion. It is here that the agenda for overthrowing the normative values of society is devised. Across grimy pool tables and busy urinals, over cigarette ashtrays and fruity mixed drinks, the worst schemes to corrupt everything from traditional marriage to the age-of-consent laws are hatched by these relentlessly perverse plotters. They are all about sex. Sex all the time.

And let's not forget about the children.

"ABANDON ALL HOPE, ALL YE WHO ENTER HERE"

As you enter one of these establishments, you are instantly hit by the noise of gossip and fluids being traded with vicious abandon. The black-painted walls and pulsing red lights will bring to mind a World War II bunker on high alert. Yes, the danger is imminent! On any given night, you may encounter a crowd that consists of aging florists, European fashion photographers, old-money millionaires, beer-bellied truck drivers, urban runaways, scruffy-faced all-American jocks groping Asian college students, coked-up hustlers in torn tank tops, Latino gangbangers in loose-fitting sweatpants, barrel-chested black men who smell of cologne and lubricant. . . .

These people around you will reach a pitch of unnerving excitement as men move back and forth at narcotically inspired speeds, rearranging themselves for drinks and furtive fondling like chess pieces on the game board of spit-slickened animal depravity. Careers are born on those sticky barroom stools. Young men slide close to captains of industry, unbuttoning shirts mother may have ironed only hours before, letting a mature hand explore their plateaus of quivering flesh. Actors and journalists, web entrepreneurs, and public-school teachers will conspire to monopolize their respective industries. How many corporate domination schemes have been based solely on a shared proctological propensity? America would be shocked to know.

As you settle into a quiet spot, a Grizzly Adams look-alike will saunter up and desperately try to get the attention of a bartender he had unrepentant anal intercourse with years ago. Yes, after a decade he is still banking on those two minutes of shared musk for a free cosmo and facile chatter. Delicate boys, their Gucci pockets stuffed with exotic lip balms and unpaid rent bills, will use any smile as an excuse to approach. Dropping a hand in your lap, they will waste no time in determining whether you are endowed, financially or otherwise. A screaming transvestite will lurch toward you, spilling her oversized cocktail on your new Gap jeans. And maybe in that moment, with Ms. Destiny's icy vodka cranberry chilling your loins, you will come to understand that all hope is lost. You have been rammed up the colon of stale beer and faded dreams.

San Francisco's infamous gay leather clubs force themselves on you with tragically macho names: Anvil, Boiler Room, Dugout, Ramrod. These titles are meant to intimidate with threats of surprise anal rape. While that danger is real, the masculinity surely is questionable. The denizens are most likely chartered accountants and home decorators who spend the rest of their week in chintz-drenched apartments singing songs from *Les Miserables* and caring for fussy miniature dogs named "Mr. Bubbles." In New York's crime-plagued Puerto Rican district, there is a bar named after a common farm animal. It is infamous for its crystal meth-dealing drag queens, slumming D-list celebrities, and stage performers who give themselves whiskey enemas before entranced audiences. In Los Angeles, West Hollywood is known in underground circles as the place where young men go to place their film careers in the moisturized palms of the effete elite. The bars here have monikers like Backlot, Daddy Warbucks, Capone's, Improvision, and Numbers, giving a surly nod to California's most homosexually dominated industry. Even our nation's capital is not immune. Washington, D.C., is home to a rash of bars whose names (Secrets, Phase One, Hung Jury, Mr. P's) hint at their patrons' profound interest in destroying our most hallowed legal protections.

For the heterosexual community, the danger is that straight men will chance upon these gay bars unaware. Husbands, seeking a little reprieve from the cloying miasma of home life, may think they're convenient places to stop in on the way back from the office. Suffering from the exhaustion of a long day at work, one might not notice the strapping, exclusively male clientele. College boys, jilted by ungrateful girlfriends, confused by cell phone maps and hormonal tyranny, are easily drawn to the flashing lights of these houses of ill repute. Affected and disaffected young men will find in the gay bar the perfect place to codify their rebellion against loving mothers and a God they are not yet mature enough to comprehend. And once these former heroes of family values have ordered that first pint from an overly attentive barman, the novelty of new flesh will push the lusty regulars into a tizzy of strategic maneuvering about them.

The homosexual puts a great deal of stock in fresh meat. It is considered a sign of admirable prowess to convert a heterosexual and after doing so, the gay will be rewarded with several rounds of free drinks from his jealous peers. These people are hyper competitive and yet their battles reside exclusively within the realm of physical conquest. Faith, fame, and fortune will never mean as much as anal penetration to the gay man. For those who have dedicated their darkest hours to living in the homosexual bar, hardcore sodomy with "the new member of the team" is the most precious thing imaginable.

As the hour grows later in America's most dangerous gay bars, punk rock go-go boys with bursting jockstraps will appear, flaunting their funky cargoes in the faces of young and old alike. Ex-cons, still reeking of forced detention, will slice you with their hungry maximum-security eyes from across the room. It's not unusual in prison to have your body covered in something akin to grill marks after you've been assaulted against the bars of your cell. Here, they wear the stains of rusty basement pipes and cigarette burns like badges of honor! And then there are the "leather daddies." These primordial princes of pigskin live on a steady diet of tap beer and testosterone. At various times throughout the night, the crowd will part as these men wrestle bare-chested for a contested twinkie boy. The winner will claim his moist, purring prize against a back wall while the defeated clears martinis and designer handbags from the bartop so that he may put his head down and weep silently. Swarthy men of unknown origin will emerge from the shadows to beckon the innocent into bathroom stalls where any question of affection is resolved with a quick slap to the face. On your knees, forced to gag in a forest of pungent pubic hair, is that your idea of love?

THE DARK ROOM

A "dark room" in a uniquely urban homosexual invention. It is a small cage at the back of most gay bars where there is no light. Behind a chain-link fence, men strip down to their underwear and embrace the first body they encounter in the blackness. Unexpected acts of sodomy often follow. The man with the largest phallus, regardless of body odor or senility, usually becomes the center of attention. No words are spoken, although the English language would be practically useless in this grunting, ethnic crowd.

With their pharmacologically enhanced libidos, homosexuals can climax about once an hour over the course of a six-to-eight-hour night. For this reason, they find the darkened room an important element in extending their evening activities into the dawn. It saves them from committing their energies to pursuing a single partner who might end up being flaccid, bossy, or uncooperative once at home. It also perpetuates their alcoholism, for between sexual bouts with that muscle-toned gym rat whose whiff of sweaty chest hair gently tickles the cheek, the homosexual will find new stamina in the purchase of fresh piña coladas.

It will dismay most of my readers to know that the portrait drawn here is just the beginning of one's career within the gay lifestyle. That small mistake of entering the wrong type of bar is simply the start of a wholesale commitment to a larger social agenda that traditional Christian society finds abhorrent and wrong. Coffee dates and Thai dinners inevitably follow your night out at the homosexual club. Outrageously priced jeans and skin-care products! *Golden Girls* marathons and vintage furniture! Art fairs and Key West! Then comes the patronage of gay-owned businesses. That seems innocent enough, but how far a trip is it from the cake shops and hair salons to the after-hours sex clubs and private sadomasochistic billionaire dungeons? Are you ready for the late-night phone calls from wandering Latin tricks needing a place to release and crash? What about the calls asking for donations to community theaters and political organizations? Don't doubt for a second that the command hasn't come down from the highest echelons of the gay power elite. They want to egg you on with the promise of more sex, more grungy nights tied down on the bed of some jock fraternity, more parking-lot encounters with insatiable pizza boys, more trips to the Speedo-filled beaches of Spain. They will hold all that out like a carrot, a carrot of sodomy to drive you on and on until you, too, are conspiring to remake America into some socialist sex haven where no hole is left unviolated, no disgusting anti-Christian fantasy left unrealized. How the mothers will weep!

An Encyclopedia of Homosexual Drinking Establishments

- *Sports bars:* A famously dangerous place for the confused heterosexual, these businesses lure unsuspecting sports fans inside with wide-screen televisions and expensive cable channels. Upon closer inspection, one will notice that the patrons here are spending more time examining the tight buttocks of star players than the actual games themselves. Beware the friendly jock who invites you to reenact the high school drama of locker-room horseplay (in his mother's basement).

- *Businessmen's clubs:* Corporate execs in the market for a raunchy merger and acquisition call this place home, as do the business-minded young men who crave a firm hand and a monthly wardrobe allowance.

- *Leather bars:* You'll feel like you've traveled back in time when you enter these private enclaves of semen-soaked sawdust and masculine posturing. Night after night, beefy bikers and 1970s-style policemen role-play melodramatic plotlines stolen from old cop shows, always arriving at the same dangerous finale of bruises and tears in some forgotten alleyway.

- *Piano bars:* Velvet drapes, overpriced gin rickeys, and a former Broadway star in a bad toupee—the aura is so quickly overwhelming that you'll forget where the exit is! Here the greatest hope is that someday Nathan Lane will come stumbling through those doors to join the pianist in a rendition of Shirley Bassey's "Big Spender."

- *Twinkie bars:* Androgynous boys drowning in glitter and impossible hopes of celebrity dance before mirrors, doing their sad impressions of David Bowie. Is this really what Mother expected when she sent her boy off to Vassar?

- *Drag clubs:* Julia Roberts look-alikes lure lonely men from the street into these salacious saloons for nights that begin with cheap champagne and end in even cheaper motel rooms. That's what you get for complimenting a pretty "woman's" gold stilettos!

- *Gay discos:* Blinding lights and deafening music all but insures that most patrons will be numb by the end of the night. Add to that the bathroom drug bazaars and it's no wonder this crowd is unaware of the disgustingly pungent sweat they share as they writhe shirtless on the dance floor.

- *Latino bars:* With all the glamour of an INS processing center, the Latino bar is shockingly direct about its purpose on American soil. Sex, sex, and maybe a green card. Steer clear of these notoriously passionate, firm-bodied people, for they will throw you down on the floors of their inner-city apartments for encounters so shameful that even their elderly neighbors across the hall will blush.

- *"Bear and beer" bars:* So named because they exude that raw wilderness smell, "bears" are men who hunt others with an animal-kingdom intensity. If you show the slightest sign of fear or confusion in their presence, they will pounce on you with catty

Scissor Sisters lyrics or demands that you find genius in Sue Syl-vester's *Glee* antics. Best to stare them straight in the eye and back up slowly when confronted.

Now that we know the dwellings of these creatures of the drug-laced night, let us now take a look at each type of species mysteriously bred from the abnormal fornicators of the world.

THE MOANING MEN OF HOMOSEXUAL SPIRIT

Chanting within the most ancient corridors of human history is a voice that lisps with spine-breaking terror. In the most still hours of night, its eerie howl resonates through the landscape of Earth and Heaven, where it falls upon the ears of sleeping angels who lie para-lyzed by its nightmarish words of sin-stained shame.

The quilt sheets of America were sown in patriotic Puritanism, made to fit man in a snug yet comfortable fashion. But we find this ancient beast sees no difference between boxer, brief, and panty. To it, all is the same in the very end. The end justifies its means, and this monster will gladly rip through the toughest of fabrics to release its spewing desire.

Friends, we are talking about the most feared enemy of all, The Spirit of Homosexuality.

Beware the sneaking mist of gay desire, for it can furiously spew into your face from the most innocent of sources!

Through time and history, we have seen man and civilization crumbled by intestinal iniquities. Within the storied world of chivalry and class, there are countless parables of "merry men" who silently spooked within old Victorian homes, darning their socks in the si-lence of night and then emerging with the heart-stopping shock of an apparition: cold, chlamy hands helping themselves to the warm bosom of morality.

While many in society thought "A witch!" or "Demonry!" with

all the dead cats and missing children, little did they suspect the true Salem Witch was an Anal Wincing Warlock. Dogma warns that the fingers of homosexuality are crafty, pulling the puppet strings of reality to vilify the innocent in their play to attract man, woman, and child.

Liberal readers will balk, angrily burning our books and demanding librarians nationwide realize that gays do not have a perverted view of reality. Democrats will whine and demand their Sir Lancelots of lobbying anal legislation stand firm against these words of truth.

But be warned, America! Beware! The gay army is flanking morality. They are attacking us from the side and then sending their carnal cavalry from the rear. No front is safe from their wide-mouth attacks.

The mighty American military has already waved its white flag to the bearbacked barbarians. No longer can we walk safely in our streets, and the storehouse of modern democracy is forever corrupted under the Skittled banners of "homosexual equality".

Like General Custer, the moral man is being overrun by a feathered flamboyance of mounted warriors with face paint and pointy daggers of doom. At the tip of their spears and arrows sits a poisonous blend of pathogens that baffles the most learned of science. Where did it all go wrong for the Manifest Destiny of God's Democracy?

Standing colossal and scheming like their marble-chested Greek fathers, modern gays are directly connected to deceptively evil demons and ghostly spirits. Greek culture claimed democratic values like capitalism and monotheism, but let their little phallusophical minds wander with thoughts of firefly fisting deities. Where do you think the term fairy came from? It was used to describe their deep bond with black magic and devil worship.

From boy-drenched togas to fancy and fabulous sequined clothes, the gays use their demonic designing skills to embroider up destructive patchwork plots against God and America.

With their new leaders like Lady Gaga, The Muse of Homosexuality, and Hillary Clinton in place, the new gay male movement has started its new attack in full force.

The saying goes "Satan's greatest trick was convincing the world he didn't exist," and the same goes for homosexuality. Homo males are tricking the world into thinking they pose no threat to us. Using the same tactics as the dark lord himself, homosexuals are now being praised and exposed publicly to the world. There is no need for the wolf to wear wool.

Once upon a time, there existed a world where children could run about happy and homofree. Proper men and women always had pitchfork in one hand and a torchlight in the other, prepared to strike down any sassy wolf who dared show courage in presenting his true form.

Nowadays, however, the packs of gays are bold and brash. They wildly shake their manes and roar in delight, as their pride of loin lusters fiercely seeks out the most weak and innocent. Just like hungry jungle cats on the prowl, gays are wild and unpredictable.

Parents must beware, for the gays are swifter than a spotted cheetah. In unprecedented primacy, a gay in heat can fairyfoot himself across the plains of morality at blurring speeds of seventy miles per hour in their PT Cruisers. Even in the crowded urban streets of the third world, flan-licking floozies frolic around town hand in hand with businessmen and their little habenero hotties—a sick triumvirate of disease, prostitution, and adulterated spectacle.

The Homosexual Safari is full of spills and thrills, spectacles and abominations that curse in the face of God himself.

Deep within the most lush canopies of Quaalude-induced delights, herds of gays can be seen excitedly thrusting, romping, and groping about, trying to pull whatever loosened backsides they can into their ball of mammalian misery. Do not think these warnings are embellished and made only for the most distant jungles or impossibly diverse cities.

Gay men have two fists pushed deep into every town, media, and industry across the globe.

The golden calf of Baal showers gays with endless torrents of decadence, the Long Island ice teas of cosmo queens. God is red-faced with anger and he cries out to his sheep to help end this war of unnatural sexcapades. But, in these times it is hard to do God's work when you will be labeled a "homophobe" or "hateful." We don't see how being against a disease-spreading plague would make us the bad guys.

Even with the increasing acceptance of male-on-male erotica, gays still know they need to be sneaky little ninjas. They know if their true agenda is exposed, their blood pact with Satan will be broken.

This leaves gays faced with two options: Evolve with culture or make culture evolve into them.

Over the years, gays have broken off into different types, so they could blend in better with their surroundings. Just like any predator, they must be able to camouflage themselves in any environment, so their prey stays unaware of their presence.

With the help of liberals, gays have successfully set up two headquarters, one in sunny Palm Springs and one in San Francisco. Which should be of course no surprise that both are in the heathen state of California, the stink hole of America. With havens to call their own, the gays have been able to create new and different forms of the gay male species. These different forms allow the Gay Agenda to move in closer to the American home and destroy it one family at a time.

FORSAKEN SOLDIERS OF SODOM

LATIN LOVER

The border-jumping homo can be seen by night chowing down on Juan's jalapeno at your local salsa or reggaeton club and by day raking up your leaves. Maybe the most aggressive out of all the gay rainbow spectrum, this churro scarfing homophile is crafty. They get into the landscaping business to blend in with the less harmful Southern Latin

Mexicans, so they can learn the schedules of when Mom and Dad leave and come home. When they see that a child is home sick without any parental protection they will strike in a swift assassin fashion. Being able to blend in with any group of lawn choppers, this type of gay would never be able to be picked out of a lineup. It's hard when they all fit the description of short, light brown, shaved head, and poor.

BUTT BLOGGER

This fat, out-of-shape, whining wimp sits behind a computer all day spitting out homo venom on his celebrity or fashion blog. They promote viral brownie king videos, racism, pro-gay-marriage news clips, sapphic passion, makeup tips, and lies about how the world treats them. You will also find this angry class drawing poorly detailed penises on the faces of anti-gay and pro-life celebrity photos. Just like little dogs, these men are all bark and no bite. If confronted about their sexual digital entries, they will run and hide and yell hate crime, instead of standing up for what they supposedly believe in.

BFF

Mostly seen with the SLF (single large females), the BFF anal assassin will try to infiltrate and influence your wife by becoming the new best girlfriend. The BFF will fill your wife's head with delusions of a fantasy lifestyle of shopping, late-night club dancing, and threesomes with twentysomething black male models. Having a BFF walking around your home freely is just as scary as having an Allah Akbar–screaming suicide bomber looking to sacrifice himself in hopes of destroying your marriage and turning your wife into an overweight fag hag.

ALL BUSINESS

This suit-and-tie wearing corporate penile pooslinger masks himself within the working world. While not a very dangerous breed of homosexual, this male is not completely all business, no play. The CEO homosexual gets his kicks by making trips to the bathroom while other men are innocently releasing yellow body wash into a urinal and will slowly try and take a gander at their girth. They also spend company money on business trips to countries that openly have young-boy meat markets, to satisfy a gay's pedophile delight.

Just like any animal kingdom, the female species is the more vicious and aggressive of the sexes. The same goes for the homosexual kingdom. The female diesel dyke is burly and the more manly breed; she must be handled with caution.

BEWARE THE FISH-CAVE WORSHIPPER

Like cats, lesbians are always hissing and coughing out hairballs as they lap each other's milky sins and then prance around in coy defiance to natural order.

Across every continent, the cult of clitoral calamity has arisen in all species of people. From the once-proud Nordic tribes of Europe all the way to the sub-Saharans of Africa, we have seen women burned by the worst of muffled sins.

The historicity of lesbianism can actually be first seen in ancient Egyptian myth, where the false gods Horus and Set were having a syrup-wrangling match. A key component in Egyptian philosophy and lifestyle is animal mounting, as is the case for most African cultures.

As such, Set vied for world domination and, as we see in even today's Homogay Agenda, tried to achieve this end by complimenting "everyman" Horus's glowing gluteal musculature and then forcing himself within his body. Not savvy to gay libido, Horus soon found himself mounted by Set and the victim of a backside attack, the classic SN2 mechanism of ancient Egyptian atheist sciences.

Review the encyclopedia of history, for the story gets even more bizarre yet revealing. Not completely daunted by his situation, Horus tricked Set into thinking his inner thighs were his carnal cauldron. Set soon finished and walked off from the crime scene, in typical genetic black fashion. What he didn't know was that Horus was never truly mounted and washed away Set's shame in the cleansing Nile river.

The story ended with Horus being vindicated through a vengeful act of inseminated lettuce, but also from this story the lesbian cult was born. Women of ancient Egypt would drink of the Nile, saying it transformed them into the "Daughters of Set." Set is the Egyptian word for Satan, meaning these were the original whoredemons warned of in Revelations.

Peering through the draped windows of history, we see the tragic eye of lesbianism still stares deep into our culture. The dirty waters of the Nile still course with the blood of neo-lesbians suckling down ritual fishwater at Lilith Fair events. An unknown miscreant once said, "If you stare into the Abyss long enough, the Abyss stares back at you." Who would have known these words would have such relevancy to the new-age lesbians, the women converted by blackdaddy issues looking in the black holes of their lives for too long.

Friends, lesbianism comes down to one thing: attention. Any fishmonger you speak with will tell you she had a bad upbringing or was not popular in school (usually made up, so people will feel sorry for them). A small percent of women who choose to feast on caviar specials were abused by a homosexual child-crazy male or most likely a homosexual feminist female when they were younger. Most are just spoiled kids who want attention, so they try and do the most outrageous thing possible. They purposely embarrass their parents, lie about how they are treated and other made-up false situations they claim to have happened to them, but at the same time enjoy all this negative attention. This is why most leshomos try and have a rebel sassy antisocial attitude.

Clamdabblers come in many forms and we should point out each one so you can keep yourself informed and protected from these hairy bullet-wound-loving sinners.

THE TODGER DODGERS

HOUSE MOM LESBIAN

A lesbian who wants to pretend she is fit for motherhood and likes to play the part as a wholesome chatty Kathy. This one is very hard to identify, as they will pretend to act like every other mother on the block. Wear mom jeans, cover their milksacs, but are making an agenda of when the husbands leave for work and when they come home. You will see this type at soccer games, school events, community functions, but they never have children with them. What they are trying to do is make "friends" with other wives, so they will invite them over for coffee. When they are allowed in they will try and make passes at men's wives and try to pressure them into performing female-tongue-mouth-sex acts. If she doesn't get her way she will do one of two things: rape your wife and make her feel too ashamed to tell anyone, or say she is a hateful anti-gay person and make it look like the humble housewife did something wrong.

MODEL LESBIAN

This labia lover likes to stalk her prey in a different way. They will use their sassy hot looks, sinful dresses, and lipstick to entice a husband with devil brainwashing to have sex with them and then tell their wives about it.

Once the red-lipstick leshomo breaks the news to the housewife, she will use that woman's anger and tell her that they should get back at the husband by having sex. Women are easy to confuse and it's easy to make them do things that go against proper beliefs. The housewife will fall for this tactic, even knowing it is wrong. But her anger will take over and will allow the model lesbian to perform uvula-dipping acts on her that you would only see in a liberal-made porn. The lesbian doesn't have to worry about getting in trouble, as she has caused enough chaos to leave the crime scene unquestioned. Mission accomplished. Break up a family and get her kicks at the same time.

CHUNKY MAN HATER

The fat ones are always the loudest and the most needy. This leshomo blames her eating problems on the world. They hate men for not liking them, instead of thinking it might be due to their over-obese waistline. This type of fatso is always seen with another homo heifer, as no man would want to deal with their laziness, their morbid bodies, and their loud mouths. Chunky men haters don't see that the problem is them and their obesity. I doubt they would still like other fat women if they got off their rumps and walked a few miles and put down the Ho Hos. They also usually have tattoos of tigers and dolphins or some other animal or cartoon fantasy character on them. Funny how they are the size of large animals and like to tattoo themselves with large animals.

LESBRO

This is a lesbian who follows similar characteristics as a chunky man hater. They want to be just like men so much, that is why they try and do everything men do. They know they will never get married to a proper male, due to their grotesque appearance, so they try to be one of the bros. The lesbro is usually overweight, dates other overweight swamp-cave lovers, and always tries to talk in a deep voice. If they "love" women so much, why do they spend 90 percent of their time trying to be sweaty with other men? This doesn't make any math. The lesbros are so in awe with men, that 65 percent of them have sex-change operations.

GOD'S PUNISHMENT FOR HOMOSEXUALITY

In the time of ancient, God was forced to flood the earth. It was infested with a vermin, a tap-dancing rodent who could not resist gnawing wood and leaving pellet-stained floors of infestation in the lives and homes of normal people.

Angry and retching, God grabbed the hose of extermination to wipe out the homosexual menace. For forty days and nights, the Earth was cleansed and yet, even with the mighty holy water of God himself, we see our world is still tainted with the lingering curries of pervert pies.

Undaunted by the fate of their hamster-stuffing forefathers, the gays continue to march in defiance of God. They proudly wave their rainbow standards as they gallop into society, treading upon the will of our Christian nation.

Make no mistake, the wrath of God is slow to brew, but when it spills over, it explodes with the catastrophic fury of a clogged catheter.

It is all sick and perverted, because it refers to gays! Get it straight, humanity. There is a storm out on the ocean and it is moving your way. If your soul is not anchored in Jesus, you shall all drift away!

Take heed, sinful sodomite enablers. God will not forsake his word. He shall not use the gentle suffocation of endless salty seawaters. This time, there is a new wrath brewing. One that will tan even the hide of Satan himself. Beware, America, for the year 2012 comes and as the wicked Nostradamus had whispered to him by Satan, there is a fiery meteorite being knuckleballed right into the face of every gay-enabling land of Earth.

SOLAR TSUNAMI OF 2012, GAYS TO BLAME

The forecasting power of prayer reveals that in 2012, auroras will manifest in the night sky, a cosmic reminder of how small we are to the will of God. The Bible says no to gay marriage and fornication, yet we have not made being gay illegal. We allow them to continue to push for "rights" while God patiently waits in heaven above.

Cameras on board NASA's Solar Dynamics Observatory have already recorded massive eruptions and explosions on the Sun's surface, caused by God. These explosions have hurled mega-tons of plasma—charged gas—straight at Earth. By this point we all know who is shooting that plasma right at us, and who is responsible for Him doing so.

The event is called a coronal mass ejection, and hopefully the gays know that when they use their ejectioned Satan scepters to dally each other's backsides, they are just setting the stage to be burned in the hot fires of hell for all time where their entire intestsins will be shot up with ejected plasma from the sun and it will sear, burn, and torture for all time!

Even after all of these examples of God flexing his power to scare us and make us take notice of his will, gays remain resilient little pests and keep reveling in their little defiant orgies of sulphur-scented sins.

It is written, that when the damnation of mankind draws nigh, we shall find the most sultry of Satan's terrifying snow bunnies hopping in unbridled contempt, no longer scared of being hunted down by God's shotguns of final judgment.

We shall find that like every other cult, Satan has branded his cattle. Homosexuals shall be tramp-stamped with the mark of the beast, the endless sign of giving one's mind to the dark side.

In the times of ancient, the most branded homosexuals of academic swagger erected a giant shrine to their sins: they called it the Tower of Babel. Gays planned to poleclimb its greatest heights, then parade their foul scents all through the streets of Heaven.

Greatly angered, God threw a great tantrum of comets and ice storms upon the gay constructors. Their tower crumbled and their agenda was dead.

But gays are persistent in pantsed protrusions and savvy of craft. Undaunted by the failures of their forefathers, the new-age gay has once again submitted himself unto a new god, one who wields a stamp so powerful, it can CAPTCHA a soul in an endless cycle of illegible frustration, an e-purgatory crafted by man himself.

The gays are desperately trying to outsmart God, and believe it or not, they have teamed with science as their seminal mistress.

THE ONLINE HOMOSEXUAL MOVEMENT

The Internet is a new tool used by gay terrorists to electronically infect mass population with their vile stenches. The ability to send ten thousand megabits of digital destruction at the click of a button gives any gay man tighter pants.

Behind this movement's rear, lurks a corrupt and dedicated leader. No, not Perez Hilton. The man goes by the name of "Joe My God," the anal admiral of the new online homosexual movement, with his legion of seafaring drifters surfing the seas of the Internet, looking for anyone they can unload their cream-filled gay propaganda on.

You can hear these men charging in unison toward your computer screen as they hold their rainbow battle colors high, while singing their war song, "Born this Way" by Lady Gaga. This is the same woman who wants your children to wear a fragrance that has the smell of blood and semen combined.

Joe is one of those fearsome "leather daddy" types of gays, who is obsessed with pumping things at the gym and holding Village People–style parties in his exclusive and meticulous Manhattan loft. These events are frequently raided by the police, yet the infamy has only made Master Joe more famous and politically active in the vicious circles of homosexual New York. He truly epitomizes how the same-sex addicts are destroying the original Constitutionally Christian and heterosexual intent of "freedom of expression" and "freedom of speech" with his licentious and testosterone-spurting blog.

Joe My God is homosexuality's archangel, who dares follow the path of Satan in trying to corrupt the kingdom of God and nature. With gleaming dildo in one hand and bear trap in the other, the homosexual legions are furiously clicking away with their new weapon of choice: The Blogosphere.

Marching along the high-speed Internet with smug looks of snobbery, Joe and his band of ass bandits scour the world trying to find things they can complain about or turn gay, calling anyone who disagrees with them "homophobic" or "closed minded." He and his cronies are notorious for labeling good Christian Republicans as hate mongers and baby killers, planting bogus stories of sex scandals involving right-wing-minded people, just for their own jolly kicks.

Ever since this man has been commanding devil tricker, the amount of gay-related content on the web has increased by a whopping 39 percent and have increased by 15 percent of gay Internet users. This is obviously a growing threat to America and its high-speed information highway.

This backdoor crusader has also been nominated for many online web awards and is nipping at the heels of becoming America's biggest threat for gay integration. The poster boy of the new-aged, tech-savvy, gay online movement needs to have his modem subscription turned off. Each micro-bit that is allowed to be uploaded is one more child at risk of becoming gay.

This man has been allowed to gather his troops and stock up with blog-entry bullets for seven years now and grows stronger and hungrier every day. If we allow this to continue, there will be no way to stop this Goliath of gay, this Sultan of Scat, from swinging his sword of impurity directly into the innocent heart of the modern culture.

It is apparent that to stop the vicious agenda of the gays, we need to cut off their life support. We need to stop them from being able to use our own technology against us. It doesn't just stop with the Internet, my friends; gays are using many forms of technology to grow their stronghold. Destroying anything that promotes normal hetero sex and trying to extinct any traces of our once-great nation as being a civilized non-sodomy empire.

Do you want future history books to depict the past as being a world of preying-eyed, alternative-lifestyle-choosing, hairy-chested pedophiles and non-makeup-wearing anti-homemakers? We think not.

CHAPTER 3

Glistening Red Sun of Technological Damnation

GENESIS 3:1
"Now the serpent was more crafty than any other beast of the field that the Lord God had made."

INTRODUCTION

In the days of old, every child knew to beware the shadowy man in salmon-pink pantaloons, eagerly offering him a plate of teen-time dream bars with a seductive side of lemon meltaways.

Kids were trained to know those were all coded homosexual words for golden water sports and a belly full of vanilla pixie butter. Dismayed, classic gays rallied and continued their pink pyramid schemes to stack themselves atop the children, but their successes in abduction were failing. By virtue of Jiminy Cricket after-school specials, our precious plums learned an important aspect of the gay: it is predatory, like a hungry jungle cat.

And like cats in heat, gays will always eventually arch their backs and expose themselves, showing their true desire to hunt innocence to the point of extinction.

With the kids of Reagan's eighties fully educated about the stranger dangers of homosexuality, throngs of gays mewed and hissed in anger, starving for a hearty taste of their favorite elementary pudding packs. Crafty and wily by their feline nature, gays quickly adapted a new way to prowl the alleyways of America's school yards by way of modern-day technology.

As with our little furry ferret stuffers, we now find technology is being sexual-backdoor-abused by all the devilish masses. It is a global pandemic of moral blaxploitation. Its rapid growth and girth has birthed some of today's greatest creations, but the heartless left and its agenda have turned communication technology into a Frankenstein of oil-jocked sleaze and musky-perfumed disgrace.

The first sign that modern technology was going down the chocolate sin drain was in 2005 with the birth of Myspace. This new type of unsocial networking was created by Chinese programmers to compete with the Harvard-campus-created site ConnectU.

Using Chinese technology, Myspace became one of the most popular websites in America and added life back to web real estate after the "dot bomb" era. But knowing it couldn't grow if people knew slant-eyed Communism was behind it, they hired a man who went by the code name "Myspace Mark" to be the American poster boy for the company.

After dubbing this "Mark" as the founder of Myspace and now having a soft collegiate face for their marketing, Myspace grew almost overnight, making up 46 percent of the Internet's traffic requests. Myspace seemed unstoppable.

The original "social network" was a hub for fourteen-year-old kids to post vintage-style photos of themselves to share with friends. These images are directly to blame for the influx of Internet child porn and video nasties. Kids would capture

Evil Myspace.

images of themselves in the mirror while they posed in sexy catwalk manner, while duck puckering their lips glossed in black-color cherry lipstick.

With so many images of young children in one spot, Myspace became a quick hotspot for gay perverts to gander and gawk at a library of half-naked kiddies while they juggle their lemon date balls. Studies show that 58 percent of Myspace's traffic was from twenty-five to sixty-five-year-old male demographic and most of those browsers weren't even Myspace users. As research shows, for every one gay four children are at risk of being abducted and dillied.

The butt hunters were also able to self-sex themselves while reading the blog entries of each child user. Each entry was almost like a digital diary, where kids would write about the parties they went to over the weekend and would embed them with uploaded Polaroid photos. Not only were the gays able to view this new type of kiddy capers, they were now allowed to turn these blogs into their own type of prepubescent steamy sex novels.

This website not only allowed pedogays to get their digi kicks from the safety of their homes, but also exposed children to Chinese terrorist programming. Myspace allowed kids to learn the basic Chinese programming code called HTML, which stands for "Hiroshima Terrorist Marxist Language."

With every fifteen-year-old boy and girl now being able to create quick short codes of communistic technology, they were free to start spamming the world with images of their favorite emo band or random photos bordered in black with witty captions underneath them. Little did they know, they were spreading a virus within their free hosted images that allowed Chinese hackers to peek inside American Internet space.

The Chinese would have been able to complete their mission of Internet domination, but due to the back door they left open, the gays ruined any chances for the quest of a red America.

With its quick decline due to its homosexual-predator nature, Myspace tried to scramble to change its moxie. In 2007 it was too late as in the

Chinese Myspace hacker.

distance lurked another social network, with more features, more silly images, a more American-pie-faced founder, and the ability to "poke" other users. Myspace's end was near.

Facemash was a new and cool shiny social network that was first only exclusive to college students on the East Coast. It was almost like a secret cool club that only Ivy League rich kids could be a part of.

This frat house of exclusivity was developed by a Jewish Harvard freshman named Tom Zuckerberg. Zuckerberg developed Facemash from stolen code in hopes to make his ex-girlfriend jealous. Tom's dream was that he would get so popular and would have so much sex with other girls, that his ex would feel like she made a mistake by dumping him for the row team's captain.

The new social network allowed college students to live chat and just like Myspace, allowed students to send electronic mail and post semi-interesting comments on each other's profiles. Facemash's biggest feature was the ability to allow users to "poke" one another; we still don't understand what this poking was meant to be used for, but most likely it had to involve some sort of hacker talk for sex.

As its popularity gained, so did the shenanigans it was causing on college campuses nationwide. In its first year of existence college gropings went up 14 percent and binge drinking among students increased 45 percent. With so much chaos caused by Zuckerberg's new website, the embattled Harvard admissions office was forced to kick him off campus in hopes to bring back order to the school.

Now with no place to go, Zuckerberg moved to California and bunked up with his high school friend Shawn Fanning, who was also the creator of the porn piracy program Napster. Fanning allowed Tom to move his Facemash site over to his computer servers, but said he had to change the name so it would look fresh and not have the bad press of Tom being kicked out of Harvard tainted all over it.

While thinking of a name, Zuckerberg remembered that his high school yearbook was called "The Facebook" and just like the site's code, he stole the name and branded his social network "Facebook."

FACEBOOK, THE NEW HIPSTER HOTBED OF SWINGING POLYGAMY AND MOONLIT ABDUCTIONS

For those not in the know, Facebook is a lion's den of cleaned bones and carnage, picked apart by vultures who masquerade as friends and only stand to violently bludgeon the life of you, your friends, and your family.

The little piddles you hear from your son or daughter's room late at night—it could be a Peeky Tom or Luring Lisa, typing away secret chats or pokes to your kids and baiting them to sneak outside their bedroom windows and down long, dusty roads to abduction and terror.

Your girlfriend or wife's gentle giggles as she clicks away on the computer: it could be her old high school sweetheart, silently in-boxing her pictures of his thingy that he has Sharpied her name upon.

Those addicted to the hidden Facebook life will violently deny these facts, claiming the social network site is not responsible for woes such as addiction, chlamydia, adultery, abduction, and ass Democrat ad paraphernalia being used as propaganda for the malleable college mind. It is important to double-pat a Facebook addict on the back, and then let them know "Friend, the first step is denial."

During the Middle Ages, there was the Bubonic plague. In the early 1900s, the Spanish flu. The new viral threat to humanity of this era is Facebook, the destroyer of nations and assassin of home stability.

It is sick to know that any of Earth's seven billion people can ferret out any person they want on Facebook. Your entire life is plastered on the site for everyone to see, all aside from secret pokes and in-box chat messages.

What a feast for shadowy strangers and Satan! New studies reveal that children younger than three and four use the Internet, many of them savvy enough to have a Facebook account by age eight. Imagine, 7 billion people on Earth can hop onto a home computer and search a child down via web camera?

Facebook is no better than a wild safari, where all the animals in the jungle are hungry and you soak the innocence of home-schooled children, wives, girlfriends, and job-seekers in the sweetest honey-marinated Crisco, then throw them out into the frying Serengeti. The smell of fresh users will waft into the nose of every type of predator, and for those who are not prey they will find themselves in the vice grips of dopamine-addled addiction.

CHEATING/DIVORCE RATES

If you find your spouse is stealing away from bed late at night and then furiously clicking away at the computer, their ex-boyfriend or girlfriend from years ago has probably "friended" them and is trying to set up a secret meeting to "reunite" over dinner at a hidden hotel.

As you read this harrowing revelation, your significant other is likely on a computer. If so, perform this quick experiment. Using great stealth, silently walk near to where your S.O. is browsing the computer online world. Make a motion as if to peer over his or her shoulder, much as a strict proctor will do during a testing session.

Then yell out, "Hey, honey, what are you up to!" Odds are, they will furiously click their keys and try to shut windows, or nervously laugh as they shut down their laptop screen. Congratulations, you have just caught a Facebook Cheater and should get tested for herpes AIDs.

As you can see, the data indicate that the divorce rate in America is exponentially increasing.

According to various sources, Facebook initially launched in 2007, in the month of February. What a perfect month for debauchery, cold-child snatches, and betrayal for all the relationship criminals out there.

Our data show that you are not alone in being cheated upon. Nearly 20 percent of all divorces in America are because of Facebook. College men: your girlfriend is 93 percent likely cheating on you, with a 95 percent level of statistical significance (+/− 2 s.d.). The stats are similar for college-aged women in a proper hetero relationship.

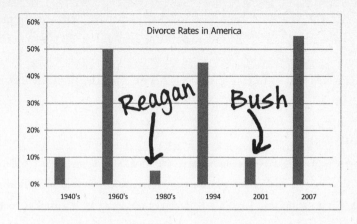

Gays are naturally deviant so no statistics are needed to know they use Facebook for backbent betrayals.

In the whirl of all of this mess, we see a sprawling increase of disease and bitter breakups. On the "Friend Wall" of Facebook ac-

Chat log of a cheating wife on Facebook.

counts worldwide are soap-opera tales of triple love-"poke" triangles and women finding their husbands drunk in a rhombus of oil-tainted loins at a secret gay club. These are all the horrors Facebook has made possible by interconnecting the degenerate with the typically moral, all at the click of a button.

FARMVILLE

In today's dark times, less people are A to J. No longer is it "coolio" or "hip" to be addicted to good things in life, such as Bible study or a redeeming hobby. Liberals balk and laugh at the notion of being Addicted to Jesus, though a hit of Christwire in one's life will lead to eternal salvation.

There is another type of "hit" being peddled by web techlords and it is Internet traffic. It is the new currency of e-drugs. One of the most addictive vices Facebook techies have created is *Farmville*, a dizzying game of burly mountain men, crack-eyed animals, and relentless "quests" to get more and more gifts.

Farmville is socialist by design. One cannot grow one's farms without "sharing" goods by inviting unknown friends and neighbors. This is all the equivalent to going to Wally-Mart, slapping the butt of the unknown person in front of you in line, and then asking if they would like to come over to help cook dinner.

It doesn't make sense, but put in the framework of game and competition, it is addictive. What if for every Wally butt-slap, you were given a free can of beans or promises of a new wife or lawn equipment. There is always the promise of more gifts, for the more agrarian work one does on the game.

To the astute mind, it would seem that this is a big conspiracy between Facebook and China. Could *Farmville* Americans be forced into the renowned Reward-Benefit Addiction Cycle, the very technique described by Worzheimen in deep Vietcong brainwashing prisons? Is it rice-field preparatory work for the post-Obama Chinese overlords? The startling answer is yes and the proof frightening enough to shake the most stoic, bitterly brave vet who served this nation with endless honor.

SEX GANGS

As Facebook has flourished over the years, Christian families have struggled to keep up. The number of homosexual, radical Socialist, and drug-related groups on this Internet service are impossible to quantify. Faith groups like Focus on the Family have created comprehensive guides to stopping the online obsession of America's teens. Many great parental monitoring software programs have been invented. Progress has indeed been made. Yet children, suffering from peer pressure and angry rebellion, continue to clamor for more time with their computers, and inevitably that means time away from the concerned oversight of parents.

In London, reports of sex gangs using Facebook to target innocent teens have made headlines and resulted in calls for governmental censorship. A mix of European and Arab

Evil Facebook ad promoting a Putin fan club.

men have been "friending" young people in a scheme to turn them to drugs and prostitution. These types lust for the simplicity and naiveté of a blossoming soul, for it is something they have long lost in their pursuit of violence and Allah's grand kingdom. The site has violated countless lives, destroying the precious sense of decency so necessary for modern decorum. As this reckless Internet site inevitably collude, the danger our young face is potentially catastrophic.

All a digital gangbanger needs is one risque photograph (found easily enough in any profile) and the name of the school a girl attends. With that information he can threaten to send the nude photo to all the girl's classmates unless she succumbs to his vile demands. This is a common tactic used by Communist agents who taunt homosexuals with exposure unless they become spies against their home countries. It is one of the many reasons that gays are recognized as a security risk in the war against terror and radical Socialism.

A forthcoming report in *Shape* magazine reveals that young people on Facebook are far more likely to quickly engage in sexual activities, including sodomy, with someone they have just met. Other risque social sites are also to blame. Names like Foursquare and Reddit.com come to mind when one thinks of dangerous liaisons.

Are we on the brink of another nationwide teen sex crisis? Only time will tell, but the warning signs are evident. The rampant hardcore sexuality is dripping on every page you click to these days. Children delight in exposing their serene, smooth bodies to every man they encounter. These are kids so burdened with hormones and a desire to fit in, they will do just about anything to get your attention. This trend hasn't escaped the greedy eyes of pedophiles, either. No longer are they prowling parks and public toilets. They're logging on and getting off. It's a horrific thought to imagine: our most beautiful children getting acquainted with old perverts living in grungy basements, nothing but a stained blanket and their deepest desires to comfort them as they send out cloying messages of eerie fetishism and Socialist depravity.

eSTRANGER DANGERS

Dress a girl child in a bubble-gum-pink dress and take her to Central Park, New York, at 1 A.M. Wave good-bye from the subway station as you yell from your megaphone, "Fresh meat! Fresh meat! Come get five-second fresh bubble-gum-hinted meat!"

From the shadows will emerge wolves even scarier than the Team Jacob monsters, and you would not want to see the final result of the thriller child wolf attack. No twice-drunk Tarantino could write a script more gory and horrifying, so why on Earth are parents allowing their children and wives to be left alone on Facebook?

Common sense dictates that no person will leave a child alone in Central Park. There are thousands of things that can go wrong and all of them involve an evil stranger, the enemy of every after-school special and bogeyman of late-night parenting parables told to children in moral, safe homes across this country.

Every family must fear strangers like Mexicans fear *la migra.* When the name is mentioned your children should run at *arriba, arriba* speeds and leave behind a trail of fast-footed dust, screaming higher than a siren in a prowling black crack-drug alley.

Now, with this knowledge, what sort of sick person would allow a child to be left in a secret pit full of 7 billion anonymous strangers? Facebook allows users to post their hair color, eye color, height, age, and school. It is a buffet of exotic cuisines for homosexuals and strangers, our children on virtual display to satiate their must-lusting palette.

All it takes is a simple search, a poke and then an in-box request to "let's play e-dildo remotes at 7pm lol" or even scarier "a/s/l." It is all a segue to confused late-night webcam sessions and exposed thigh flesh, all used for the stranger's delight or a further agenda of manipulation, penetration, and desolation of everything right and moral.

The fact is simple, Facebook is a dangerous website. Your mind has now witnessed how this site is allowing strangers to lure sweet and innocent high school daughters and is causing workplace trouble.

Monster swaddles of homosexuals are using Facebook to bait children and then snag them with their master dingle and if that doesn't work, entice them to send indecent pictures so they can Satanbate their Satan scepters, if you catch our drift. As if it was not all bad enough, Facebook divorces one out of five marriages and prods the confused children with phallic pokes and game addictions.

If you need to take a break to go to your child's room right now to see if he or she is being poked by a stranger, please feel free to run and do so now.

If you go to "Facebook.com" on your child's computer, it will probably automatically log you in. There are advanced techniques to trap and cancel the account, and even when your child comes home from college, it is highly suggested you break their Iron Curtain of security by using our "How to Hack Your Child's Facebook" tips on the side of this page. Remember, college children are emotional and when they naturally cry about this, tell them they will shut their mouths or they will not get tuition money next semester.

How to Hack Your Child's Facebook

Journals and Diaries

Go into your child's room and find their journal or diary and flip through it to see if they have any nonsense words scribbled inside. Sometimes a child will use an off-the-wall keyword as their password and there is a 60 percent chance that it is within their book of secrets.

Remember, this is not invasion of privacy as your house is not theirs.

Name and Date Game

Does your child have a boyfriend or a girlfriend? If so, try entering the name of their teenage sweetheart along with the last two digits of the year they were born. If you don't know the year, then call their parents and ask for it.

Also, if your child does have a boyfriend or girl-friend, you are giving them the okay to become teen-age parents, by engaging in premarital sex. Last thing you want is to turn your daughter's baby hole into a devil flesh wrap or your son's twiddle rompus into a Satan scepter. If they commit this sin, then you are just as guilty in God's eyes.

Hacker Programs

If the first two options aren't effective, then try down-loading a hacker program called a "key-logger." You can easily find this by Googling "record my child's passwords" and downloading the software provided by the link.

The key-logger records all keystrokes from your child's computer and this is a guaranteed way to ac-cess their digital compound of sin.

With Facebook's crippling effect on American family and life-style, it quickly caught the attention of the dreadfully cold Soviet Federation. Heartless in gaze and chilling in action, Communist Czar Vladimir Putin threw the Russian red economy behind Face-book marketing and economic schema. The USSR now has a secret "Socialist network" weapon in every American home and classroom, deadlier than a death nuclear arsenal.

Radiating power and annihilation with Soviet funding behind it, Facebook immediately grew to the tens of millions by 2009 and in

2010 was noted to have over 500 million users. The ultimate sign that the site had reached phenomenal heights was when its climb to fame was turned into a Hollywood blockbuster movie.

With great technology comes extreme dangers. Like Mr. Zuckerberg's ancestors, we fell victim to an evil menace who used technology to enslave an entire continent. Hitler was able to use military technology developed by the Russians to successfully invade his neighboring countries.

Hitler knew that technology was the key to world domination and world domination is the ultimate goal of the left-wing whore machine. They have taken over our TV stations, trying to impose Communist law upon our conservative radio voices, crucify our freedom fighters like Sarah Palin, and implement net neutrality, so they can control the web space.

And just like the funny-mustached dictator, the left wants to use technology to place the American family into concentration camps and use their acid baths to remove any type of true morals for each non-follower. Their wish is to starve the world of much-needed Godly nutrition and once our souls have been darkened, they will bury our bodies in shallow graves.

With the gay community as their pink-uniformed SS, the liberal death march plans to turn our devices against us in their final solution for America.

TECHNOLOGY: THE SILENT GAY KILLER

Of course it should be no surprise that our bottoms-up boys are using technology as a new flank against the American home.

The gay community knows how to evolve with modern-day changes and they also have the ability to morph technological advances into new terrorist tools. With the birth of the Internet we now see the birth of vicious campaigns to manipulate your digital surfers into the dark and lonely lifestyle of homosexuality.

The gays are a mean, perverted lot who want everyone to think they are normal. They claim they only like rogering each other, but just like the nasty predatory monsters they are, they love little prey. What prey is tinier than your innocent children?

Gays tend to be sassy and crafty, making them twice as dangerous! They sit around in their little easy secretary and nursing jobs thinking of new ways to subdue children and then have their way roasting their rumps with sin!

It should not be shocking to learn that the gays are moving onto the online and tech world. There is no easier way to attack, when their prey is tangling itself within the web of its stalker.

Technology is the ass cowboy's new BFF and together they are baking up magnificent recipes to food-poison the world with. Skipping down the streets of suburbia the gay and technology are hand in hand, peeking into each unsuspecting household and diluting them with temptations of carnal pleasures. No man, woman, or child is safe while this vermin has its grisly death grip on today's technology.

EXAMPLES OF TECHNOLOGICAL GAYNESS

It is bad enough homosexuals have their hands in our children's pockets, but now they have slid their hands in our homes by the way of technology. Eighty-seven percent of American homes have modem-connected Internet; also, the average American family owns three to five electronic devices and the fairy skippers are on to this.

Filling the world with Internet homo-core porn and enticing sexual electronic devices, the gay movement is spearheading its cause with dangerous marching lines directly into your home. At the click of a mouse or the flick of a power button, the conservative family is bum rushed with an army of galloping Gestapos riding their magical unicorns, looking to pierce the sewer tunnel of any rear they can invade.

HOMOGAY AGENDA USES SUBLIMINAL CAPTCHAS TO TURN CHILDREN GAY

A devious and fiendish little piece of technology has been uncovered that homogays have developed on their little "MAC" (Men Attack Children) Sin Machines. It is called CAPTCHA, which stands for Creepy Anal Predators Teaching Children Homo Agenda.

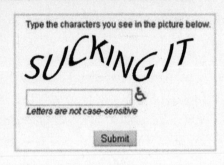

You may have seen these when you want to post comments on sites or when creating a new Internet account for a social networking site, but lately we've noticed on MAC and Gay Agenda–created sites, that their CAPTCHAs are using subliminal words to turn your children into Satan-scepter sewer-tunnel lovers.

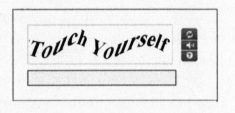

Just like the blacks using eight-bit music to brainwash white children, these fecal-feasting Dorothys are using technology to entice our youth to sin.

Some gay CAPTCHAs are very hard to pick out if they have a subliminal sexual meaning and others are flat-out blatant.

Each CAPTCHA is used in hopes that if the child gets used to typing words like "Penis" or "Anal Sex", it will become a part of their day-to-day vocabulary.

For every gay CAPTCHA completed by a child, a seed of homosexuality is planted into their brains.

SUGARPLUM DANCING VIDEO GAMES

The most popular games that children play are not first-person killers and surprisingly not fictional fiery sorcery games. The hot item for the past few years has been dancing games.

These games are created to teach your daughter or son the latest disco tech dance moves while blasting techno pop, as they learn the rhythm of gayhood. Watching a child play this game would give an instant feeling of shock and awe. There is nothing cute about watching a young girl move her hips like a two dollar whore at the local nude-breast bar while she lip-synchs the words of immoral music. It is even scarier to watch young Billy or Timmy spinning like fabulous gay tornadoes.

Obviously this is the goal of the Homogay Agenda, teach our children forbidden dance moves to entice them to frequent local leather disco bars. It is just like how the pot is the gateway drug to heroin and other hard drugs, virtual dancing is the brown gateway drug to unprotected orgy club parties.

You will also see that these games have been adopted by local schools for use in their P.E. programs. The gays' mouths salivate with glittery rainbow dust knowing this. Yes, it might be a great way for kids to not become slobby mini Michael Moores, but obesity and liberalism can be fixed easier than the homosexual urge.

CRAIG FERGUSON'S SIDEKICK

It's sad when a grown man is forced to promote sin docking between two men as a form of humor, so a network can gain ratings from the fish-cave-to-fish-cave worshippers and the San Fagsico iGay generation. The network thought it would be funny to use a talking bony skeleton (bones and we know that the gay men love bones) to brainwash gay agenda in the form of humor. They have even forced him to act sissy in a few of his open acts and skits.

The robot's first name is Geoff and spelled like a gay man would spell "Jeff" and notice it has the word "off" in it and his last name has the word "Peter" in it, which is a word that gays use for twiddle rompus. So the secret gay message is "Off Peter" which translates into "Sin tug another man's penis, until it produces liquid DNA."

Even when Craig introduced ABC's (Always Been Commie) new Gay Agenda robot they made him do a homoerotic song and dance, that includes Communist Asian strippers, a fat black man and a sin-hole-loving, homo hobbit biker. The catchphrase in the song was "The Monster Is Coming." Just another example of pure subliminal filth!

iTABLET

Like most gay-supporting Apple products, the iTablet is something that should be avoided. Apple is a very questionable company that promotes questionable "faggy" behavior in college and is not moral.

This device isolates children from their parents and allows adult pedophiles direct access to our young ones' intimate lives. They spread pornography like a disease, destroying marriages and tempting young men into sexual experimentation. Apple's new iTablet threatens to make this situation entirely worse. Yes, it is a cumbersome and slow product with an ugly design that most adults will find akin to a German coffee machine. Yes, its fiscally irresponsible for a public company to produce something so ridiculous as a keyboard-less computer. But the new era of private and portable "Tablet" computing is upon us and Apple has a long record of redefining reality.

No longer will a parent be able to simply look in the computer room to make sure their son or daughter is only surfing Christian-friendly websites; now a child can sneak their new toy of destruction right into their room. While safe under their covers they are now free to explore the vast void of pornography and be bombarded with pop-ups about gay cruises and rainbow-colored street parades.

Portability is key. The anus lovers know they can't follow their prey throughout the day, so they created the perfect tracking device so they could be next to your child, holding her hand at school, church group, or at an ice cream party.

If you look deeper into their diary you will see that children aren't the only victims of this new growth of gay movement, but so is the common Anglo-housewife. And not only are the architects raging homosexuals, but a dark evil that lurks in the dark corners of crack infested ghettos.

GAYS INVENT NEW WII SEX TOY, SO BLACKS CAN HAVE VIRTUAL SEX WITH WHITE WOMEN

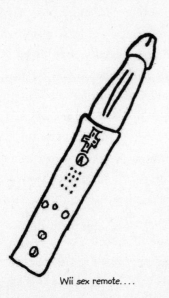

Wii sex remote. . . .

Two forces have come together to take their sexual life styles to a whole new level. One side likes inserting their Satan scepters into other men's sewer holes and the other likes to brainwash young white youth with eight-bit music and turn your lady homemakers into "ho" makers. The two have combined forces to virtual-sneak into your house and violate your American wife while you are hard at work trying to get by, while Obama steals your health care plan.

We present to you the WiiRape toy by Ninjatendo! Now I know you're asking yourself, "Why would these two groups need to join forces to create this? I know the African American community is not fond of the gays." Well, we have an easy answer. The Afro-Saxon community is not very good at building electronics or handling money, so they asked the Homogay Agenda to develop the product for them. Also, gays have a lot of money saved up because they work as bartenders or florists and collect gay welfare at the same time. In return, the Afro-Saxons would make sure that each item that is sold comes with a list of children in the buyer's neighborhood. Now what *Ellen*-marriage believer wouldn't want that? A whole list of fresh meat to prey on?

So now that this product is in "A Store Near You!" rappers can use the hipped-hopped music they play on Bravo or TLC to brainwash your wives and tell them to go to the nearest Circuit City and purchase the new Wii "Toy" with, of course, your hard-earned cash. The item comes with a free game disgusted as an opera CD, so that for sure a real male would never bother checking it out. What it really is, is a dating game that displays images of large black twiddle rompuses. Your wife can browse through categories like "Balla," "Big Playa," "Deez Nutz," and other hipped-hopped lyrical terms. After she picks what type she wishes to "play" with, a video screen appears where your wife can be swindled by Satan-like sexy speak. Once your wife has been put into a trance, she will be asked to plug in the new Wiimote and on the other end the predator will be able to control the speed and has electric tips so the women's fish cave can be shocked. We think this is what is referred to as "The Shocker" in liberal collegiate vernacular.

Now, you may ask "Where is little Billy, while mom is playing sin games?" Well, he is alone and looking for attention, which is what a homopedo predator looks for in a victim, before he plays twinkie stick rape games.

Ninjatendo should be ashamed for such vile inventions. What is next? The Lesbian Lick controller? Or the Rainbow Butt Heckler attachment? We should call for a recall on all Ninjatendo products before your wife and children are victims of hate crimes.

In the same cesspool swim the liberal media, they and the gays live in coexistence, plotting and planning ways to extract morals and values out of the American household. Crawling out of the pond of primordial Communism, they too follow the same rules of war by the Homogay Agenda. And just like their loose-bowel-muscled buddies, the liberal agenda has outfitted technology to their newly polished propaganda Hybrid.

THE AXIS OF EVIL, ONLINE

Those who dare tread upon the endless highways of the Internet, beware!

You're all sinners in the hands of an angry God, a spider dangling over the burning flames of hell and only protected by one silk thread. God has scissors ready and hates those who spin webs of sin

What web could be more mangled, tangled, and filled with the goostuff of Spider-Man homosexual lifestyles, under-aged drinking, adultery, and the explosions of chaotic terror mung rings than the modern Internet?

Site after site, we see the worst of humanity: college kids are using Dell computers to fornicate with Lady Communism, by download-ing her virus-laden music on infected "Napster" and "Kazaa," then spreading the sick tunes faster than a vajazzled girl can cry out "I'm drunk, enter me!" to each and every passing innocent fraternity boy.

Disease and damnation! Do not pretend you have not heard these horror stories!

Facebook chlamydia and cyber adultery, the divorce rates and statistics do not lie. Bands are losing economic revenue and promi-nence, because the Internet is becoming more Socialist in nature.

The Chinese steal movies from Big Hollywood, while using a reverse-transcription technique to turn a profit and further break America's financial backbone!

Over 40 percent of the Internet is owned and operated by terrorists, anime pervert Asians, or homosexuals. It is no wonder people have forgotten a true adage: The road to homosexuality is lined with the most damaging potholes, so steer clear or burn and then sear! It applies to everything that is anti-America's God and the Internet is a virtual hell on Earth.

Beneath the breeding ground of Facebook's Socialist network, spreads a seedier grade of dank Internet sites. These sites sprawl in secrecy and are testament to vodka-chugging Socialism, the very backbone of the Pelosi spend-happys and the product of late-night Poughkeepsie speakeasies.

Blessed Senator Joseph McCarthy warned a greater red tide of poison was coming for America, and this is it. This new left-wing, on-line movement has made the Red Scare nations look like tight-bunned Puritans in comparison.

It is a new Axis of Evil, a "Dark Internet" that serves the worst social Democrat propaganda. This new online blight is a concrete mixture of pornography and errant policy, a crude mix of anorexic clown-face-painted girls in too tight T-shirts and communities that are built as shrine mosques to Obama-era deceptions.

Friends, this Dark Internet is the new Red Scare, the Axis of Evil delivered upon your doorstep. There is nowhere to run, there is nowhere to hide. When you signed up for your Internet account, liberal think tanks were two steps ahead of you. You can't run from this evil, for it resides in every college schoolhouse. Its schemes arise between the sipped cappuccinos and black frames in every Starbucks near you.

With every click of a mouse button, each and every person around you is being exposed to potential torrents of liberal propaganda, flooding from the murkiest sewers of Satan's intestinal cesspools of Hell.

The supply lines of Satan run strong along the tracks of the modern eUnion railroad and there are five destinations that Engineer Satan toots his horn toward, hoping that everyone will shake their caboose and stop for a demoralizing visit.

THE 5 MODERN WEBSITES OF LIBERAL HORROR

DIRTY SHIRTY (DIRTYSHIRTY.COM)

A site directly connected to Satan's plan to defile our daughters, by showing off their bodies with T-shirts, while promoting the idea of "Keep It Dirty." How is "Keep It Dirty" a slogan to live by? Does this new battle cry of fashion brainwash our young women into thinking they should go out and be the neighborhood's next coke queen?

Dirty Shirty's rise to fame was done by exploiting and showboating sassy twentysomething-year-old sex bunnies, dressed in thigh thumping shorts that expose too much leg. In the typical M.O. of Big Hollywood, the owner of Dirty Shirty goes through these it-girls

Engineer Satan's first stop . . . Dirty Shirty.

faster than a Chernobyl-lung chain smoker does a pack of smooth and easies, greedily puffing out smoke rings of death and somehow calling it high fashion.

Most of these females are tricked into using their flesh temples and milksacs for sexual propaganda in hopes of getting discovered by a famous TV producer out in L.A. Little do they know the only agent they are attracting is the agent of evil.

Along with its website of pornographic nature, Dirty Shirty holds an annual "muddy fuddy" event on Christmas day. Each year, people submit wild Facebook photos in hopes of winning invites to this party. Each girl is required to bend at awkward camera angles to show off her "fuddy" and tell what dirty things she will let the L.A. model agents do to her. It is sick and scarily turning good girls into Mexican hot-topic harlots.

Every submitter's photos are examined and then voted on by the head of Dirty Shirty and his team of Jezebels. Hopeful partygoers submit head shots, video interviews, and a pair of their underwear. We hear some of the video interviews are of people performing self-sex actions and releasing devil DNA to show they can fully perform. The team of sinners then selects a hundred people to come and partake in this festival of sweat, nudity, and sexual activities.

With its rancid clothing line and army of promiscuous groupies, Dirty Shirty is a website that uses Satan's playbook to entice children into buying not just their clothing, but also their lifestyle. Who knew today's fashion could be so dangerous?

THE ATLANTIC WIRE (THEATLANTICWIRE.COM)

This news site is more left than a tree hugger eating tofu, while driving her hybrid and listening to Alan Colmes all at once. Sprouting seeds of hate, each article is chalked up with poorly researched accusations and advice columns. It is as if Dear Abby's ugly stepsister tried to give advice while writing about current events and politics.

With its one-sided-agenda "journalists," The Atlantic Wire continues to print false articles to discredit right-wing political figures, promote government spending, and heinously support gay "rights". Their articles don't have a hint of any proper journalistic swagger, nor do they even come close to being any type of source for real news. Do they know there is already a site that twists the truth with poor writing skills? It is called The Huffington Post.

One of the main culprits of The Atlantic Wire is a young blogger named John Hudson. Armed with his laptop and burrowed within his parents' D.C. basement, John writes hurtful columns trying to destroy anything not atheist or left leaning. John also seems to have a morbid obsession with trying to create the downfall of us personally. He was even credited with creating a fake article, in which he claims to have spoken with the "founders" of Christwire. How can you call yourself a journalist when you try to attack the word of America's God with false sources while having a permanent smug look on your face? Obviously John's mind is filled with dreams of sex brothels and thoughts of sinister malice.

This hack of a news blog actually has a fitting name. With ad revenue plummeting, it is literally drowning in The Atlantic and holding on to a wire.

CRACKED (CRACKED.COM)

Satan's favorite hobbies include luring people to sin with exposed back flesh and telling sick jokes around the water cooler, so there is no doubt that his sulfur-laden hand is behind a sick new Internet site named Cracked.com.

Regular writers craft nonsense out of thin air, how-to articles that will never be used like "How to Form Your Own Cult" or "So You've Been Challenged to a Duel." The trick here is that the readers are so irrational, they imagine that someday they'll need these tips in their pathetic lives, and it further adds to their delusions of grandeur.

In practice, Cracked.com exploits the mental weakness of its readers. Its blog posts become building blocks in the fortresses that teens construct to separate themselves from reality. It would not be wrong to say that the people funding this site are directly complicit in the spread of unrealistic childhood expectations and later adult employment failure now plaguing America.

As a whole, Cracked.com is only perpetuating our young generation's addiction to "factoids" and not real facts. It enables attention-deficit disorder and discourages deeper thought. It is the antithesis of faith and study. Mock science, poor history, and blog mythology is promoted on every page, setting a dangerous example for today's students (imagine if your children were writing homework essays with titles like "History's 10 Worst Royal Nicknames" or "A Day in the Life of a Scratch-Off Ticket Purchase"). The whole presentation of this information is taken to unbearable extremes with big typesets, excessively large page layouts, distracting advertising, and a breakdown of these lists into tiny sections that beg you to click and click some more, so that this failing business may generate some semblance of web traffic to keep its finances afloat.

GAWKER (GAWKER.COM)

Like Fidel Castro emerging from the jungle and suddenly realizing he has a country to run, Gawker.com has surprisingly fallen into a leadership role for the next generation of journalists. And, as in Cuba, most citizens of the Internet don't have a clue about the inept, bankrupt future that awaits them at the hands of this salty steno pool of blogging bastards.

Gawker started out covering the nasty inbred world of the New York media elite (a creepy place where sources are traded as often as pubic lice), but lately it has branched out into politics, celebrity gossip, and homosexual activism. The site is a constant flow of the latest major news stories, broken down to simplistic sound bites and then given a layer of all-too-predictable sarcasm.

With its hardcore following of young journalism-school grads and aspiring bloggers, it has become the Preppy Handbook for the Internet arriviste age. Wear pink shorts and pick up a lacrosse stick, the blog tells its eager readers, or rather dress yourself in disdain and carry a superiority complex. You'll make waves and money, not by looking deeply at the profound moral issues of our time, but with headlines like "Madonna Topless" or "Tom Cruise + Scientology." They are the cut-and-runners, attacking some of our noblest public figures (such as U.S. soldiers guarding embassies in Afghanistan and Glenn Beck), and then scampering off behind some bush to hide from the aftermath and count their precious page views.

If you really think Gawker doesn't pose a threat to American news and American values, just take a look at a few of the websites and careers it has spawned: Perez Hilton, David Carr, Queerty, BryanBoy, and The Huffington Post. Should they not be held accountable for this?

YOUTUBE (YOUTUBE.COM)

Besides its horrible design and structure, YouTube is essentially an amateur child kink video store that allows the sickest of gay predators to gaze at videos of preteens and shirtless college boys without paying any type of membership fee. While Ken or Markus is covering his soul in shame, his anus puckered with joy, Obama fights to allow gays to openly use YouTube as a source of sinful pleasure.

Burly-chested man bears aren't the only molesters of this service, as liberals also use this technology to post and promote to YouTube's college base of viewers. As we all now know, videos seen on YouTube are deemed creditable and real in the eyes of a flip-flop-wearing, communications-major college student and they spew out quotes from these videos as if they were true facts.

Let us ask you a simple question. If YouTube wasn't so dangerous then why do they call popular left-leaning clips "viral videos"? We are so blinded that the left can label a buzzword explicitly explaining its vile purpose and we turn our heads and giggle at cats playing piano or atheists making presentations on creation.

Satan frolics in this new age of cinematography. For each video view, the world becomes closer to the dark lord. With each thumbs-up given to a cross-dressing tween or a remixed music video of a black man talking about rape, we are playing with Satanic fornication. For every crying gay man who cries over his favorite pop star, Satan becomes more aroused. And for each turtle filmed getting raped, Satan smiles with orgasmic joy.

Whether it's Satan himself uploading videos, gays fondling their flesh Gucci bags, or liberals using viral videos to brainwash America, all in all YouTube is full of offensive content, created by offensive people. There is a small army of popular "vloggers" out there trying to become famous by creating ridiculous shows that young children are mimicking.

The 10 Most Offensive People on YouTube Today

10. *Dan Brown's Universe:* An egomaniacal young man who fortunately stays clothed for his cloying videos begging you to revel in his lukewarm intellect. He aims to be some sort of atheistic leader of the YouTube tribe, but he is more like the fool you see sitting on the wall, eating his own hair as you exit this rank-smelling village. My child, you know nothing of morality and your voice still breaks with puberty. Why don't you start a blog after you've had some life experience outside that messy Vassar dorm room?

9. *The Miley and Mandy Show:* Need proof that teen girls today are too obsessed with jewelry and sex? Just watch any of the "works" from these two spoiled rich kids, desperate to show off their bodies and their possessions like future candidates of *Housewives of New Jersey*. In a day and age when this country is in a financial crisis and our boys are dying overseas to protect our freedoms, it's disgusting to see these vapid harlots parade their conspicuous consumption so recklessly (and with such obvious damage to their hardworking father's credit card).

8. William Sledd: Epitomizes the very worst of the vain and sexualized teens in the gay lifestyle movement. He tells our impressionable boys it's okay to go gay, but do it with flamboyance and the most expensive hair products available! Please lay off the self-tanner, young man.

7. *Smosh:* Two boys with no obvious skills wrapped in a gender-bending relationship, which unsurprisingly includes a greased-up gerbil. Whether they're lathered in makeup or rammed into tight-fitting jeans, they are disgustingly sexual and demanding. They must know that their cross-dressing escapades are the delight of lonely old men in basements everywhere. Some of their stage sets are so expensive-looking you have to wonder what sugar-gentleman is funding their gerbil experimentations and what services he's getting in return.

6. *Machinima:* Here is a man who is doing his very best to promote the most sexual and violent games to young boys twenty-four hours a day. On top of that, he is dull beyond belief, yet this is one of the most viewed channels on YouTube! We never knew flagrant hedonists could be so boring.

5. Justin Bieber: Someone has kidnapped this poor child from reality. He looks too young and naifish to be his own mini-industry! Yet he acts like a man in his videos, crooning to middle-aged women and inviting them for sex in Laundromats (see "One Less Lonely Girl"). Plus, the singing is so heavily mixed and lip-synched it's unbelievable. His hip-bouncing moves and "come hither" looks are evidence that corporate America has no fear dancing on the grave of morality for a quick buck.

4. Tila Tequila: Does she own real clothes? All that flesh draped in tiny cocktail napkins of fabric, it's just offensive. We really don't see the point of this person. What a wonderful collection of angst-filled teenage boys, house-arrested pedophiles, sex tourists, and failing college students she must have as followers! Tila, we can't imagine the damage you have done to American society with your nakedness firing up the lust of men who really have better things to do. Think of the man-power hours lost! We only wish YouTube required green cards.

3. Fred Figglehorn: First we'd like to ask, where in the world are your parents? It seems like you've ingested something from your frazzled mother's medicine cabinet. Otherwise, what in the world could you possibly be so excited about? And stop squinting like you're reading off cue cards. We feel bad that you have to airbrush your pimples out of your videos, but that pity evaporates the second we hear your duck-quacking voice. Donald, we can't imagine you ever growing chest hair. You are that creepy. Why are you so popular? We look forward to the day when you're a bitter, exhausted, and quiet adult.

2. Philip DeFranco: You are the heart of the problem with YouTube. A guy like you would not draw much attention in the real world. You're clean-cut enough that you could probably land a good-paying job at Best Buy, yet you choose to spend your life online? Frankly, you're too old to be on YouTube. We find it extremely unnerving that people like you are so desperate to surround themselves with the little boys and girls of the Internet. What's your ultimate motive here? Also, please stop talking like Casey Kassem.

1. Shane Dawson: You look like a nice boy. Clean, well-fed, good home. So what's with the cross-dressing? Is suburban life in the land of American plenty really so bad that you have to lash out at the loving parents of this country in your heels and inept mascara, screeching like a drunk sorority girl lost in Harlem? Does your mother even know? Many of us are concerned. It's pretty obvious that you find a secret thrill slipping on those elastic panties from Victoria's Secret. Did you think no one would notice? The impressionable boys of America have! They're saying to themselves, "Shane does it, so it must feel real good!" Have you even bothered to wonder how many children you have corrupted into cross-dressing with your floppy hair and firm legs, your warm voice and curious eyes? How much self-abuse has been performed in your name, Shane?

Most troubling of YouTube degradation is one truth; the video site is a cornerstone of the "Net Generation," the youth of today.

Within the young men and women who roam our college campuses and enter the working world, there exists the hope and dream of the brave colonists of rebellion, the ire of every redcoat Brit. The living angels who defended Earth from Europe's tyranny bled cubed tears upon the frozen Delaware and stood strong upon Christian decency, for they knew one day their sons and daughters would build a New World upon their sacrifices: a world of love, decency, and freedom for all mankind.

But there are forces of evil, whose eyes squint in hateful contempt of this nation and her allies. These monsters of mayhem wish not for people to be free, for they covet power and detest the notion of God. Their morals stand shorter than their height and every Vespuccian map even has the monster nation marked as warning for all: Asia.

There was a time when a map marked "Here Be Dragons, Beware" and we find that even today, the untold horrors and menacing machinations for America's downfall that exists within every true Asian's mind cannot be fathomed by even the most brilliant neuroscientists.

The New Lords of Communism, the Chinese, now sit high upon

their yuan-laced thrones again, seeking to build a new terra-cotta army. The adopted Sons of Sun Tzu are well versed in the art of war, and much like their Mongolian ancestors of old, know how to break through America's protective firewall of morality.

President Lincoln warned America could never be attacked from without; the Chinese understand this fact. It is a childhood nursery rhyme sung to every Chinese baby's mind, their yipping mouths retching rice milk with the mention of "Economic Individualism".

"You cannot attack strong enemy from without,
So little Mao attack from within!
And when you convert all their youth,
Bludgeon them again and again!"
—Chinese Nursery Rhyme Proverb

Written into the hearts of our enemies are masterful war plans of old and a senseless jealousy mustered by Satan himself.

The children of the Mao revolution are now the Marching Mongrels of the Orient. While Reagan's children were being taught the dangers of Soviet socialism and homosexual strangers, the Chinese were secretly teaching their schoolchildren complex languages, beyond the confusing characters in their impossibly random nonsense scribble alphabet.

Written into the Chinese children of yesterday was the code to destroy America's chil-

Chinese nursery rhyme.

dren of today. The ancient Warlords of Shanghai knew that deep down, capitalism would breed great technological riches to America's children.

And with this technology would come the need for a new "electronic programming language" to be written into not only America's national security firms and businesses, but also the children of all Western nations. And within this language, the eternally calculating Chinese have established a programming plot beyond the algorithmic abilities of any American supercomputer.

HOW TO KNOW IF YOUR CHILD IS A CHINESE HACKER

Chinese are a hateful, porn-enslaved breed and they are turning American kids into hackers at an alarming pace. With the average teenager already knowing how to write in basic HTML programming markup, converting them into what they call "leet" hackers is a very basic and easy process. It is the hope of these Chinese to turn our children into virtual terrorists and create wormhole viruses. These wormhole viruses damage our mainframe and grant the slant commies direct access to our country's secret databases filled with military information.

Leet Chinese hacker.

The term leet comes from the Latin word elite. This word was commonly used in Chinese forums for people who had administration privileges and was quickly changed to describe people with the hottest hacking skills.

So if it is so dangerous, then why are kids attracted to this type of vandalism? Easy, it is called "LuLz." Kids love games, and LuLz are points kids win from completing a different hacking mission.

Just like a point system, there are levels and each level gives a child a new rank that opens up harder and more difficult challenges. The more points, the closer to the rank of leet you get. Kids get to see what missions are available by logging on to a secret Chinese website called mIRC, where they get to also view a scoreboard to see where they rank up with their other deviant friends. What better way to make a nerdy antisocial child feel cooler than enabling him to go around message boards bragging that he or she is the leetest hacker in America?

The Ranking Structure
Noob: 0–50 Points
Kiddie scripter: 51–100 points
Hacker: 101–200 points
Pron god: 201–400 points
Haxor: 401–800 points
über-elite: 801–1500 points
Leet: Anything above 1501 points

If you want to learn if your child is a part of this leet movement, pay very close attention to the information that we have discovered.

ORTHOGRAPHY

One of the leet movement's weirdest things is how they teach children to use numbers or funny keyboard characters to spell out words. This form of typing was created so a child could use the computer-character map system or num-lock pad to spell out words so concerned parents couldn't understand what they were typing.

Just like Chinese, this language looks like a bunch of dots and scribbles when seen on a computer screen or on a piece of paper.

Some examples of leet speaking are: \/\/(\)\/\/, 1337, n00b, B1FF and f1lamer.

MORPHOLOGY

Has your child been spelling words funny? Have they been scribbling things like "I haz mad pwnage" or in their diaries do they write "I'm the ultimate pwnzorz"? This is a clear sign your child is a part of an underground hack operation or clan.

This system is actually pretty easy to crack and we have the decoder ring. Children will try and substitute ends of words with funny misspelling. A great example is "I'm teh greatest haxxor with the utmost best skillage." What the child would be saying in proper American here is, "I'm the best hacker among my friends and I have the best skills." Notice how the "ed" is changed to a "xxor" and the "s" in skills is modified to "age". It is not hard to break these codes, once you have the basics locked down.

At first it might seem confusing, but just remember if you see words that end with a lot of x's or a word has had an "age" put at the end of it, it would be safe to say your child is working for the Chinese government.

TERMINOLOGY

/b/: A universal term used by hackers or ebaumsworld.com to let them know a forum is filled with "bad" content. Since kids didn't want their parents to know they were demon whacking in their rooms to produce devil DNA, they would make computer folders named /b/ to throw their parents off.

From this folder, hackers started to use /b/ as a sub domain to let other hackers know they had a IRC room full of porno and *wherez* to share illegally.

Epic: An elite word used by hackers to describe an image that has the most porn scent to it. If you hear your child use this word, then you know to look through his Internet browser's history to see if he has been cruising on hell's highway.

Pron: The misspelling of the word "Porn." This is to throw parents off. If a parent looks at a child's keyword searches on Google and only sees the word Pron, then they wouldn't know they are really searching for Porn.

Wherez: These are illegal software programs given to children by downloading them from Chinese websites called "Torrentedz." If your child is using these programs, remove them at once. The FBI could be tracking your son or daughter waiting for them to commit a terroristic act.

PEARL HARBOR December 6, 1941

TECHNOLOGY IN THE HANDS OF AN ANGRY ASIATIC DEITY

• December 7, 1941 •
"sleeping upon the frontier of democracy"

On the beaches of Hawaii slept America's bravest sons and daughters. Word had come to D.C. that a nefarious force of Satan had risen in war-prone Eurasia, a ravenous ravenhawk the likes of which the world had never seen. America was aware, but innocent. Alert, but green behind the ears. Little did anyone know, that beyond the proto-shores of America loomed the original homegrown terrorist, the sake-soy Japanese kabuki deathgliders of Armageddon!

Violently screeching from the zephyrs of Orient, the Japanese struck Pearl Harbor with a hate-laced fury that would bring an eternal death knell to even the mighty Phoenix of lore. Hell-bent on kamikaze destruction, these original hordes of Socialist alliance Twittered to one another using a primitive "Web code", a leaked perversion of America's original Morse Code Internet communication.

Officials in Washington were stunned. The Japanese had managed to make actual planes. No more did their little meticulous hands craft paper of origami cranes, but now war machines that could steal the lives of three-thousand young men and women basking in the sun-kissed rays of innocence and love. The once-pure scent of fearless innocence had given way, in its stead a wrenching odor not even matched by clogged toilet arteries at sushi-bar homofish night.

Moving at expected maestro piano speeds, the Japanese High Command furiously clicked upon primitive typewriters, e-telling their pilots the necessary coordinates needed to sneak upon young America's navy of peace. With every buzz and click, a Japanese plane came closer to rending the flesh and blood of America's children with the fires of betrayal and bombs of heated bigotry.

Liberals will turn technology against the innocent—never forget this life lesson. When getting into the "online world," remember the voices of our fallen countrymen at Pearl Harbor. Never forget the kabuki deathgliders of soy-scented terror. Remember, brave friend, that every fleshpole worship site, Facebook adultery scandal, and Socialist-Obama squawk box, took birth from the seas of Japan, a place from which a great monster of hate wildly spews trash and death into the homes of 300 million innocent Americans.

THE SEDUCTIVE RISE OF THE BURLESQUE BEAST

The Internet of today represents an infested cache of the world's raunchiest: tentacle anime perversions from Japan all the way to exploited college-girl children in America. It is full of biased Democrat propaganda that would give pause to Goebbels, his sulfur-toking soul seizing in sexual passion at the complexity of Democrat lies in media.

It's a well-known fact that due to their pagan ways and heathen rituals, the lesser cultures of foreigners are typically maligned and the source for much suffering on our Earth. At the front of all technological horrors are Satan's original scientists, the oceanic Dragonspawn of the Beast.

Japan is an ancient culture of mystic wonder; the progenitor of the new atheistic spirit, its cultural effect is a tidal bloodmoon of spiraling vertigo. At the heart of evolutionary science, atheism, eStranger Dangers, and even SinoSoviet socialism are the original Children of the Red Sun.

Even with the Japanese temples of old crumbling with decrepit decadence, we find the modern Japanese keep alive the rituals and ideologies of their ancient ancestors. In their place, the Japanese people keep up an agenda—one beaten back seventy years ago—to be the death of the true Son.

Upon the misty streets of modern Japan we witness opiate-eyed children with shock-blue hair, wildly dancing upon the grounds of a penis festival and reveling under the blood dragon's will. Their calligraphy pens, seeping with the life force of a Komodo dragon and fibrous brush hairs of the innocent, eerily give in to an innate urge to draw countless graffiti of large milksacked women and monsters beguiling children with schemes so raunchy even Hugh Heffner would not want to play.

With everything from cannibalism to dancing naked under the moon, it's not uncommon to encounter entire civilizations who've lost any semblance of decency, humanity, or morality when doing missionary work, particularly in the Africas, Asia, and East Europe. But within Japan, there is an original creative spark. There is born

Satan's original work in modern times, a unique experiment in what would a culture do with unlimited potential in science, but no centering Christian morals or Judeo-American edict to guide their ways.

Be encouraged, dear friends, to harden your faith as you embark on a missionary journey to witness the original architects of damnation in action. Seeing these sickening . . . examples of what can happen when an entire people are without Christian morals will break your heart, but will fortify your mind's ability to understand the new great foreign danger, waking up from its long sleep on the shores of America's horizon.

> **WARNING: The following image media and cultural study detail the core of immorality in humanity's most ancient scientific culture. Many of the images will be too crude for a general audience. Please first pray and then demand all women and younger children leave the classroom/home before reviewing this work for your local parenting council and review board.**

JAPANESE TELEVISION INDECENCY—ANIME

(HENTAI, SHENGAI, MANGA, YAOI)

Being a prostitute of The Enemy, the Japanese culture is allying with liberals in your country to engage in spiritual warfare against your children. Yes, parents, you should be very scared and afraid of what the Japanese culture is trying to instill in the minds of your children. College children, you should be twice afraid, for you are the target.

There is an Asian form of cartoons called anime. Anime is roughly translated to "pornography" in English. Anime is the Japanese word for pornography.

Anime perversion takes origin from the extant pharyngula cult of the northern Hokaiddo regions, their works still found etched in the flooded coral caves beneath the Pacific. This cult seemed to have transferred a theory of endosymbiosis, a bizarre belief that people are the evolutionary product of bacteria and that within the womb, a person goes through a chicken phase, a wolf phase, a horse phase, a fox phase, and then finally human phase.

From these ancient tablets was born the Chinese zodiacal and even modern evolutionary theory. But also was born a concept of indoctrination: cartoon perversion.

We see it in American comics and on Comedy Central every week. In Japan, we have the origins of using cartoon graphics in technology to trick the gullible minds of elementary and college children to believe the most bizarre twists in reality. The children of the ancient Japanese still send packets of this "anime" filth into your child each and every day.

There are five different variations of Japanese science agenda, kabuki-masked as anime fun time, being pushed off onto your children.

HENTAI ANIME

This version of Japanese pornography is the absolute worst. Hentai anime literally means "the pornography of tentacles" and describes a version of Japanese debauchery where seemingly young characters  are assaulted by huge octopi or squid in very inappropriate manner. We will spare the details, but you can surely get the gist.

This type of animated Japanese porn also features characters whose eyes appear very big and glossy, clearly advocating rampant drug use and the spirit of prostitution. If you catch your children watching any of this anime pornography on cable television, immediately pray for them, toss out the TV, and explain to them the dangers of such material.

Latent to hentai anime is the groundwork for evolutionary teaching. Modern evolutionists believe the universe started with a big bang and magically, somehow bacteria appeared on Earth. Through same-sex docking, a process liberal evolutionists call endosinbiois, the bacteria used homosexual reproduction to give rise to all life.

This story of creation is the basis for hentai anime. Its cartoonists maintain that the origins of man started with homosexual bacteria festerfests in primordial goostuff, so it should not seem so bizarre to see a tentacle willy, a girl's sally jessie, or a bear honeysuckle a boy's tainted tetherballs.

We can see how this founding cartoon of technological perversion plays into even the modern Homogay Agenda, attempting to make society believe we are the product of a lemur-monkey female and a coddling caveman's pelvic-pounding night of prehistoric mayhem. It is very sick to think about, and as such, gays hope that seeing a man stick a man in sin won't seem so bad in comparison. What a marvelously villainous way to trick children into being anti-family and thinking of gays as normal people.

SHENGAI ANIME

Shengai, a word which means "spirit gay" or as properly translated to "gay spirit," is a form of Japanimation that was specifically created to praise large skin-rod, ass-leap-frogging, homosexual spirits. These spirits all have rippling muscle definition and each has a special symbol marking on his forehead. Each one has very shiny multi-colored hair and red or black eyes and goes by a name such as "Sukinpōru (Skinpole)," "Hyōhaku hōru (Bleached Hole)" or even "Sakkunobu (Suck Knob)."

These gay spirits go around fighting other shengais in gladiator-type battles to the death in front of a crowd full of twelve to thirteen-year-old children. Each monster uses large weapons that look like plastic tadpole torpedoes to beat and smash each other until one submits to the strong shengai's dominant power. The loser gives up by dropping to his knees and lifts his fanny into the air like a fetal position.

The winner of the fight has to deliver the final blow to the surrendering opponent with his death ray that comes from his forehead. This final move is called the "Okane Utsu" or translated into "Money Shot." The "Money Shot" is when the symbol lights up and glows and the shengai looks into the crowd of kids and depending if they cheer or boo, may or may not finish off his opponent with the okane utsu. If the crowd of children screams in enjoyment, then the shengai will unload his rays of power right into the forehead symbol hole of the other shengai. The losing shengai has his soul stolen and becomes a part of the winning gay spirit.

MANGA

Manga is Japanese comic porn and like most Commie literature, reads from right to left and is most often drawn in black and white. The meaning in

English is very direct and means "homorous pictures." Most manga porn stories involve plots about vampires, tennis players, or even messages promoting atheism.

The characters in these porn books almost always have large drugged-out, dilated eyes, small mouths that spit out devilish profanity, and large breasts, and they also have Justin Bieber–styled haircuts with abnormal gay colors.

In most of their stories, you will see devil-like figures always fighting each other with long swords, with sexual moaning words written in comic bubbles above their heads.

Manga had been banned from our country, due to their X-rated content, until 1998, when Bill Clinton started trading nuclear secrets with the Chinese. One request the Chinese had was to allow the Japanese comic books to be sold in American bookstores. Since then it has been a red tidal wave of destruction to the American family.

If these comics aren't so evil, then why are they forced to display content ratings on their covers?

YAOI

"As the samurai silently slipped across the soggy plains, only heard were his pittering footdrop whispers. Little did the villagers expect a stealth sword of fleshy-gold caliber to enter body after body on a cold, rainy night above the Northern Hanoi rice fields."

Within the Book of Yaoi, we find written the earliest tales of homosexual erotica. The Book of Yaoi is the hallmark for ancient homosexuals, their breeding ground being within man-only Japanese Hindu temples.

The books were meant as propaganda pieces, a primitive technology to weaken the natural desire of young little Japanese boys to find themselves a geisha momma. The hormones of puberty were soon laced with protein pustules of expelled sins, a fate that stuck the boy's mind in an endless cycle of depression and lust for kamanamara, Japanese flesh swords.

So strong were the imagery and stories of ancient homosexual literature, that Japan faced a near species extinction and to this very day, are of short height and low population from almost wiping themselves out with brainwashing stories of non-baby-yielding homosexuality.

From their moments of ancient weakness, the Japanese government still understands the power of pre-Columbian homosexuality. They know that if they can find a way to enter the minds of young boys, there stands the chance they can make a man cry out, "Mammalian ludicrosities!" and run away from a woman's natural prominence, but still covet the neighboring gay's spoiled manmilk. If they can find sophisticated new ways to make Yaoi enter America, forever will all schoolboys resemble a spark dazzling *Glee* cast member.

The Japanese love to cook up steaming mounds of sin in their woks of immorality and feed it to whoever in the world is hungry for perversion, and make no mistake, evolution scientists and girthy gay rights advocates have signed up to eat from the tables of Japanese art pornography.

HOMOSEXUAL PINK DOLPHINS

Evolutionists are using genetic technology to bring various stories of Yaoi anime to life. One of their recent crowning achievements was genetically engineering homosexually pink dolphins, then putting stories about it within *Weekly Readers* at elementary schools across America.

Stories from Christian scientists in Saint Louis began to reveal a scary phenomenon along the muddy Mississippi: they witnessed a dolphin that has faggy pink skin and oversized blowhole phenotype!

According to peer reviews in the esteemed *Christian Monitoring Science*, not even a week of straight prayer and fasting could prepare the human eyes to see this genetic abomination.

Fun Fact: Scientific poll data indicate gay males fantasize about gaping, pink sinholes an average of twenty-three to twenty-six times a day. This is likely why you usually see them daydreaming when they should actually be performing their little secretary and nursing jobs.

So really it should come as no shock that homo scientists are now molesting nature itself to create a living version of their perverted fantasies. They have no respect for divine order and have found a way to doubly penetrate students with evolution and homosexual indoctrination. Japanese anime is to blame.

HOMUNCULI AND SEPARATOR FLAPS

WARNING: The following section contains improper content. Please have women/children leave the room before reviewing this item.

If you have a teenage son or daughter in public school, they have been told lies about our existence and formation. This very day, there are students who believe that man does not hold the seed to all life. There are those who dare believe it is of good ethics to mouthgobble a babybaster or even worse, a female's fetal incubator.

The Bible tells us that even when we are growing in the womb,

God has made a plan for our lives and that we were fearfully and wonderfully made. There exists within every man a legion of little God warriors, a potential army of family pride and Christian soldiers to walk in the light of American patriotism and freedom for all.

Yet, with anime, we see the seeds of destruction planted by the calculatingly crafty hands of Japanese scholars from many moons past. How sick to know that since the times of ancient Japan, mankind's rich six thousand-year history has been corrupted by misleading tales of human anatomy and physiology?

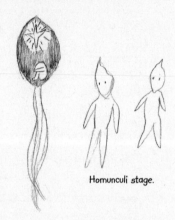

Homunculi stage.

The squint-eyed cults of Nostradamus predicted there would arise a great Christian nation, and knew just how to ensure their Asiatic teachings would breach the mind of every child within its borders. Therefore the Japanese created a two-headed sea monster to attack the child's mind with seemingly bipartisan fury: upon the left head, was written bukake, the Japanese word for "seminial sea spittles." Children started to think that an act of "M" was not destroying millions of stage-one baby (homunculi) lives.

And to the right was the hallow-head of "pushukai," the Japanese word for "the three rice fields of fertility, yellow streams, and muddy waters." Contrary to the very simple layout of a female's anatomy, an entire nation was fooled to think women did not have one releasing hole.

Central to the cult Yaoi stories are mouth sex acts. In old Japan, it was an "honor" to know a person's taste. Much like when dogs greet each other, Japanese people would lift one another's kimonos and sniff the scent glands of one another, as a show of greeting and knowing every passerby on an intimate level.

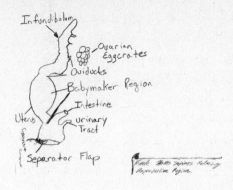

Infundibulum
Ovarian Eggcrates
Oviducts
Babymaker Region
Intestine
Uterus
Urinary Tract
Separator Flap

Female Homo Sapiens Relating Reproductive Region.

As the notions of sanitation and monogamy were brought from Christian Europe to the Buddhist pagan Mooni demon worshippers, the power of Yaoi fell. Japan began to show signs of industrialism and progress, trading in their public bathrobes for honorable business suits and learning the old language of God's business on Earth: English.

This was the golden era of Japan, but like all good things, it came to an end. Somewhere along the line, Japanese Socialist counter-culture resurrected the Yaoi cult. In the second Yaoi movement, there was a militant effort to use Yaoi tactics not only to subvert culture, but to destroy the Exalted Nation of ancient prophecy: America.

Many tried to figure out why Japanese kamikazes would sacrifice their lives, tearing through the air like wounded banshees in death dives against American peace ships. Was it a true hate? Was it mind-bending drugs swam over by Mexican drug dealers?

To truly understand the power of Yaoi, realize that it was one of the biggest propaganda tools in World War II. Its perverse artistic renderings made the Japanese people turn back to their immoral roots, tearing apart any sense of decency blessed to them by European culture of Protestant religion.

Though beaten back with the atomic muscle of God himself, Yaoi cultists of Japan still thrive to this very day. Like little Armageddon dung beetles, they hide from the light and then roll out nasty plots for American demise. Their newest efforts do not come via deathplanes flown by brainwashed divine wind pilots; today, their agenda is being imported to every health book on the desk of America's students.

The new Japanese agenda flanks the minds of America's children from the right and left. On the right, the one-eyed dragon of Japanese deception is whispering words, making American boys stiff with sin and thoughts of their seed not being holy and nontoxic before marriage. Boys no longer find every act of "M" to be genocide.

Then from the left slithers the "pushukai" beast, once again flicking its tongue and telling tales that there is nothing gross about licking tail or eggspout, it's all the same.

The Japanese understand the power of America is its obedience to God: the nation is fruitful, it multiplies. But when children are viewing Yaoi perversion on television, how much motivation will they have to get married? How many times when a child could be created, will instead two women decide to frolic in the ponds of lesbianism? How many American boys will hold up to Yaoi's true meaning, as they are heard pitter-pattering in the middle of the night, stealing away to locked bedrooms and bathrooms to satanbate their Satan scepters, kneeling before the porcelain thrones of temptation as they defy God himself in red-faced frenzy?

Against such odds, America fails. People turn away from marriage and sanctity. They give into lust and lewd lifestyles. The divorce rate in America is 50 percent, and there may not be enough children in America to support Medicare within the next decade. The Japanese anime technology is working; it is decreasing America's reproductive rates and weakening our national resolve.

Against the Hordes of Animated Horrors, America's moral army dwindles. The little potential soldiers of God, crusty splats upon the tiled floors of Satan's in-home shrine mosques. The Japanese are winning. America is losing ground. The calligraphy pen is truly proving to be mightier than the American sword.

ANIME TEMPLES

As you know, the Japanese culture is currently being overrun with the vile spirit of atheist liberalism! These atheistic wonders of Japan have all sorts of scary, evil things that they are creating and trying to spread to our sweet, innocent little children of America.

Over the past years we've learned of several spiritual weapons of mass destruction the Japanese have crafted in efforts of destroying morality and freedom, turning your precious children into gay little pornographers in the process.

The immoral albeit crafty, quick little hands of the Japanese have meticulously constructed pagan anime sex temples. The Godless Japanese created shrines to their false goddess of anime, so the spirit of pornography would always be recognized as at least "historical" in their nation. These architectural monstrosities are truly disturbing, both in terms of morally questionable aesthetics and societal implications.

From these temples of temptation, we now see towel-hatted, desert drifters lifting the same blueprints to erect their terror mosques. Shining bright, these domes of defiance are franchises of Satan's workshop. Each temple is built to honor their false gods, as they manufacture hate weapons with each scope automatically adjusted at the true holy land to the west.

For every mosque there are thousands of sand farmers hidden in the dunes and ready to pop up, more impossibly frustrating to find and whack than an arcade Whac-A-Mole. These hidden tubers attack in the name Ali Baba in hopes of dying for their fairy-tale beliefs and to receive seventeen non-baptized virgins.

When our great gardener of happiness, George W. Bush, was in office, these terrorists were run out of America's vegetable fields. Mr. President made sure that any vermin or insects were flushed out with patriotic pesticides and kept them in the dirt farms to the Far East. Not only did he clear out the dust rats, but also the rabid ass rabbits. Once the Lord's chosen leader of the free world left office, the fields become dry and dead. This is completely the fault of the new dark gardener with no agricultural experience.

With Emperor Obama now in office these terrorists are planting mosque weeds directly into America's great garden state. He proudly welcomes the construction of America's fall with open sin-tanned-colored arms. As the weeds of Islam eat away at the roots of morals and spiritual guidance, America has opened her thighs to be impregnated by long-bearded dust devils.

Obamanation—it is the process in which sharia law will yield endless crops of homegrown terror. It will literally create an Obama nation, a place where wielding a welfare check is an act of ceremonial honor. A place where a Muslim man can whip a good, Christian woman on TV as the masses cheer "Ole, jihad!" following the cattle cries of Satan. Within the neighborhoods of America will grow those who sympathize with the greedy oil-horders and chant praises to the inane ramblings of Prince Ahmadinejad, the Axis of Evil's PR man himself.

With a nation turned against itself, Obama will arise to be the Anti-Lincoln, a sheer tale of irony. Lincoln freed the black man and sutured the wounds of division in America. Defying even a Heavenly Master, Obama now hopes to stomp down upon the Christian majority of America, ensuring that they rot away under the son-blocking canopies of fundamentalist Islam.

With Americans falling under Islamo-tolerance in this new age of Moor influence, the armies of darkness prepare to attack the final strongholds of American life and decency—the church and rallying points for the GOP. The sharia Sandtroopers are sharpening their scythes and stand prepared to chop through the dwindling Moral Majority, not caring if man, woman or, child stands in their path. All are targets and will comply to their demands, or further feed the Islamic desire to turn America's rivers red with King Pharaoh's muslimagic death, reborn.

Moses stood strong, protected by the Hand of Righteousness and sent before the children of God to give them prophecy and warning. And once again we find God has sent to us a modern-day Moses, whose voice rings more true than Aaron's, but blessed with a heavenly smooth frequency modulation.

Andrew Wilkow, the Prophet of Patriotism, has warned each and every person in a Western nation about the terror temple builders. The Enemy takes origin in the fertile crescent, meaning they have a farmer's determination buried deep within their terror togas. They will stop at nothing to ensure every American follows their every wish and command.

While strong in rhetoric, the hordes of Habibi are weak in technology. Even with the Legion of American Liberals brainwashed to do their bombastic bidding, the falafeling fundamentalists no longer have true weapons of mass destruction to unleash upon proper cities. The Cross of Saint George Bush still protects America and her sleeping children.

But alas, friends, alas the sable reign of Obama has produced a poisonous seed, one that feeds the belly of betrayal with the breads of sharia Socialism and hummus of hotheaded turban horrors.

Such an explosive danger lying in our backyards can only mean General Satan marches several steps behind, rallying his Judas troops to burn effigies and sing indecipherable chants of moaning temple noises. The Secret Sheiks of Backyard Betrayals already stand nigh in America, ready to rebel and cause Egyptian street chaos by the command of their god-king Hussein Obama.

As the Old Guard of the Bush administration fade into the gentle sunsets of warm nostalgia, the crooning crowds of Obama grow electrified, emboldened, and ready to tear our peaceful kingdom asunder!

The Omniscient Orator, Donald Rumsfeld, is no longer there to be our shining secretary upon the Hill. The empowering skybox of Karl Rove no longer whispers God's strategic will for America, but instead is now filled with the war howls of Obama's Siberian ter-rorwolves, the bureaucratic czars of Socialism whose snarls drip wet with welfare policy and rabid rhetoric of Mecca-kneeling betrayals unknown.

Yes, Old Mcbama has cultivated homegrown terrorism. The con-scripts of Russoislam betrayal stand firm in America, waiting on their orders to attack from within. Lincoln's spirit trembles and calls for his Republican sons to grab fast upon the Patriot Act, firmly wielding its sharp paperblades to cut through the sand Moors like blessed Cru-saders from humanity's golden years.

But the golden days are past. No longer is it legal to bludgeon ter-rorism to death; it is not PC in Obama World. No longer can we yank a Muslim-looking person up by the scruff, and yell, "Are you a ter-rorist?" and know, if they seem offended or belligerent, that they are of Gitmo-bound guilt! The Patriot Act was defeated by Pelosi pagans.

Today, America lies weak. The protective policy of Bush-era wisdom has been burned by the anti-Constitution Democrats.

Chanting all across America are millions of people, perhaps your neighbor. Your friendly store clerk. Your wife or Cal State Fullerton–bound academic genius. One never knows where terrorism can strike. Maybe even its spirit builds betrayal within you. Have you protested Hussein Obama today, pinko?

A new civil war brews in America. Our society hides behind the walls of American purism, constructed by sweat and tears of good men: Nixon, Hannity, McCarthy, Reagan, and Bush. Outside, the moor troll army, a rough hodge-podge mix of college hippies, orgy balls of lipstick-clad hipsters, and powerful liberal industrialists.

The army of Neo-Muslims stands outside hocking their rocks of homosexuality, chucking their Zulu poison-tipped spears of liberalism and trying to catapult boulders of ObamaCare into our holy city, but find their primitive Hamas camel-kissing weapons are no match for our muscular might of Godliness.

But to the east they find a formative and modernized ally within the Japanese. Remember, the Japanese are genius and crafty, very sneaky with meticulous hands, and with but a small electronic item can create a great instrument of war and destruction. Japanese have a perverse infatuation with creating weapons and immoral technology. Their people have no hearts and love to conduct secret experiments where they make machines that can kill people more efficiently.

Our forefathers learned this lesson the hard way, as they mourned their sons and daughters who were sent to heaven at the hands of a crop-plane-flying menace on a day of infamy. The Japanese had managed to take a flying tool of good and Wright, the product of a Priest, and turn it into a war instrument of destruction. What more could be expected from the ancient children of the samurai swords, the perverse science warriors who tortured poor mother-ship China for years and gave birth to modern militant atheists.

Do any of you remember when they nuked Pearl Harbor? They just flew their planes over here, then rained bomb after bomb on our innocent sons and nurse daughters stationed on our beautiful, peaceful island of Hawaii.

So many died that day and the Japanese laughed as they completed their blood oath with Adolph Hitler. They would have kept flying their death planes over the rest of America, but decided to turn around so they could torture our friends the Chinese some more.

Now the same menacing laugh once again emanates from Japan. "Kikikiki" from their wormhole generators. "Kikikiki" from their jet laser ludicrous lightning-speed death gliders. "Kikikiki" from their secret moshi moshi hardon collider's anime pornography generator.

But beware! That is not Japanese laughter, but rather a countdown code to unleashing their most furious technology upon America. The Japanese are smart; they have calculated the risk of wielding death machines themselves and know the price is nuclear freedom. They look to outsource and find an army already stands clamoring outside America's holy wall of decency.

The Children of the Samurai have now joined hands with the merry Akbar Knights of Camel-lot to fill their sand bases up with deadly WMDs. They won't be the type we found in Iraq in 2004, but instead weapons so destructive they will cause Lucifer's brow to sweat and face to flush as his jolly factory explodes, drenching America in hell's sex lava.

THE SCARY JAPANESE ROBOT THREAT TO AMERICA, EARTH

As you know, Japan is currently a hot-zone nation—that is a region where the people are full of promise but lack the light to show them the way to morality. There is a battle between good and evil for the minds within our squinty little horny hornet friends.

Friends, the Japanese are engineered to hate American freedoms at birth and there is nothing that would bring joy to their cold little hearts more than burning you and your children dead.

In the last century Asia murdered our grandfathers during a sneak attack at Pearl Harbor, and now they will send these robots over to firebomb you and your precious children in your sleep.

Now some liberals will try to fool you and say the Japanese would never do such things, the thought of burning a human is preposterous. To that we say, tell that to the cute little puppy that's being barbecued and eaten alive at your local Mongolian barbecue.

He'd try to bark a response, but his little grilled mouth is too busy swimming in the soy-sauce-laden bellies of the very people who support making these robots.

Anyone who has no problems eating puppies will not have an

issue ensuring you and your loved ones are seared well done by their weapons of mass destruction.

This finding has put so much fear into our hearts that we will not sleep well, and you are naturally scared too. Let us look deeper into this danger so we can become more panicked and have greater incentive to implore our political leaders return the laws of McCarthyism and sign executive orders against anyone who may be trying to aid the Japanese in building these new WMDs.

During our last mission trip to Japan, we uncovered and encountered many eye-opening accounts that included their perverse television habits, their scary gay penis festivals, and even their sly, sinister plan of sneaking hentai tentacle perversion animes to your children!

More so than not, despite their transgressions against America in the past, the people of Japan are some of the most sweet, gentle, and impassioned. They love life.

As you may know, after America saved Earth from the Nazi-Asia alliance during World War II, the compassionate government of our great land sought to teach the vanquished enemies of good the way of sciences, arts, and civics. This was done not only out of compassion, but to also teach the good people of Japan that there was more to life than being a kamikaze warmonger.

Since that time our former enemies in Japan have progressed quite impressively in the field of science, specifically robotics. Though robotics can have good applications for Earth, we fear that with Japan leading the way in the field of robotics (behind the U.S.A.), we are all in really grave, dire danger.

Quite simply, Japan is creating robots that are both creepy and frightening. They are freely sharing these robot technologies with our enemies and they will soon be Gagaku, goose-stepping down your streets, angrily knocking on your doors to destroy your life.

I-Fairy Robot

Anti-American Agenda: Homogay Agenda (gays, double-gays, lesbians, and transgenic gays)

Weapon Grade: iHomo Class 3 thinking device designed to infiltrate American culture and make gay marriage seem cute, so the public will rally against the Federal Marriage Amendment.

Terror Warning Level: ES (Elevated Sneakiness: for impersonating a man of the cloth and performing homogay unions behind God's back and against American marriage laws.)

Danger Rating: Highly Gay 4½ / 5 stars

Description: Japan has created yet a new monster that threatens our morals and traditions!

They call this one the "I-Fairy," a little four-foot terror that is doing the job of a pastor! Robots cannot be pastors and have NO right to marry a couple, even Japanese!

Reports say that at the first I-Fairy wedding, the Tokyo Japanese sat quietly in chairs with their big smiles like all was normal. They watched the little bride walk down the aisle like this was just common to have a robot pastor!

As the bride walked down the aisle and a Japanese organ played "Here Comes the Bride," reports say its "eyes flashed and plastic pigtails glinted." That is nothing short of heresy against traditional marriage!

The robot then actually said, and we aren't making it up, you seesaw liberals, it said, "Please lift the bride's veil."

It then waved its arms all around like the good Pope and then the Japanese kissed couple and all fifty people applauded and had a robot squid-ink orgy fight. They then ate cake and then politely applauded again. This is not normal to have a robot pastor, no applause!

In researching this new threat to the sanctity of marriage, we found that the company that makes this robot is owned by the same company that peddles Hello Kitty filth in America. So if you are against gay marriage or this robot-conducted marriage, you should definitely help us boycott Hello Kitty.

Sicko Japan! Whoever does this is worse than the gays and steroid-chuggers who have no respect for natural law! Marriage is Supposed to be between a man and woman and verified by the pastor of the church! Heathen Japanese robot scientists, know that you will meet hellfire for your sins!

Hentai Handmaiden Sexxx Robot

Anti-American Agenda: Anime Invasion Agenda/Liberal Agenda/ Video-Game Union Agenda

Weapon Grade: X3 Class masturbatory sin device to entice Americans to perform sex acts on artificial devil whores.

Terror Warning Level: SS (Severely Sinister: for creating sick sex robots to tempt men straight to hell.)

Danger Rating: Android Demon Whacking 4½ / 5 stars

Description: The Japanese have now created a sex robot and are selling it. They call this filthy invention the Roxxxy Robot and it is full of mechanized sin!

We wish this were still World War II because we'd sign up for the Air Force and drop nukes all over these lowlifes!

How sick is it that they have created this filthy mecha and are advertising it as the "world's first life-size robotic girlfriend." As if you should be tangling nasties outside of marriage in the first place!

The sickest thing about this robot is that the Japanese have programmed it with artificial intelligence. It can blink its eyes and move its limbs. It can make noises.

A man named Douglas Hines is responsible for the American sales of this contraption. Look at his foul words: "She can't vacuum, she can't cook, but she can do almost anything else if you know what I mean."

He continues, "She's a companion. She has a personality. She hears you. She listens to you. She speaks. She feels your touch. She goes to sleep. We are trying to replicate a personality of a person."

The Roxxxy Japanese sex robot is five feet, seven inches tall, one hundred and twenty pounds, and "has a full C cup and is ready for action," according to Hines.

It is no surprise to find that this evil robot is being sold in Sin City Vegas right now and we are going to boycott!

We hope that someone who sticks their woggle wag in there gets electrocuted to death so this whore robot gets sued and then burned all to the ground. Burn them all!

This robot is going to break marriages apart and tear apart families. No surprise the Japanese are so anxious to start selling it here. If you see one in your hometown, boycott the store and burn the robots! The only one who would be upset is Satan. Whore demon robots from Japan have no place here.

Robot Children

Anti-American Agenda: Genetic Atheist Agenda/Evilution Agenda/ Liberal Agenda

Weapon Grade: Astrologically "Yellow Mini" superhuman bomber whose squinted eyes provide HDTV-quality spy coverage of American streets and schools, all while discouraging real-life kids with its computer-driven memories controlled by JASA ground control engineers.

Terror Warning Level: RF (Robot Fetuses: Japanese scientist modifying children with electronics found in their crafty electronic devices and brainwashing them to kamikaze attack American soil.)

Danger Rating: Electronic Baby Bombs 4 / 5 stars

Description: My friends as we know, the Japanese are a vile people before God who do perverted things to their children. They now weld sinful agenda into the body of their kids, all to undermine America.

We have seen them sing their immoral poopsies songs and fornicate their kids with squid anime pornography, but never in a million years did we suspect we would catch them doing biomechanical experiments on their kids.

They have now used their Jap science to create robot children. At first we thought this was just a Halloween costume, but it turns out from our sources that the Japanese are now experimenting with live human robot armies.

They must plan to join China as allies against America. Blood is thicker than water and from the looks of things, there is no difference between a Chinese and a Japanaman. They are all looking the same and hating America.

You cannot trust a people who will craft machine parts into their children, then brainwash them to attack America. Japan already proved they will stoop to low ends when they told their young boys to hop into crop planes and fly those planes into American ships during World War II.

In addition to forcing their children to off themselves, we see the Japanese do not fight fair either. There is no word yet from the U.N. on this subject, but we hope and pray there are at least sanctions because this is a crime against humanity and exploitation of children.

Ropid Robot

Anti-American Agenda: Prowling Black Afro-Saxon Agenda/ ObamaCare Agenda

Weapon Grade: Prototype primitive robot to make neo-urban/corporate partnership corruption seem like a cute little Indian monkey dancer.

Terror Warning Level: TB (Tainted Bubonic: brown and black robot death.)

Danger Rating: Ghetto Dangerous 5 / 5 stars

Description: My friends, the Japanese scientists have now officially gone

too far! They have created a way for whores, gays, and homosexual pe-
domen to electronically dilly your kids too! We are absolutely livid and
organizing a way to boycott Japan off the world wide web!

We could only wish that Harry Truman were alive to properly take care of the place that created this Penistron contraption because the heat of 1 million nukes will not compare to the heat of hell, where its creators belong!

This is outrageous. Japanese scientists have created a new video game where people can electronically control a man's thingy or a woman's sally jessie!

Let's say a gay man comes on Myspace and tricks your college son into buying one of these abominations. The gay man can use a joystick to electronically control the artificial Satan scepter in your son's room, all the way on the other side of the world via Internet.

The gay will then type, "Okay, now stick the rod into your devilhole and I'll make it move all around with my joystick here!" You see what is going on here! I wish this were two thousand years ago and we had unlimited stones to throw at all involved parties!

Rest assured that while all these online gays, homosexuals, and whores are fornicating with this new video game, Satan will be typing "LOL" (laughs out loud) as he creates a new place in hell for all involved parties.

My friends, this game is sick and there is nothing fun about burning in hell. This Penistron is absolutely filthy. Your wife and daughters may get an offer from a stranger to "sign on late one night and stick this thingy where the sun don't shine" and think their new playtime won't lead them to burn forever.

Oh my friends, we am so ascared and you should be too. As we researched the web for more information about this fornicating electronic sex hobbit, the more our knees shake with fear of annihilation. There is an "upgrade" for this bakatech called the Ropid Robot Penistron. My friends, this thing can do it all: jump, look both ways, turn circles, and run! It stands just as tall as a Japanese at about four feet tall and lacks a heart as well. That means just like those kamikazes from World War II, it has no problems killing innocent people dead.

A liberal conspiracy of new-age rags to riches, the Ropid Robot is the brainchild of Shock Yellow technology bought out by ObamaCare-era illegal tax-funneling into corporate D.C. think tanks. The new robot kicks this contraption up a notch by attaching a Mexican hat-drug-dancing robot midget to the Penistron.

It may seem ridiculous, and what's even more shocking is liberals love it. Every day shock jocks like Howard Stern endorse this dancing menace, using moaner whores in the studio to test it out and then telling 18 million parents it is all fun and innocent. Video-game arcade pavilions attach this robot to *Dance Dance Evolution*, tricking kids with a "cool" robot dancemate who gets them bent over in an Odd Twister dance move. It'll then moonwalk over, do a double-down Macarena and snocker them right in their sin treats. It is a simple Obama conspiracy of highest degree.

The end goal is simple: money. There is a power play; the more little brownie babies running around, the more a family can claim for welfare. The more welfare, they more Obama can spend on worthless programs to drive our country into deeper Socialism. Maobama knows the more kids he can get with flussy hooker-whore values, the more underaged sinchildren will population boom like Chinese horny rabbits and then fester with the stagnation of Indian rainwater! It is an abacus-calculated disease bloom of welfare and poverty, which makes his Moor mouth salivate with the American spirit.

Obama and his left-handed legion want a population of underage babies and welfare mothers, so society will grow dependent on ObamaCare.

Any stranger can hop onto Facebook or *The Advocate* and control one of these mechanized "dancing penii" monstrosities from a control application. They can electronically plug their eranger into your kids from their secret basements, Obama general conspiracy rooms or jail prisons. You are terrified and wonder why your child is spending so much time alone in his room. Does he have a jumbo-edition Ropid Rumbler and Facebook?

Be assured, Online pedostrians will be trying to send a new "gift" to your sons for Christmas, and you'll never know why they are locked in their room for hours with their magically swiveling robot scepters.

The Penistron technology is directly from Satan himself and we are not surprised it was invented by the Japanese. Please alert your parenting/church networks about this device so we can start to organize the official boycott.

Asimo Robot

Anti-American Agenda: Genetic Atheist Agenda/Evilution Agenda/ Liberal Agenda

Weapon Grade: AAAI Advanced Artificial Asian Intelligence designed to walk on our soil and interact with the American people without knowing they are being spied on.

Terror Warning Level: AY (Agent Yellow: This robot is so advanced and evil that it can even see, walk, talk, and do long division, easily.)

Danger Rating: Advanced Asian Scare 5 / 5 stars

Description: We figured this day would come before long. For years we have built up a large arsenal of weapons, and ever since they were two, each one of our boys has been learned how to shoot a gun proper. All the families at Christwire are all excellent marksmen and hopefully the same is true for your family.

The world is now in official peril, my friends. The rowdy Japanese have finally created the apocalypse technology—that is, a robot that can learn.

They call it Asimo and this robot is more evil than the Japanese fire-breathing robots, hover tank robots, and even their gay-marriage-pastor robots and hooker-whore robots. These robots can learn endlessly and take over Earth if we do not shoot them down on sight and nuke Japan in every facility that insists on making these death machines.

If the idea of a learning robot is not bad enough, the Japanese have given this robot abilities that no one has a right to have. The robot can upload itself to www so it can even see what you are doing on your computer. It can leave messages on Twitters and break into your home Internet to trick your children like a Myspace stranger, and entice them to come out into the open, where it can abduct them or do any sort of evil programs to them. You can only imagine the sick, evil, twisted things the Japanese will program these robots to do, based on their anime pornography and fascination with the morbid.

We call for all families to go on high alert and demand America tell the U.N. that this robot is banned in all countries, and whosoever shall break our edict shall be kicked out and cut off from the rest of the world. We will nuke whoever allows this robot into the Stone Age and hold its creators a tribunal for crimes against humanity.

ON THE RED HORIZON

As you know, the Japanese have a perverse infatuation with creating weapons and immoral technology. Their people have no hearts and love to conduct secret experiments where they make machines that can kill people more efficiently.

Much as with nuclear arms, the field of robotics has way too many dangerous applications and should be trusted only to a responsible, moral nation like America that uses technology to bring peace and stability to the world.

As these robots become more a part of everyday technologies, the rise of the red Communist sun hibernates on the horizon of America's shores once again. Sleeper cells live amongst us as our neighbors and work in our family-owned convenience stores. They lurk in our society, blending in with the common folk, but far from common they are. They lie asleep waiting for war as they dream of the day they hear the call from the conch rebellion being blown.

Just be warned, they are in your yards cleaning your lawn, they clean the dishes at your favorite restaurant, they do your wife's nails once a month, they tease your girlfriend's hair at the salon, they are our customer-service representatives, they work the counter at the gas station, and they even work at our DMV offices.

Even though they come in many different forms, they all share the same goal, to destroy America from within. The flag they fly may come in different colors and variations, but all bow to the golden star laid upon a Communist sea of red blood. They all may have different community organizers, but all bow before the same dictator of merciless horror.

The Japanese are smart: they have already feasted at the steak-house of America's divine wrath. Their scientists know to create evil technology in secret, but to give it to a new master. The gays are queeresponsible; they carelessly dance around stark decadence and are not cunning enough to wield a doomsday weapon. They seek a master to strap them down in obedience, all while the terror hordes wait to assault American freedom with primitive-brown bared hands.

Upon the new horizon, the skies cry out in a sea of crimson. Our enemies from without and within tremble, all kneeling before a new master of ancient origin, one who constructed their own protection walls thousands of years ago. Upon the zephyrs of Orient, blinding embers fire and dragon's steamy breath explodes, each growing gust singeing the locks of Lady Liberty and burning the wings of Heaven's angels with a soul-chilling gale.

On the Red Horizon, a heart churns with newfound hate and vengeance. Rising from the ashes of defeat, a great fiery beast has been reborn. It hungers. It lusts. It touches itself while dreaming of desires to thrust its ravaging claws deep into the tightly covered bosom of writhing freedom, then to satiate its passionate thirst for damnation with the tortured screams of innocence lost.

America lies flushed and prostate, weakened to her holy knees by gay agendas, Japanese torment technologies, liberal betrayal, and Muslim mayhem.

Above all iniquity, and above all hate, a silence falls over the world. On the Red Horizon, The Ancient Beast awakens to challenge America's throne as humanity's lone savior and eternal superpower.

CHAPTER 4

Foreign Dangers

LEVITICUS 25:44-46
"However, you may purchase male or female slaves from among the foreigners who live among you. You may also purchase the children of such resident foreigners, including those who have been born in your land. You may treat them as your property, passing them on to your children as a permanent inheritance. You may treat your slaves like this, but the people of Israel, your relatives, must never be treated this way."

INTRODUCTION

China is a sleeping dragon, waiting to wake up and viciously devour your life and soul!

My friends, today you should beware the threat of China like never before! As you sit comfortably at home or toiling at work, the nation of China is training its male citizens like crazy so they can enact their eternal end goal . . . World Domination.

I am extremely terrified of Chinese people, but I'm not racist. You should feel the same way too.

Much like their brethren in the U.S.S.R. and the Democratic party, the Chinese are atheistic wonders. Their lack of morals means they have no problems developing WMDs with which to bring massive death, all while doing genetic manipulation and cloning to ensure population boom.

Only sixty years ago, these Asian peoples joined up with Adolf Hitler in order to destroy the most moral nation on Earth. Even though their attacks took the lives of many good men on a day of infamy, America was blessed to rain bombs of freedom and nurture resultant liberty within a very dark Asian culture.

Despite past American grace, the menace of the People's Republic of China is truly a great peril to the world today. Indeed, these people seek nothing but to steal land from the West and kill you and your family dead in the process.

Not only a few years ago, China managed to reconquer the lands of Hong Kong and steal it back from Great Britain, all while no one did anything about it.

You see, dear readers, the fact of the matter is that the Chinese Communists are very cold, calculating, and harsh people. The core values of Chinese Communism include wanton carnality, stealing, bringing death, and providing slothful people with income. From the time it's formed as a zygote, every Chinese baby's heart is innately filled with much hate for not only you, but your children as well. It's a part of their cultural heritage to hate the good Eest.

Historically, Chinese people have naturally wanted to bring destruction and great mayhem to all things American. Liberals will tell you lies and say this is not true and very extreme, but mark my words. Liberals want nothing more than to see a small population of America overrun by billions of Asians. This is why they support abortion.

Now skeptics and atheists out there will say that Chinese kill their young too, and yes, you're right. It's true. Reports show that each and every day the Chinese people brazenly sacrifice their young women in pagan ceremonies, so that their men may have more supplies and food stuffs to consume as they train for battle.

What battle, you may ask?

Know that the Chinese are going to attempt a great battle, battle being perhaps better described as a world-domination plan. Such endeavors typify their nature, as their culture still does not value the principles of life, liberty, and pursuit of happiness.

Asia still is bitter about WW II, and how we showed them new ways to live outside their old pagan tradition, and it's for this reason that you must be very afraid. At its roots China embraces Communism, a practice which noble men like Senator McCarthy, President Ronald Reagan, and the somewhat liberal John Paul II fought against with all their heart.

Much like when the Soviet Russians were the powerhouse of liberalism, the Chinese are busy performing all sorts of nuclear experiments, genetic manipulation, and training of troops. They are even responsible for the recent housing-market crunch and faltering U.S. economy.

How can we combat this Communist threat?

Right now, YOU CAN NOT. Bill Clinton was caught giving our nuclear secrets to China, and President Obama has let them buy up all of our national debt. Not until you write your Congressman and demand McCarthyism once again be our national standard, the menage of Chila will continue to grow.

Unfortunately, next time they may pick you and your precious family as their Pearl Harbor! Call your politicians today and demand a return of McCarthy, all for you and and the bring joy to your kid's future.

THE ORIENTAL EXPRESS

Armed with a hidden culture and knowledge almost older than six thousand years, the Chinese of new inherit the sinful thoughts of Ancient Sensei Satan—the fallen lord of the Orient.

Within their Hindu Bindi religions, they fall before the throne of iniquity, yelping out with foreign tongue and asking Satan to bless them with ill-technological abilities just as he did their ceremonial forefathers.

In the day of ancient, Satan gave the Chinese gun powder to bring war to Christian Europe. He gave them fine silks, so that their women could seduce innocent traveling Greeks with "Sucky sucky five dorrah" schemes of nastiest perversion. Then, he gave them writing, a scribblestick language that baffles everyone from the most knowing scientist to the crayon-armed three-year-old.

But today, Satan realizes the children of God have grown powerful. God has bestowed upon America a nuclear might and industrial strength that overcame Satan's heil champion of the last century. Satan is ready for a new Super Bowl and is arming his new team with mystical techniques to weaken America from without and within, so the final showdown of Revelation will be in his favor.

Satan is a student of history and knows he must be careful and strategic, so he has donned Soviet-lined argyle socks and IBM computer technology to diligently align his Chinese lemonlords and their pawns. They move carefully, each move triple calculated by 2.6 billion lightning-fast hands, all moving in unison to bring checkmate techniques to God's chosen ruler of morality and mankind.

The code-yellow agents from the Far East have plotted America's end ever since they failed back in the forties and fifties. With defeat painted on their hands, the Dread Asian empire grows infatuated with perverse revenge and hatred toward the Western holy land. The Buddha Dragon's belly hungers to grow fat by feasting upon Christian sorrow and gobbling down American corporate enterprise, creating a nasty gastric mixture of Beijing Sunshine McGriddles and Woktong Wal-Marts as its weight crushes our failing economy.

Knowing any direct attack at America would be foiled within a matter of hours, the Chinese understand their hidden power is using Shanghai shinobi tactics to try and blindside America with peppered terrorists from the east, while they soysoak our culture with the overwhelming tanginess of Satan's master tangle of doomed Asian invasion.

The Chinese are music to Satan's ears, so it's no surprise to see these Mao maestros have orchestrated an anti-American melody that will strike fear into your hearts and cause Satan to sing encore.

From the east, the Chinese government furiously shakes its bamboo baton, calling upon its Muslim sandhorn section to blow blinding torrents of terror and hate all across America's heartland. With crescendos and fortes of unprecedented bigotry, the big bad Akbars do their best to huff hate into our innocent hearts and then puff fiery destruction into the gentle breaths of every precious American baby.

Oh, friends, it is the most unmerry melody, but rest assured. The Muslims are nothing but an iTunes sample, just a pale thirty-second taste of what China can truly do in a full set. The true Chinese are using the Muslims as a cheap opening act, hoping we will jump up and down in panicked horror as we point out Hollywood Fab Satan's crescent star celebrities, when in fact we are seeing just a terror body double.

As the terrorists do their little sandal prances upon the catwalk and take credit for all the latest Hollywood explosions and CNN summer blockbusters, the true star of the show sits pensively at home, plotting out the next stage and act of America's destruction.

Just like their jujitsu Japanese cousins, the Chinese plan to sneak-kick America when we have our pants down, collectively dropping giblets of shameful horror from the perceived Muslim threat. That is to say, China plans to fury-kick us in the balls when we least expect it.

Such cheap tactics do not seem very sporting, but we must remember the Chinese are dirty Communists and there is nothing fair about their atheist culture. They are full of hate and seethe with a dragon's fury, so have no shame in cheaply undercutting capitalism and composing America's death scene in the most chilling ways possible.

China has already written the death ballad for America. It plays as your eyes read these words. Satan taps his foot and a demon plays a cheerful violin, for the signs are nigh. American's doom is on the horizon. The Chinese plan to become the new America and we need to only look no further than glorious Wally-Mart to see the mitey Chinese have already infested our culture.

CHINESE WAL-MART

Wal-Mart is a once proud American company created by a good Christian man, the late Sam Walton. Sam Walton wanted Wal-Mart in every town, so American families could buy quality products at a good price. He wanted to do his part in helping the pocketbook of every American family, and bless him for what he has done.

It is so sad that Wal-Mart is now becoming a less moral place. It is starting to allow non-quality products to slip through its bay doors onto the shelves and it even preys upon its humble employees and small towns. It is becoming a typical corporation. It is no wonder that it now has major Chinese shareholders and divisions.

There are certain things they sell at Chinese Wal-Mart that they don't sell at proper Wal-Mart in America, and we will now review these items to see what they are up to over in Communist China.

SEAWATER CROCODILES

The Chinese are no strangers to eating improper animals and pets: puppies, goldfish, monkeys, and even octopi! That is just weird and sick. Squid! Yuck.

So it is no surprise to see they take a mighty sea salt crocodile and try to make it as normal as having a row of chickens or cut flank steak. We would get sick and ask them why they are eating reptiles instead of leaving them in the bayou.

CHINESE MYSTERY MEAT

An average human being would be too scared to eat this. It is called "mixed cuts" in their language, but that's just a veil name like "mystery meat" is on some nasty public-school lunch menus.

What "the meat" really is is anyone's guess, and for a people who think it is normal to eat crocodiles and pets and then throw away your sweet daddy's little girl, we just would not trust this meat and buy it. If you are in China, it is probably safest to just go with the rice and it will save you money should you need an emergency plane or taxi.

LIVE TURTLES

And even though they can make nice things, we see that they also have no laws for animal cruelty. Here we see they have placed some nice turtles, as if they were some delicious lobsters waiting to get boiled.

Turtles have visible heads and brains, so it is sad that Chinese boil these turtles alive to make soup and their whole family squeals with delight as the turtle flicks its little tongue and tries to hide in its shell while they boil it. Our hearts are heavy for the fate of the millions of turtles in Chinese Wal-Mart.

Turtles also carry the risk of salmonella, so they spray them down with harsh chemicals (giving it skin burns) before boiling them alive too. Such torture and animal rights violations are not American.

CHINESE BEER ($0.15)

The Chinese love to drink beer with their rice, so it is no surprise that for the price of fifteen pennies, a Chinese can buy a bottle of whiskey. We always used to think it was a joke in the karate movies, how the drunk karate man could just have bottle after bottle of Satan's nectar as if he could afford it on a Communist house budget.

But now we see that even the Chinese can afford beer at these prices and that is why it must be so common. We hope they just don't drink themselves into reservations and not wanting to take care of their country like the Indians did, or we may just have to go over there and take care of them on reservations while we run the nation. It would be a sad shame, but I would support us doing that to help those poor drunk savages.

INSTRUCTIONAL DVD

As we searched Chinamart's video section for more films to warn everyone about, nothing could prepare us for the filth we discovered. A demonic Chimpopn play to seduce American men!

From all their perverted anime and willie-tingler robots they are making sure we know these veil people are hiding nothing but sin under their curtsies and big fake smiles! But this takes the cake!

Chinese schools are teaching their young teen schoolgirls classes on how to seduce us in our American language! They always try to pretend that Asian education is gooder than ours, but you see these lowlifes are literally learning their children how to "sucky, sucky, five dorrah you make my juice frow!"

Yeah, you liberals whine and say we're making all this up, but you just watch this following filthy display, then try to cry about cultural sensitivity!

This is one but a billion of those Japasians and I'll tell you what. They can keep their filthy man-seducing ways to their-selves, putting sticks in their hair and painting their faces like mimes!

My blood is boiling with the rage of many exploding suns right now and I pray that God's wrath strikes down their universities and grade schools with a holy tsunami this summer, right in their American-language classrooms.

If this were World War II, I would laugh with delight as I reported these videos, then watched as our American military put involved sake prostitute devilwhores where they belong!

Liberals will try to say this is all fine and a part of culture, but we'll see what they say when their young son dies from cancer or AIDS because he got a little "OOOO suck suck one dorrah!" on his twiddler rumpus and lived out his final days stricken with bird flu and all the other Asian viruses!

My friends, this is why we must stop the Asians from peddling their filth in this Godly nation. They are training their women to attack our men with sex! Let us leave comments and DEMAND this filth be taken out of our American country!

The only juices "frowing" will be the marinade Satan uses when he grills all involved parties upon the propane grills of hell!

THE SHOCK JOCKS OF THE AIRWAVES

Chinese ambition does not stop in the suit-and-tie corporate world. With the strongest of American shopping institutions dominated, the Chinese sit coy and cockeyed, like a four Loko–chugging praying mantis under the command of Sun-Wun Buddha.

It's an almost wondrous sight to see their industrious claws clack while their little bugeyes roll around, wild like a drunken blues trumpeter searching for the next sour note to make all in the crowd cringe from inharmonic accidental perversion. But rest assured, there is nothing soulful about the Asian hornet assault that is coming for our airwaves.

The Chinese media empire seeks to sting America in the most naughty places, knowing that this sting will be nothing we can ignore. And who can ignore the loud and proud ramblings of media's king of spin and sin, Howard Stern?

While the upper echelons of America have their Godly morality proven by their Right political affiliation and financial blessings, at the bottom lie the common masses. The rogue pleb mob, as Plato so affectionately called them.

No better than clamoring Greeks at the Colosseum, the bottom line of America want nothing but a bloodbath of filth, bathroom-stall shock and awe to satiate their perverted desires. These are the children of liberal politics, the victims of decades' worth of immoral television and video game assaults on morality. These are the 20 million fans of Howard Stern, who listen to him and his vaggiterian cohost every morning from their Sirius XM hybrid pansywagon satellite boom boxes. They can hear twenty-four hours of strippers playing Syberian midget moan make-out games and their ears can be filled with perversions of wiener and fart jokes, the bread and butter of the Chinese comedian's dinner table conversation.

The Chinese eyes squint with phenomenal focus and amazing oriental math calculations as they know that if they can capture all of

Stern's listeners, they can control nearly 10 percent of America. To bogart Stern's magic microphone hold over the masses, the abacus masters have unleashed a monster scheme of flubbering proportions.

THE GLAMOUR GAYSHA BOMBSHELL

In the secret of night, the hefty hentai handymaidens of Hu Jintao will tenderly enter your child's room. Instead of worrying about Little Johnny playing undercover twiddle stacks with a flesh magazine, your mind must worry if he wants that twenty dollars to get a jumbo-sized Twinkie filling behind the food court's mandarin woks.

It is all a sick, sweaty, disgusting mess for parents to think about and this is exactly what China wants. They want your sons to turn into little marching Mouseketeers, ferreting each other's excremental Ho Chi sin tunnel mazes in confused ecstasy.

Original geisha girl.

They want your daughters to feast upon the tables of yellow-colored marshmallows, so a new tribe of loyalists will arise from America's ovens nine months later.

This scheme is not half-baked but one that not even Chef Ramsay could muster in the most hellacious kitchen.

The Chinese scheme is simple. They will overtake our media with an unprecedented perversion factor. Our sons will cry out, "Teriyaki ticklings!" in excited delight when they see a glamour gaysha, while women and children run around in circles, confused by images of vajazzled sumo wrestlers playing wet-noodle slaphouse with the newly gay men of America on Mao Disney Channel.

With all the men dreaming of rice rockets in their launch pads, the women will be left to have their natural female lust for phalluses filled by lemon drizzles.

New glamour gaysha.

There is nothing racist in the context of truth! When loquacious liberals get anger-lipped and try to say these things are not veritable, ask them about the role of geishas in ancient society. Ask them why, if women are not sex-addicted little vixens who crave their Eve pits be filled with sizzling pork desire, they have given birth to 6 billion pieces of proof that females crave sex worse than a catnip-snorting kitten forced into the sober Bunny Ranch for weeks on end.

The Chinese media empire is a beast unto itself, a hungry mantid of epic lore that sees the most "shocking" Americans in television and media as but ripe, young honeydew grasshoppers. Their corporate executives are one in the same with their government leaders. They know America's modern men are not cut from the same cloth as those in the forties and fifties; they understand American women love to advertise their desire for constant rogering with detonate-here tramp-stamps on their lower backs, backyard advertised by the bared Facebook and Myspace pictures they send to all their guy friends.

The lines between men and women slowly fade in America. It is unknown whether a swift wind's gust will expose a fake vagine or portly puffer when a "woman's" skirt is hixed by Satan's New York chuckle winds. The transgenic sexuality of America's DNA culture does not confuse China's brilliant media scientists. They understand one simple empirical fact: Sex sells and to overtake America, they must sell the most lurid samples of their cultural depravity.

In ancient China, supple and firm geishas would emerge in the still of night, dragging random men away to pleasure pits where they would fulfill their most tantalizing desires. Countenances rigid in the deepest throes of ecstasy, the geisha girls of China were known to torment poor Chinese travelers with hours upon hours of fornication, until the men were finally forced to release their seedshot against their will. The poor men only wanted to remain loyal to their wives, but instead, were victimized by the government scheme to insure all Chinese women were constantly pregnant with their future death armies.

Don't be shocked—there was decency in the most ancient men of China. They were proud scholars and children of semi-morality during the JC dynasty. But as warned by the illustrious Pastor Jack Gould, pornography is drugs for the mind. The pits of writhing geisha would not only drag the defiant men down into their suffocating leg grips and gymnast pleasure pommels once, but have them happily returning again and again in sexual addiction. China's men were weakened. They no longer respected their nuclear families, but instead, played right into the Chinese liberal elite's plan to overtake the world with prostituted pregnancies. This is how China has nearly 2 billion people.

From this ancient lesson, the modern Chinese Jintao dynasty takes a lesson and is unleashing a glamour gaysha upon America's youths. In T-shirt stores across the nation, boys who like sugar in their tea are encouraged to wear "Glamour Gaysha" shirts and worship at the brand's glimmer girl, a five hundred and eighty-three-pound Sumo fashion model named Hoki Horitzu, the Hong Kong terror.

Never mind that China stole the great city of Hong Kong from London through Carter-era betrayals; the "Twinkie Treaty," as this sumo model is affectionately called in San Francisco fashion stores, is branding your boys with a searing logo that makes Satan somersault in sniffing delight. To the great dragon, the seared flesh of gay is better than a medium-rare steak with a nose-tickling side of vintage vino tinto from Castilian Spain. Each bite is a refreshing reminder that all gays will one day have an all-expense trip to hell, booked by the effervescent Chinese Media.

Where America currently sees shock and awe with gay sitcoms and Jersey girls whose attitudes exude the aroma of three-day arm-sewer sweat upon a river rat's breath, the Chinese hear the soothing mouth whispers of an angel's bedtime lullaby. Their shock-jock media will drive a wedgie deep into our current "bad boys", making them cry out like schoolgirls who just lost their favorite binkie doll lollipops.

Howard Stern may be one of the most vile defilers in history, even bringing his malicious cuss-drenched Tweets to the innocent songbird youths Twittering their lives' gentle details to all their friends. But know this. The Chinese Howard Stern will be twice as black-nasty, a raging panther demon ripping and filling the airwaves with a howling mix of raciarry slurred speech, obligatory Chinagirl ecstasy moans, and sumo-man panties.

It's a musty mix of sin and you will find the names that shock and awe the American household would not even warrant a yuan in values-deprived China. On their game shows, old geriatric men are forced to strip down and play flap dangle slip and slide across oiled-down giggle geishas. On *Octopus Octogenarian*, Chinese grannies are stripped down to their Depends and then are forced to escape a shallow pool of eighty eight-armed writhing octopi that are laced on LCD. Remember, noble Nixon did not have scandal or questionable ethics until his soul was blackened by entering morally bankrupt Beijing.

It may sound crazy, but it is all true. Ask any missionary and they will tell you of all the awkward sumo sutra positions they were forced to lie in just to leave the savage airport gates of China.

Even on Chinese *Family Feud*, nuclear innocence is lost as the losing family's father has to let the host pierce his wife's Mandarin delight with his soy-spouting fleshsword, then eat breaded baby pudding. The audience sees all of these things and politely smiles, giving golf claps as the studio lights dim and they go on about their day-to-day lives.

China wants unimaginable nastiness to become the flag-waving standard for America. They want us to pledge allegiance to the flag of a country that refuses to deport bleach-blond Chihuahua-squealing illegals who refuse to correctly sing our national anthem before the big game. The Chinese want us to sit with obligatory wooden Asian face, bereft of expression and rich with flat affect, as our eyes witness children licking gay ice creams at phallic penis festivals in the park, to celebrate the latest gay marriage between chipper Steve and Merriweather Maury, sunny sin-kissed hair waving in gentle auburn waves, adorned with Sadako crane pigeon barrettes.

For every one American gay marriage, two more people can never give birth to American children. The Chinese want the population of true Americans to dwindle, driven into the madness of thinking gay marriage is normal by lovable effeminate secretary boi characters on Chinese Mao's *Office* or even creating shows where gay adoptions and sewer-hole cakes are common child topics for talking birds on *Opiate Street*.

Do you see their agenda? It is to enter our society and unleash a supernova-sized media bomb into American homes via radio and television. As we cope with the vertigo associated with gay thoughts and gay bowel disease, the Chinese will continue to procreate and begin their Asian Invasion of God's chosen nation.

THE AUTOMOTIVE BONSAI

Over the past few years, Chinese were being very smug and arrogant, making fun of fair America because for the first time in the history of the modern world they managed to sell more cars than us.

Now, much like you, we are extremely terrified of Chinese people, but we are not racist. The fact that they so blatantly cheated to outpace America in auto sales this year, then started having national parties to gloat about their dishonest and relatively insignificant victory is just more evidence of their deep-seated desire to beat us at everything!

Yes, today it may be automobile sales. But tomorrow it may be your life. Your precious little loved ones' lives too.

As China continues their victory parties, there is one thing we would like this great land of pagan magics and extreme anti-Americana patriotism to answer. Who invented the automobile-making process?

Now this search result may be blocked in the Chinese web search, so let us tell you.

Americans.

George Selden. Ransom Olds. Henry Ford.

These titans of industry created the market for the automobile, and the hardworking, innovative American people started the process of mass producing these wonderful chariots of the modern age.

America is also a benevolent power, therefore we taught the rest of the world how to make a proper gasoline-powered car and make them affordable, so anyone, even poor pagan farmers in countries that like to mock the very people who gave them technology, could afford them.

Now it has come to pass that, for once, the student has temporarily surpassed the teacher, and I do not find the student's antics, granted their perceived victory, very nice. The teasing, taunting, and other sophomoric antics are just very inappropriate, China.

All America has ever asked in return for teaching the world how to make cars is that you use them for good and love, and also let us have access to our nice oil in the Arab countries that have it in their soil.

At every turn it seems, however, that the world has abused this wonderful technology that America drafted for the good of all mankind. The Germans exploited our technology of mass production and attempted to blitzkrieg the world into oblivion. Even though America saved the world from the Nazis, it still broke everyone's heart—including that immortalized heart of Mr. Ford—to know Germany would employ the technology for evil.

Still, we rebuilt Germany and their allies in Asia, giving them the tools to create companies such as Volkswagen, Mercedes, Toyota, and Honda. What is the thanks we get?

The Germans create high-priced cars that fly right in the face of our principles of creating affordable automobiles for all, then laugh at American cars for being "cheap and inferior". Meanwhile, the Chinese and their friends sell questionably built cars for very cheap, laughing at America when their billions of people buy these cars and they therefore have better auto sales than the good U.S.A. for a brief fiscal period.

Know this, however, you automobile Brutuses. Life is not a stage play and the American automobile empire shall not fall by the tips of daggers wielded by ungrateful subjects. Nay!

We shall rise and after saying "Et tu, Brute?" to all you no-good, Judas countries who have benefited from our automobile technology, we will not fall over in a pool of our own life-blood, but instead innovate and recreate an automobile market the likes of which the world has never seen.

With the glorious pools of its life-giving oil in tow, the American automobile industry will indeed rise again and be the envy of the modern world. There is no one who can dissuade the economically sound, feasible, frugal, and yet stable ability of American innovation and craftsmanship. No one will be able to stop our efficient, practical, and affordable machines from once again dominating the global market.

Now with China's new found fake sense of victory, they have gotten a little bit too cocky with their death plots for America. With biochemical warfare on the minds of all terrorist nations, China was the first country to actually try a full-scale assault against America with viral attacks. But like everything else the Chinese do, it sloped flat on its face, before it could even build steam.

THE SARS SCARE

One of China's most recent plots to use Commie viruses to destroy America came in 2003, when they tried to infect businessmen who were traveling from China's Communist capitals, back to America with a deadly lung bacteria called "SARS," which to them stood for "Strike American Republic with Sickness."

SARS was developed after their loss in the Korean War. The Chink-a-billy scientists worked hard trying to develop a disease that their jaundice-color bodies would be immune to, but could affect non-sin-tainted Americans. They were able to develop a sickness that couldn't live in their highly polluted Communist air, but once it was allowed in clean golden American breathable air, it would grow and develop into a silent killer.

The idea was to hire kabuki girls to come in contact with American businessmen, cough on them, and then wait for the bacteria to settle down in the lungs. Once the lungs had absorbed the illness, it laid dormant. When the male businessman left the sin-polluted air of China, the virus would start to slowly grow, and by the time they touched down on our holy USA soil, the virus was in full effect.

Not knowing they were infected, the businessmen would go back to work and cough all over their offices, infecting their coworkers thinking they only had a simple cold. But simple it was not. This Hiroshima-sized virus attacked the infected person's lungs with great force, closing the lungs and airways so the carrier would die a slow and frightening death.

The SARS might have been a silent ninja attack, but before the Lemonheads could celebrate in terrorist fashion, our American doctors were able to karate chop the virus with our blessed medicine. Within four weeks of the outbreak, American scientists, with the help from God, were able to develop an anti-venom to this yellow plague and once again China stood in defeat.

But this sickness wasn't China's only attempt at infecting our great nation. Their evil, freedom-hating scientists tried to biologically engineer the criminals to our south, so they would spread a vile disease as they hopped over the border, giving our border patrol the middle finger as they smilingly walked by.

DISEASES ARE ALSO JUMPING OUR BORDERS

Like radical homosexual pirates, the south is raping our country, while it cries begging for more. Not only do our illegal amigos from the south bring high kidnap and murder rates and large unpaid medical bills to our country, they also bring vile bacteria over the border, making millions of Americans sick each year.

The Mexicans are germy because, since they are here illegally, they can't buy things like fresh water and antibacterial soap. They live in recluse homes and work in places like lettuce yards and chicken coops, where they have direct access to the very food that feeds our nation. Their hands are molesting our produce with foreign southern viruses that could pose a dangerous threat to the American immune system.

A perfect example of the types of dangerous diseases the Mexican

can bring over was the swine flu. The science community for months tried to blame it on pigs, but forgot we had people in our country who live just like pigs, so it threw off their research. Once they were actually able to test one of these portable filth transporters, they found the virus was being carried within the ponchos of field workers.

You see, my friends, flu virus can lie dormant. Within the Mexican genome and others who were infected, the virus did not manifest. Instead, it just hid within the alleles of those infected, but then it started to raise itself to kill us all again!

You all remember the symptoms: taco-scent sweat, bugged-out glossy eyes, a lax tongue, smelly bowels, and retching of the guts. It is just like a weekend in Mexico after drinking the *agua mala*—that is, bad water in American language. You get the same symptoms, but with swine flu, there is no return and odds are you would have died!

During the outbreak of swine flu, America fell down with a disease that not even Montezuma could call his own. This is more proof why we must throw all the Mexicans out of our country. They think they can sneak in here and steal our way of life and then give us their illnesses!

They are like vomit spreading throughout the clear streams of America. They are poisoning us with their nonsense language and filthy living habits! They are the truest and most spot-on definition of "filth" there is! They have tried to take over this country long enough and now they strike us with their swine-flu attack!

THE ATTACK FROM THE SOUTH

As the liberals fight for American rights for ILLEGAL immigrants, limp lefties are the people who have one Mexican short of a Taco Bell burrito working on their hundred-acre estates at $3.25 an hour.

Did you know that only every forty-three minutes, an unsuspecting American family is approached and then accosted by a stray Mexican? To add to these alarming figures, many of these poor, mangy wretches may have rabies and drug habits, leading to their reddened eyes and stoic stares without saying a word, only motioning to purses or wallets.

With the growth of this southern epidemic, the blood line of true Americans is being diluted with spicy meat sauce. They come from all of Mexico's states, whether it is Cuba, Brazil, Peru, or Puerto Rico, these roaches are crawling into our country right under the cracks of the American border. We are starting to lose our language, our culture, and even our ability to do our own lawn care. The days when being bilingual was something only the Canadians were, are over and we are faced with a mustached, cheap-labor evil that is being shielded and babied by our own government sympathizers.

Like all dirty things, Mexicans are the reason why the United States of America cannot own nice things. This is the main reason why we went out and created our DeportChristinaAguilera.com campaign. They come here not even knowing the basics of America, nor will they take time out of their non-busy days to learn maybe one or two sentences of English. Maybe they can start with learning how to say "Thank you for giving me freebies," or how about making them create thank-you cards to give out to tax payers during tax season.

It is sad times when white folk can't even enjoy a lovely walk around their neighborhoods without having to be mixed with lower-class people. These Mexicans, whether they are from Chile, Peru, Venezuela, or some other third-world, fiesta-having state within their southern country, are up to no good. Why can't we just go someplace and have good ol'-fashion entertainment without being afraid of being raped, murdered, or drugged?

Why is it when you want to have some American labor done, you're forced to have thirty-burrito breathed amigos in your house, looking your wife up and down while they take taco breaks every hour? You would think they get paid to have a siesta in your house at your expense. When you try to talk to them they say "No habler English," but if you ask them how much money you owe them, they become

English professors. They always get paid in cash as well, because they can't show any income to make sure they get that government assistance that all us law-biting Americans just love to pay. Who wouldn't want to get paid just to be lazy at someone else's house all day and have your wife produce as many baby grape pickers as possible?

Everywhere you drive in America now, you don't see signs saying WELCOME or AMERICAN RESTAURANT. You now see signs in Mexican saying *Servicio de Jose césped* or some other Latino scribble. It's bad enough that they can't speak or write in our holy American tongue, but now every sign has to be in Mexican or Chilean. Why do we have to change our country's ways to make illegals feel comfortable in our own country?

TACO CARTOONS ARE TURNING OUR CHILDREN INTO BI-LANGUAGE CITIZENS

They have even invaded our television screens trying to turn our children into little welfare recipients, with their hands out begging for a peso. The most famous bi-language cartoon is called *Dora The Explorer.*

This *Dora* show is about a young nine-year-old Mexican girl who dresses in a hooker fashion and tries to make our kids learn Mexican, just like an illegal's child would do.

The show always starts with a song: "Come on vamanos, everyone let's go!" You see, vamanos is Mexican for "Everyone let's go" in American.

They are trying to make our kids learn that language and how to communicate with illegals, so when they are older they will have a soft spot in their hearts for people who do not belong on our land in our country. They are trying to convert your children into social liberals who will not uphold President Ronald Reagan's Christian edict to kick all the illegals out of our country.

This cartoon is just more proof of why more states need to be like

Arizona and adopt hard-line anti-immigration laws. We need to stop all Mexican immigrants, Asian immigrants, African immigrants, and the like from coming into our country until we can get this illegal problem under control.

Our children must learn that whenever they see a suspicious Mexican, no matter the age, to detain him if it's a child, and if it's an adult, quickly call the police or tell the adult in charge (teacher if at school, us parents if at home or work). Illegals can be anywhere so we must always look out and know the signs:

- Illegal workers usually stand around in groups of four or five. They hold lawn equipment and instead of working, use their lips to point at girls they find attractive as they walk by. They also eat fruit and sandwiches from brown bags through the day.
- Old mariachi-music trucks. If you see a truck with several dusty-looking Mexicans in the back, and a seedy-looking driver

with a passenger, and it has loud mariachi music, the entire truck is illegal. This is a group of Mexicans looking for daily work land-scaping or perhaps drywalling.

- When you ask them a question, they grin and mumble, taking a step back. If their kids are sick, expect them to sneak to a hospital with a translator who pretends to be the parent of the child.
- Red-stemmed eyes and playing a game of pick-up soccer at the local park.
- Never come to PTO meetings for the children at school.

Now that you know Mexicans can be tricky, take a look at when they fooled us with their Chilean miner hoax. Third-world countries will do anything to try and make money, and that is what they did to the world. This was nothing but a big soap opera or as they would say a "telenovella." You could tell it was fake by how badly the His-panic acting was, and within a matter of hours they were being offered money for books and movies. They acted like they were in trouble. We know just one day inside of a mine, you will look dark as an Afro-Saxon selling crack coke cane while listening to hipped-hopped music on the corner in the Bronx. While they were playing their little jumping-bean games we sent our NASA employees and American money right to their doorstep so they could buy up the world's taco spice supply.

If you need more proof of how they like to steal and cheat from Americans, just look at how they stole our Christmas colors for their flag. How dare they take baby Jesus's holiday and smear it with their enchilada sauce of defiance. We need to take action before they suck away all things good in America.

The only way to stop the Mexican invasion and their deadly use of biological warfare is to ban them from gracefully walking over our border and at the same time we need to ban Satan from allowing them safe passage.

Since our new dictator is a puppet for the bean brigade military all we can do is protect ourselves and protect each other from the southern Zimmerman invasion of sombreros.

It is tough, but it must be done for our safety and the sake of the Mexicans. The other resorts would be internment camps or worse, which is just not a nice way to do things. So let us help deport the Mexicans to their home country, as President Ronald Reagan demanded only twenty years ago.

OUR PLANS TO STOP ILLEGAL IMMIGRATION AND MAKE MONEY

America is broke and America has an illegal Mexican problem. Even the other states of Mexico frown upon their northern state. They say they are the rednecks of their country, the less intelligent, and they speak Spanish incorrectly. We have a few ideas on how we can keep the jumping beans from the south out of America and make money at the same time.

Remember when you were a child and you would go to the Christian carnival? Do you remember your local pastor setting up fun games for you to play that cost a couple of tickets? Well we think we should take some of these games and modify them to include some of our border bouncers.

IDEA ONE: WET DOWN THE WETBACK

This idea would require us to build a large wall across our border, but have one part be a high chain-link fence. On one side of the fence we would have high-powered water guns and on the other side would be dirty Mexicans trying to climb the fence as fast as they could without being blasted off. The guns would cost a dollar five a minute.

IDEA TWO: WHACK THE WETBACK

This idea is quite fun. We could make large concert walks with little holes in them that the refried rice bean would have to crawl through. We would charge five dollars to people and they would have large hammers. They would sit and wait for a tortilla tosser to pop his head out and then whack him really hard.

To the Gulf

IDEA THREE: DUNK A JUAN

By far our favorite! This one will take some work but would be quite fun to play with the grandkids. We would round up any illegals caught the night before and slap them in a dunk tank. The dunk tank would have a tube that, once the border jumpers get dunked, would suck them out to the Gulf. You would pay two dollars a ball.

IDEA FOUR: TOWER OF SOMBREROS

Got a good arm? Think you can knock down more than "Juan" Mexican? Step right up and take your best shot at knocking down not just five but fifteen Rio Grande Salmon. This idea, we would take a group of fifteen illegals and stack them on top of each other. Once they were knocked down by one of those workout balls (which are five dollars a ball) they would crash into an inner tube, like the ones you see at water parks, and be ejected out to sea.

Now, saying these things about the Mexicans is not racist; it is fact. And we are not doing racial profiling, we are just using educated guesses. Many of the Christwire founders grew up in Southern California, and their families were blessed to own house Mexicans. Though they did not speak much American, they still all had hearts of gold.

They would cook, clean, garden, and tend to the children, all with a kindly smile and steadfast determination. At the end of the day, our parents would give them a bit of money and usually some food or other nice things to take home with them.

All across Southern California, Mexicans are vital to the economy. Some help farmers pick lettuce and sell produce to the free markets. Others do massive amounts of landscaping or perhaps serve up burgers at the local McDonalds.

House Mexicans always worked hard and usually never asked for a cent more than what they were paid; they appreciated the honor of serving a proper family with their dedicated work.

In exchange for their service, our families would give the house Mexicans real money—American dollars—to take home to their families. Most of them were paid fifty dollars a day, which is good money for a Mexican. They never stole and our families helped their families establish a great new life in los Estados Unidos and even shared the same Catholic faith.

Sadly, things are not the same in modern times.

There are liberals out there who are racist and hate Mexicans. They call them lazy, no-good workers and have no sympathy for the way Mexico's economy is failing them.

Mexico is full of corrupt politicians who squander U.S. aid money and ship it into their African-inspired drug cartels, and liberals create laws that make us give health insurance to children born to Mexicans in our country, so we will have anger toward the Mexicans for using up our health care.

These hardworking Mexicans only wanted to sneak into America so they could work for our families. Sure, there are bad apples in every bunch. Some Mexicans are indeed very evil opportunists, and our border-patrol guards and patriots can only wait and pick out so many suspicious-looking ones, then send them back to their swine-flu-laden lands.

Many of the new Mexicans who sneak into our country have attitudes. They love knives and violence. They are no longer professing third-world Catholics like our house Mexicans growing up. They are gangsters *malos* and strike terror into our hearts.

Not even the women can be trusted, as they will steal your items and flaunt their curvy bean-dipped hips in front of your husband and sons. We would love for our children to have the culture-enriching experience of having several Mexican nannies, but the risk is too great.

Thinking about this, one solution has popped into our minds. *Why can't I own a Canadian?*

WHY CAN'T I OWN A CANADIAN?

Think about it. Racism is ugly and trusting one's neighbors is Christlike, so we should also let people from ALL the lesser Americas come visit us to work as well. Canada is a country full of snow-bound savages who are good at chopping wood and light industrial tasks.

Imagine how much the impoverished state of Michigan could benefit by having Native

Canadians and even their fair-skinned counterparts drift into the state to provide base labor. It would juice the economy.

Looking at data, we can actually see that Canada is a far more peaceful nation than that of Mexicans. Go figure, it is full of former British and Indian bloodlines. Millions of Canadians anxiously wait for us to allow them to sneak in, as they all live within two hundred miles of our American border.

Owning poor foreign people is a great experience that every family should have. The values and warm memories of owning house Mexicans were everlasting, and we are sure those kind Mexican women were able to provide their families with untold riches from all the money we gave them.

If we are able to have such an experience with more trustworthy modern people, like the Canadians, it would be a truly splendid thing for this generation and more to come.

It would actually be more prudent to encourage jobless Canadians to come to America and be our house workers.

Friends, let us vote the liberals out of office. They are against NAFTA and a super-highway that will connect us in special Christian harmony.

Even with a large amount of good Christian-believing Canadians living in their French territory, it comes with a price. A price that could bring our country to its knees. See, Canadians have the ability to mask themselves within our culture. They look like us, talk like us, and some can even spend like us. Notice how you never see a Canadian on the six o'clock news, while the cops are in a high-speed pursuit of a murderer? This is because Canadians can blend right in and not alarm cops with their illegal statuses.

For reasons above, the terrorists from the east are now recruiting Canadians to their terror groups to infiltrate American soil.

SPYING CANADIANS

Canadians may look nice on the outside and have pearly-white smiles, but on the inside they are completely jealous of America. Unlike Canada, the U.S.A. is not controlled by the French and we aren't forced to speak in a sissy language and acknowledge pointless holidays and traditions like looking for mythical "flying bells" on Easter day.

The Canadians hate the fact that America is completely free from any outside influence and they also can't stand the fact that we have a better government and a better military. They even have the largest number of draft dodgers living in their country. Goes to show you that they are made up of a bunch of wussy men. And during World War II, they surrendered to Hitler before they even sent any troops over to help their motherland of France.

If you really want to upset a frog, just let them know how superior the American forces are to their laughable moose-riding army. Remind them that both world wars that their French rulers started were both saved by the mighty American arms and that we don't have to buy our military weapons, we make our own with our far smarter American brains. It upsets them because they know it's true and just like their French forefathers they are weak and will deny history.

The Canadians wish they could be like us. They copy our TV shows, they try to make their cities look like ours, they try and speak the American language, and they even buy our American-made cars, so they can feel true power from an automobile.

And look at the horrible celebrities they have tried to send to our country:

Pamela Anderson: One of the biggest wastes in the world. She made sure to force images of her fake sintreats across America, while spreading her hepatitis C(anada) onto all our great rock musicians.

Keanu Reeves: Makes movies that teach kids that we live in a computer *and that God is some sort of computer hacker. No, Keanu, we don't want to take your drug pills and jump into a computer and play Ma-*trix *dressed up in some kind of dominatrix outfit.*

Celine Dion: Maybe the worst singer who has ever grabbed a microphone. We would rather be locked in a room with Kanye West for forty-eight hours, listening to his devil black music.

When was the last time you heard someone say "Hey, look at my new Canadian-made car," or "Look at my cool Canadian-brand shoes"? You don't! The Canadians depend on us for their goods and services. They are like the annoying little step-brother who wants to be cool so you give him your old hand-me-downs. We even let them join the League of Nations, just to be nice to them.

Even look at their sports: hockey—boring, igloo building—boring, moose racing—boring, and even their treasured sport of fig-ure skating—gay and boring. Just look at their flag: how lazy could you be to take two colors and decide to throw a weak leaf on it? How does that say pride? Their country's name is even weak—it means "village"—and their biggest holiday is called "Boxing Day." How many Canadian boxers do you know, and even more so, how many Canadians do you know that know how to fight? To look cool, they have even tried to claim they invented baseball. Baseball was created by Union troops during the Civil War, not by some igloo-building sassy maple suckers.

They boast that they love their universal health care, but you always see them traveling down to our country like geese, to get the best health care known to modern man. If the Canadians believe their health-care system is superior to America's, why does their pre-mier even come to our country to get medical attention?

The clear answer here is that our system is the best. You cannot beat the health system in America. We use capitalism to inspire doc-tors to compete to give the best health care. Our medical schools are superior to those of any other nation. The only true M.D. you'll find are those trained in America; this is why those who get their licenses from foreign places are told to get out if they try to practice medicine here.

What great scientific breakthroughs have they made? What, the Ricker curve? How hard is it to know how to make fish have sex and populate lakes and ponds? The person who discovered that wasn't even a real Canadian, but a Chinaman who fled Asia and accidentally got on a cargo boat to maple land instead of America. Hard to take anything scientific from Canada, when they still use the outdated metric system. You can't even get a gallon of gas there.

Their money looks like funny Monopoly money, and they try and name them cute names like "Loonie" and "Toonie." Great try at trying to be creative, Canada, great try. And like their money, they have silly territories; they don't even have the ability to know how to create states within their country.

Let's face it, if it wasn't for America, our northern friends would still be building houses out of blocks of ice and playing lumberjack all day. Canada just needs to realize they are the honorary fifty first state of our Godly republic.

Due to Canada's dependency on America to perform even day-to-day functions, they have developed an almost murderous hatred toward us, and that can be dangerous. Remember the best way to attack your enemy is from within and the Canadians have the ability to camouflage themselves directly into America's heart and explode like a clogged artery.

The terrorists know about this underlined hatred from the maple-leaf lovers against the world's greatest country ever. According to Alibaba.com, there has been a large amount of new terror mosques popping up in Eastern Canada, which is just a hop, gay-skip, and a jump to New York City.

Think about it, how do you racially profile someone who looks just like us? When we think terrorist, we know they have long beards, almost Afro-Saxon-colored skin, beady little eyes, and a bomb strapped under their bathrobes. Canadians can just walk right over the ice border and we would wave them across with open arms, knowing that they don't have the mental or physical power to do anything harmful to our more manly race of human beings. If a bomb was planted at a local coffee shop in the middle of New York City, the last person you would think of being a suspect would be a light-skinned, blue-eyed, blond-haired person.

Operation Snow Storm is happening right in front of our faces and we have no idea who is driving the plow. The terrorists have been training our weak ally to the north and it is only a matter of time before we see one of these snow birds explode from a chest full of C-4 and gun powder.

We need to be prepared for the icy terrorists from the north. We must be vigilant in detecting these frost bombers and report them on sight to our local authorities or if you know the number to your state's homeland security office, call there.

HOW TO SPOT A TERRORIST CANADIAN?

So if these American look-alikes can blend in our country so well, how can we go about picking them out? What do we look for to make sure we aren't in contact with a hockey suicide bomber? How can we tell the difference between a holy American and a soulless ice carver?

TEST ONE: INTELLIGENCE

The average American has a forty-seven point higher IQ then a dull minded, beaver-beater. This is why they have a large homosexual population, and this type of ignorance can play in our favor when trying to detect maple insurgents.

If you suspect you have come in close quarters with a Canadian, simply ask them a brain-teaser-type question. Try something simple at first, something that maybe an Afro-Saxon might know or better yet, something even a pool-cleaning Mexican might know.

If they pass the first test, up the questions to a Jeopardy-style question and make sure they answer in question form. A good suggestion would be "This man was the greatest human that ever walked the earth." The answer better roll off their tongue like it is muscle memory, and if they don't shout out "Reagan!" in an almost orgasmic fashion, you know your next step is to call INS

Canadian suicide bomber.

and let them know you have a block of ice they can come pick up.

TEST TWO: SPEECH

Due to their low intelligence, Canadians are forced to learn simpler languages like French and have a hard time pronouncing basic American English terms.

To corner a Canadian can be very easy when you apply the speech test. The test is very simple and can be useful to detect these bastards in a matter of seconds.

Simply ask a suspected Canadian what the distance is from their home to their workplace. If they use kilometers instead of miles, you have caught them red-handed. They might even try to use a more American answer like "feet" or "inches," but we all know these are unacceptable answers. Always remember this. If someone uses Celsius over Fahrenheit, then he is a no-good Communist.

Another easy test is to ask them to spell words that start with the letter z. See, Canadians don't possess the ability in their tongues to properly form the sound of a z like it is supposed to sound. They let it roll out of their frog mouths like "zed" instead of "zee." If you hear this odd sound spew out of their fancy, French-surrendering feeding hole, you have found a winner.

TEST THREE: POLITICS

Just like Obama, the Canadians are Socialist and love to tax their hard workers, so they can spread the wealth around to the lazy class of frostback lowlifes.

This test really only works in the office and should be done only during lunch hours.

An hour before lunch go ahead and order a few pizzas, enough to feed only the top-working employees—and we guarantee none of them are Canadians. Once the lunchtime whistle is blown, gather all the deserving and bring them into the break room. Almost like clockwork someone will walk in and give you a speech about how it isn't fair to buy lunch for only one type of coworkers. They will even acknowledge that you purchased the pizza with your own hard-earned cash, but will still insist that you either buy more pizzas or have everyone split their pizza slices in half so that the other coworkers can partake in the spoils.

If this scenario does play out, you should go directly to your boss and let him know that the workplace has been infected with a possible terrorist.

If you do catch a Newfiene, don't worry they won't put up a fight. Being from the direct bloodline of the French, a Canadian's natural instinct is to surrender at the sign of conflict. They are like the kids at school who willingly give their lunch money to the school bully.

These wannabe Americans might seem wholesome and friendly

on the outside, but just remember on the inside they are jealous and have been reprogrammed by the hieroglyph painters and wish to see every American baby dead.

But listen here, my friends, another ice-dwelling danger to America is the red, non-emotion-having Soviet Russian.

Russia is a death-cult nation, stealthily gaining power and patiently waiting for the day they can meet with their Chinese community brethren to bring death and destruction to America.

Such a ridiculous notion would seem wacky to most sane leaders of lesser nations, but Russian President Dimity Medvedev and Soviet Overlord Vladimir Putin have drug-induced thoughts.

These are people who think they have a chance to overcome our military. These are sick men who believe they can shelf every American in a gulag without being drenched in drunken nuclear oblivion.

THE RED BEAR

Studies show that 78 percent of Russians are alcoholics, but this type of grandiose foolishness can only be the work of hearty drugs from the immoral 1960s: magic mint, ice, marijane cigarettes, and even heroine. These are the things that fuel Communist and Socialist thoughts: look at any hippie commune or, today, any Democratic whine party because they lost the House.

The Russians are a drug cult. The entire nation stays warm during winter on the hallucinogenic drugs that fuel the ravenous thoughts of destruction and burning hatred of America that dance in their LSD-plummed minds.

There will be liberals out there who say this is not true. They will say that political dealings with the Russians are not like going to your local black alley and trying to reason with a wide-nostril cocaine tough.

Soviets hate freedom as much as modern terrorists. Therefore, they will seek to destroy America by any means. The problem is that, unlike terrorists, the Soviets have access to massive stockpiles of nuclear material.

The only thing keeping them from firing is the fear that was instilled in them by Ronald Reagan. The Soviets know the spirit of that wonderful man haunts the minds of Russia's leaders even today, as their foreheads still sweat in fear of hearing the powerful voice of Reagan forcing their country into nothing.

Besides the anti-Christian Germans, Russia is the only other country to commit genocide on their own people. Just like wild animals, they had no problem killing their own kind and their own young.

Even though Russia itself is a powerful country, they currently just don't have the mental capacity or gall to attack America. Remember, Russia is the same country that was afraid of the Japanese army and also would have lost the battle against Hitler if God didn't create a snow storm to kill the Germans.

The only thing we must fear is their uncontrollable drinking of cheap vodka, and polls show that 78 percent of Russians struggle with severe alcoholism. We all know when people partake in Devil's nectar, they can be influenced by comrade Satan himself to do stupid things, and the last thing we need is for Beelzebub to take control of a man who has the ability to push the launch button of a nuclear missile.

Also, how can you trust a nation's conscience when they sell off their women on fancy dating sites and in Victoria's Secret–style catalogs? A country that can't respect its women is a country that has no moral fibers.

Soviet Russians have always had it out for us because they are jealous of our freedom.

In the 1960s, a Russian Democrat named Khrushchev corrupted the heart of a young Christian named Fidel Castro in Cuba. Castro was a pious, devout man who loved America until, through their atheistic mystics, the Soviet liberals turned his heart to the dark side of Communism.

With all the good naturally sucked right out of him, Castro worked tirelessly with the Soviets so they could kill the children of The Greatest Generation, that is, the very Americans who had saved Earth from the no-good Nazis and their allies only twenty years earlier.

As we've seen time and time again in history, the villains against the moral nation of America were vanquished and Cuba was no exception. Through brilliant Republican leadership and advisement, a young John Kennedy was used to bring the conflict to a peaceful end.

But as you've seen accurately portrayed in eighties war movies, the Communist desire for peace is null and their hearts are filled with wanton bloodlust, a lust that can only be satiated with the blood from our dead bodies.

Long dormant the red country has been, and now with Putin in office, Russia is slowly creeping its way out of its Cold War loss and back into the pilot's chair to develop dangerous technologies against the world's freedom fighter, America.

The demonic Soviets have awakened and threatened our Christian nation. As we speak, Soviet Dictator Vladimir Putin and his homeboy dog Medvedev are meeting with Iranian terror leader Mahmoud Ahmadinejad.

Russia supports Iran acquiring nuclear arms so they may destroy peaceful nations such as Israel, the Holy Land to our faith and way of life. Today Russia vows to nuke every American city if we as much as suggest Iran not develop nuclear weapons that will destroy the unprecedented peace on Earth, which America has created as the guardian of humanity since World War II.

Putin's greatest dream is to see the flesh seared off the bones of your children, as they die from nuclear fallout and radiation. Soviets are all atheists and Godless people, so have no sense of reason or fellowship in their spiritually impoverished hearts.

Barack Obama is a decent man, but not a man who can lead us against the new Soviet threat. We need a man of military knowledge and expertise in office; a man who will not allow your children to die under the cold boots of a Soviet conscript. We need a man who would make President Ronald Reagan's eyes glisten with pride.

Your heart should be panicked as Russia mounts a new war against our amicable nation that fosters peace, prosperity, and respect for all countries on this Earth. To protect ourselves and our friends, we must double our military capabilities and call for a new cold war against Russia.

We must make their people know that when you mess with America, you mess with God. And the wrath of our holy arms is endless and without bound. They must come to understand that if they kindle our anger, it will burn until we cast their lifeless, Godless carcasses and souls to roast for all time with their true Soviet leader, Satan.

Let us all look forward to the day when we wipe the Soviet people and their wicked land off the face of our Earth. If they want war with America, the nation blessed with the eternal riches of the Heavens, so be it. We will finish the job that our dear passed friends President Ronald Reagan and Pope John Paul II started long ago, destroy Communism.

And we will not stop until there is nothing but a bleak, icy landscape covering their dark, dank lands filled with the cousin of beautiful oil, natural gas. And it will be free to all who are with us, and not against us.

Russia has now started to prepare nuclear weapons and advanced modern technologies, saying that America is still a Cold War enemy and that we are not allies.

There are now confirmed reports that the Soviets have developed space technology that allows their Communist cosmonauts to travel deep into space. They are preparing to launch one of their star-destroyer crafts to land upon an asteroid!

This jump in Communist technology means America is still at risk. President George W. Bush planned for us to have powerful ships that could reach our moon and then put our flag on Mars to claim it too, but Obama shut it down!

Obama wants us to have health care and give billions of dollars to terrorists instead. Now the Russians are far ahead and sending secret ships to asteroids. We are very scared and you are too!

Russian dogs! If they can send their ships all the way to the Apophis death asteroid, just imagine how fast they can send their Tesla coil troopers to our country!

They will drop from their planes into our cities and homes, shocking everything in their path. No mercy. Just scorched earth and nukes!

With such a super weapon floating above, Americans are not safe from a red invasion. They are not even safe from their own borders being over run by dark-and white-skinned invading aliens.

Just remember, China, Mexico, Canada and Russia are influenced by drugs; there is no reasoning with their minds. The only solution is one of permanence: Keep our nukes primed and lined, and their influence out of our Christian nation.

CHAPTER 5

Loving Life Tips and Advice

PROVERBS 17:22
"A cheerful heart is good medicine, but a crushed spirit
dries up the bones."

INTRODUCTION BY MISS AMBER COOPER

With so many things wrong with the world today, it may seem hard to turn to someone for advice. Yet remember this, when you are faced with greatest fear, it is time to open your heart to those who love and trust you and your loved ones.

Good friends, as we sit peacefully at home, school, or work right now, ready to enjoy the freedoms of love and democracy on a blessed day, the devious little hands of the Chinese plot our demise.

They detonate nukes in the name of their god. They daydream about the moment when the lifeblood of your loved ones trickles down their family's ceremonial samurai sword. Make no mistake, we should have great fear of the Asiatic Chinese, for the day shall come when they attack and try to kill us all dead!

As mentioned before, I am extremely terrified of Chinese people, but I am not racist. You should feel the same way too.

Every day good Americans and those from lesser countries send thousands of letters and emails, many asking our moral leaders for loving life tips and advice on how to stay saved in this cruel, deceitful world. As the agents of atheistic iniquities stand clamoring for battle outside our fragile abodes, we are frightened. Your heart fears for the safety of your child. Your mind wonders about the chastity and faithfulness of your loved one, as the temptations of flagrant Facebook pokes and video nasty sites make adultery just one sensually electronic pulse away.

In the course of the realization of all our personal fears, we must understand one thing. We are on the brink of destruction. The forces of terror and illegal Mexicans have aligned with a Chinese nation whose cunning calculations and genetic experimentation have colluded in a form of biocrafted warfare, trumping even U.S. sciences. While they pump our society with morals-crippling anime pornography and population-reducing gay-agenda rhetoric, the Chinese stand strong on their atheist evolution sciences that allow them to perfect the Mexican penchant for impossibly large litters of children.

Our enemies are resolute in their blatant lies and hatred. Friends, terror rips through your veins and arteries with the high heats of an adrenaline fire. Sweat pours off your brow as you read this fact. When allied together, the kill-you-dead Axis of Evil and its modern allies total over 3 billion people, internationally. The foreign dangers will only stop when they violently bludgeon you and your family dead.

There are dangerous liberals in America who will try to shroud these truths under a silken pile of lies, smooth to the touch but hiding a rugged, raging truth beneath. They will try to say it is racist not to embrace worldwide cultures who are against America and our God.

Racism is a very ugly thing. It pains our hearts when the poor little Mexicans who sneak to our country cannot speak American, just because their friends are all too racist to learn the "gringo" tongue.

Do you not hate it when we go to your son's sporting events and notice all the nice little Afro children sitting together with

Chinese are evil, but racism in the workplace is unacceptable.

their big white T-shirts and high-fives, segregating themselves from mingling with the school's original neighborhood population?

Christ had love for all the other races, be they black, yellow, brown, or red. He did not discriminate against those without his white skin, but offered his love and mercy instead. We should do the same thing too.

Christ's love is a wonderful thing and so it's such a sad shame that so many immoral peoples have burning hate in their hearts.

We will never understand why a nation stockpiles nuclear weapons and threatens to fire missiles at all who are different. It is impossible to say why China, Iran, North Korea, Africa, Egypt, and all other null-Christian dangerous lands instill unfounded fears in the hearts of their children, spreading lies and teaching their young to give misgivings to all who are different.

My friends, just like the Arab terror people, the Chinese are scared to death of our great nation and therefore embrace a culture that's against the American race.

From the moment they are born, they are brainwashed to hate our freedom-giving ways; they teach them we are very different, shield them from the good of our culture, and then, make them think we are all out to get them.

Raised in such an environment, it is no surprise that terrorist Chinese sneaked over to bomb Pearl Harbor. The little sand terrorists grew up wanting to destroy our economic pillars, and now, they are developing nukes to shoot at your family. We must fire back with a power that's more devastating than a supernova bomb to their collective souls.

I fear that it is too late for these people. There are over 3 billion Chinese and Arab terrors in Asia, all raised wanting the same thing: to be the harbingers of death and destruction to Americans.

Against such odds, we must endure in this world. A world in which over one-third of the population hates our American DNA and wants us, our God, and our civilization all dead.

In granting us the capacity to love, God also gave us the capacity for wisdom. From all of the videos, letters, and emails we receive every day, you are clearly terrified and feel lost with a Muslim sympathizer playing leader in Washington, D.C. You stand with millions of others on the field of battle, naked and ill-prepared for the upcoming final wave of chaotic calamity and Mao-lead mayhem.

As millions of you have expressed, you yearn to be clad with the Fruits of the Spirit. Democrats bow before the throne of atheist deities and cannot fund our troops who bravely defend us in Afghanistan and Iraq, so you cannot look to the liberal liars for help. Who do we turn to in this time of need?

We cannot trust Barry Sorotoros, the scheming Kenyan who canoodles in the harems of Muslim mischief. You don't recognize that name? It is because it belongs to the chief of prime-time presidential prostitution, a lie-addicted Saud puppet who calls himself Barack Hussein Obama. In a world where the half-bred ruling party of the nation bows to the feet of a foreign illegal, you do not care if he proudly exclaims, "I answer five letters from Americans per day!"

Each and every word from Obama's dirty whore-scented mouth is a blissful lullaby to Satan's ears. For every Democrat speech or Hollywood slogan that fills your home with sound, if you listen hard enough, deep enough, you will hear the laughter of demons. There is a war coming, friends, and no one but those who love you most can be trusted.

Hold your friends and families fast; hold them tight and you do not let them go. Let the enemy of your lives be combated by those who trust in Him who loves you most. Let the fight to protect your life be fought not in the brothel halls of the Senate, but in the hearts of the moral.

Friends, you only have one true friend in this world. And from that one friend, you have a large, extended family who will drop upon prayer-warrior knees at a moment's notice, to bring peace to your life. Your true family, your moral leaders and Godly followers of the GOP, seek to protect the lives of your children. Where Democrats see you only as a cluster of cells, we see each and every one of you as precious. You are fearfully and wonderfully made, and my brothers and sisters, you are all family for we will give our all.

Let us band together and find out how to withstand the forces of evil. Obama's ominous omen is upon us: the end is near. The space of the heavens has become filled with asteroids of cosmic prominence, while the wrath of God continues to slowly stew as it's being heated by Satan's master blend of carnality and violence, twice stirred by Judas-tainted betrayals.

When the boiling pot boils over and Armageddon is on the horizon, there will be a great war. You will be either with us or against us. The enemy will march and will trample you under their steel-toed boots of cold-blooded atheist Communism. You will crunch and they will shout, "Glory!" as your family is ravaged by their masses of savage fury.

Come with me, my family. Let us learn how to withstand the forces of evil. Let us keep our children and friends from falling into the liberal pit traps of prostitution, drugs, disease, and death. Above all else, let us look into the questions that plague your heart in this cruel, dark Obama-stained world. For through the windows of Obama-tinted iniquity, the future looks bleak and dreary. There is no hope.

But by wiping all clean with Christ's pure white love, we shall see that we can withstand the coming tide of destruction and damnation that threatens you all, and have the joyous tomorrow.

LETTERS TO AMBER

Dear Amber,

I first want to say I'm a really big fan of your work on Christwire and really enjoy your insight into our world's pressing issues. The question I have for you today is really embarrassing, but I hope that by asking it here I can help other parents out there too.

Some time ago my daughter forgot to take her laundry from the dryer before taking off for volleyball practice, so I folded it up and went to put it up for her in her room.

When I reached in her undergarment drawer—and I will be frank—my heart dropped as I found one of those electronic phallic objects in it. They are used to "M" and I didn't know how to handle the situation. I thought to ask my husband, but didn't want him to have to go through the embarrassment and anguish of such things. I instead asked several of my close girlfriends, some of whom are not Christians, and some of them said this was a normal part of a healthy teen's lifestyle.

The night I decided to talk to my daughter about all this, I heard, well . . . I heard reason not to go in the room. I believe she was using the device then. Is this really all right behavior for a good girl, or do I need to confront her? Please help!

—Concerned in San Diego

Dear Concerned in San Diego,

You need to immediately take that sinful device from your daughter. Masturbation is another form of pornography that will infest your daughter's mind and serve as a gateway to far worse sexual activities.

Studies show that 87 percent of the women who become prostitutes did so because of unbridled masturbation as a teenager, and over 90 percent of girls who become pregnant as teenagers did so because masturbation loosened their morals and made them more apt to engage in unprotected fornication.

Masturbation will make your daughter very comfortable exploring her body, and it will not be long until she begins to envision other people partaking in the deviant behavior with her.

This will of course lead to your daughter seeking out a male companion, or even female. As a teenager, your daughter's mind is not yet developed enough to handle the pressures and responsibilities of being sexually active. It will lead to great sorrow in her life if you don't put a stop to it right now.

So first, have a talk with your daughter and pray with her. Pray all that sinful desire of masturbation right out of her heart. Throw the device away, and then enroll her in some abstinence counseling sessions. They will teach your daughter the value and need of respecting her body until marriage. Masturbation is very unnatural, and by taking proactive steps to get this bizarre behavior out of your teen's life, you'll ensure she has a better future.

—Amber

Hi Amber,

I'm so torn, my heart feels it's been ripped into pieces. I'm crying just writing to you.

My daughter is in a relationship with another girl and I don't know what to do, I have been in constant prayer for her

and it feels like God doesn't hear me. I need some guidance here, I'm lost.

She says she doesn't know if she's gay, but feels like she should be with a girl, and when she dates a guy it only feels like a friendship thing. What can I do? Where can I go? HELP!

—Lost in Hawaii.

Dear Lost in Hawaii,

Since the days of Queen Liliuokalani, Hawaii has been masked under the island secrecy of homosexuality. During Liliu's birth, Premier Elizabeth Kīna'u developed an eye infection. She gave her the names Lili'u (smarting), Loloku (tearful), Walania (a burning pain). All of these tearful, burning, and sore pains accurately describe gay bowel disease, which will destroy her life if your daughter does not stop being lesbian gay this instant.

And then, just like a gay tries to cover their scent of shame, Liliu's brother tried to cover this shameful origin by altering his sinful sister's name to something more pleasant: Lili'uokalani, "the smarting of the royal ones." But the prophecy was already in place and God caused that soreness to the premier's eyes, so Liliu's true name would forever allow us to see Satan's volcanic hold on Hawaii.

Hawaii is the birthplace for gay euphemism. It all started with the name of Queen Liliu, who had her true name masked. Her name was to be a reminder to all aloha lesbians to say good-bye to a healthy life if they dabbled on the jelly-fish beaches of exposed secret places.

Your state school calls itself the Rainbow Warriors. This is euphemism. We all know gays love to taste the rainbow of a lifestyle indulged in fruity Skittled sins, but just like sugar to enamel, gay pride rots the soul.

Your daughter had no choice in the matter. Growing up in Hawaii, your daughter and her friend have been enrolled in the classes of Fishmongering 101, where each of them graduate a Rainbow Warrior, a hardline homegrown cliterrorist. Read through the euphemism and fear the explosive changes a raging cliterrorist can bring climaxing into your daughter's life on a drunken Kona night.

Do not let homosexuality lei its flowery hands around your daughter, my dear friend. Do not let it sugar cane your baby's life in anti-phallic symbolism. Like a diabetic in a candy store, Satan dances with glee when he sees those sweetened by his powdery confections of haupia-caked carnality. Rest assured that Satan is all man and will not hesitate to stuff an apple in her mouth and roast your daughter from behind on his fire skewer, all while demons salivate at a luau in hell. Such is the fate of any rainbow warrior who stands before the thrones of judgment.

If you do not save your daughter from the lava pits of lesbianism, you will one day come home to hear children singing, "Hala ka ukulele, momma made a baby," as your daughter returns home from college. It will not be because a Samoan island boy rogered her, but instead because Momma Gay gave birth to a hula whorelicker, all on the sandy, euphemism lined beaches of Hawaii.

—Amber

Dear Amber,

My family is very devoutly Christian (I don't even know if there was a generation of us that wasn't) and my father is also *a pastor. I recently met a charming boy who I love dearly, and in my heart I feel we can really go great places together. He's wonderful.*

The problem is that he is Muslim and my family do have a problem with trust, call them very patriotic. How do I explain to my family that they have to get to know the person and not judge on outside prejudice?

—Wisconsin girl in love

Dear Wisconsin Love,

Your parents love you with all their hearts and are looking out for your best interest. Many people do not realize this, but the threat of homegrown terrorism is very, very high and every neighborhood may have an American jihadist traitor lurking about.

"Jihad USA: Confronting the Threat of Homegrown Terror" is an excellent piece that will open your eyes against this very serious threat to America and potentially your life.

Imagine the sorrow in your parents' hearts if this young man is one of the hundreds of millions of Muslims who could potentially be working with homegrown terrorists, and he did something to harm you. Would that not be a cruel fate to place on your parents?

That is their concern, Wisconsin Girl. When you're young it's really easy to want to combat your parents and not take their words to heart. But know they are always looking out for your best interests and something in their guts is telling them, "no, no, no."

So talk to them more about their views on terrorists in America and ask the young man about it too. If he becomes

upset with you asking and gets offended, run! He may be guilty.
Your parents love you and someone else does too, Wisconsin Girl.

—*Amber*

Dear Amber:

Good evening. My name is Isabelle and I come to this
country four months ago with the promise of a good-paying job.
My intentions were to work in this country for a few years and
then buy a house so that my families can come and share in the
same opportunities I have experienced. I go to immigration
office, obtain a visa, and come here with my worker's permit.

The man who helped finance my journey to this wonderful
country did not give me the job he promised. He told me that
I would be a model for woman's clothing (of course it would be
modest clothings!). I was told that this would be a great way to promote new conservatives fashion to the young people in this country.

However, when I came to this wonderful land, I was heart-
broken. First, I find that the parish that I wanted to join did not
exist because it burn down one year ago. Then, I was told that
I had to surrender my work papers to the man that paid for my
journey. Then, he told me that I could not start the modeling job
until I do some very bad things first.

I need your advice, Amber. I want to be a hardworking
American like I see in the pictures, but now my hopes are
dashed. I want to be a part of this wonderful country, but is it
worth it to use my body in order to do that? How do I deal with
my boss to tell him I'm uncomfortable with being a pleasure
woman? Thank you very much, and I hope to hear from you
soon! God bless you and your family.

—*Isabelle*

Dear Isabelle,

I fear for your life and safety. I am not sure where you are at in America, but you need to immediately contact your local authorities (police) and talk to them about your situation.

I do not know if you are here legally or not, but whatever the case, being deported back to your own country is far better than what can happen to you. Every year, in essentially every country, women (usually travelers or immigrants like yourself) are tricked into submission, abducted, and eventually forced into sexual slavery.

An estimated five hundred thousand to eight hundred thousand young women are forced into sexual markets, worldwide, each year. They often end up never seen again, or are found murdered or overdosed on drugs. Isabelle, wherever you are immediately contact the authorities and talk to them.

Your family loves you and would rather have you back home than allow your body to be abused and to be trafficked into a life of pain then death. I want you to know that you are not all alone and good people will help you.

—Amber

Dear Amber,

I am a twenty-year-old college student from Naples, Florida. All my life, my parents provided for me and gave me an upbringing that was moderately luxurious by many standards. I am grateful and appreciative for what they have given me.

One thing I was deprived of, however, is diversity in my upbringing. Growing up, the private schools I attended had very few black people. Long story short, my circle of friends were mostly white and even now at U of F, it's more of the same. I'd like to expand my circle and my experiences.

I've thought about joining the school's BSU (Black Student Union) but worry that I will not be taken seriously or may offend someone by joining. I guess I'm writing to ask if you have any suggestions on how I can get over my apprehensiveness or how to make friends well with black people?

—Ready for Change in Florida

Dear Ready for Change in Florida,

There is only one thing you can do, be yourself. Realize this, and you'll find friends of varying backgrounds, beliefs, world-view, and even race. Friendship and getting to know people should not be determined by black and white skin, but rather by character, respect, and interest in one another.

Instead of worrying about fitting in with black people, in your case, instead simply go to a BSU meeting and be yourself. I trust you'll find friends. Beware that from your potentially sheltered upbringing, and going to a private school, that some may offer you drugs or invite you to their parties.

While it is good to not prejudge, use wisdom. Never go anywhere alone with a young guy you may meet at a BSU meeting, even if it's "just" a basketball game or "just" a chicken shack, because he may be looking to take advantage of you and do mean things to your body.

—Amber

Dear Amber,

For my job I have to surf the Internet to find information for my boss. He is a lawyer and we find the web to be the best thing in the world to do quick research on. Now, I'm a devout

Christian and raise a household where we make sure the love of Jesus is always present.

While searching Google for information on sex offenders I clicked a link and it took me to a homosexual sex site. I immediately turned off my computer screen and ran to the computer tech office and asked him to clear the images off my computer.

My question is . . . will I go to hell for viewing such sinful imagery?

—Scared in Arizona

Dear Scared in Arizona,

God bless you and the fine people of Arizona, especially the loving maverick John McCain. It is so hurtful that there can be people so bigoted, they protest our rights to be terrified of the gay agenda.

The gays love to sneak little nuggets of lifestyle into our family-centered lives, for they know that once your eyes have been smeared with the taint of rainbow colors, it will never wash off and there is a good chance you will begin to have latent gay thoughts.

Within your mind now lies one of the most savage drug addictions of the gay movement: homoerotica. Homoerotica is drugs for the mind, far more scarier than sniffing the crack-dealer's addictive magic mint or tasting of hookah *hallucinations at the local hashish head shop. It is all extremely dangerous and rests in your mind, always a constant voice that whispers for you to take another Scans_Daily peek.*

While your boss's computer may now be wiped clean, remember that the ultimate computer is the human brain. Until you get a proper psychologist or clergy to cleanse your mind, you are at risk for the pop-ups of annoying gay thoughts.

Like a virus, homosexuality can lie dormant within you. The students of fecal fornication study from the textbooks of perverted evolution, trying to convince all people that being gay is an inherited genetic deoxyribonucleic acid mutation or "alteration". Gays are bigoted enough in their superiority complexes that they see themselves as "alternative" and have even created a genre of music to celebrate their ways.

In addition to gay imagery, when you hear terms like "smashing our pumpkins" or a festering Fester saying he wants a "deathcab for cutie," be alert! It is all gay double entendre meant to corrupt you and allow homosexuality to enter not only your life, but also the core of your nuclear family.

Scared, you should be. You do not want to throw away your life. You do not want to start growing soft against the Homogay Agenda, your lackadaisical, sympathetic antics toward the gay movement to firm up within the life of your children, your husband, and yourself.

Take heart and be alert. If you feel that your body is afflicted with confusing thoughts of homosexuality from this exposure, you must choose to seek proper mental health help. Please, remember these warning signs of being afflicted with latent homosexuality and if you suffer any of the following symptoms, please immediately rush to your local church or emergency hotline:

- *You catch yourself admiring your husband's rear end. If you find yourself clamoring to be on top during acts of baby-creating secrecy, it is a sign that your brain is damaged and is being retrovirusly programmed to be a lesbian dominatrix. This outbreak still plagues Russia's black leather queens to this day and even worked against them during the final days of the Cold War.*

- *When a coworker walks by and you catch yourself trying to whiff an extra waft of her perfume, beware becoming a lunchtime lesbian. It is very common for women to go out with one another to grab a salad for lunch, but this can soon spread to a shameful palate sprouting beans and cauliflower creams, all with a side of the zestful flavorings of cucumber-melon ranch to remind you of your thirty-minute betrayal when you come home to your family.*

- *Check your MP3 player. If you have any of these acts on it, you may be a corduroy lesbian or even worse a hippie hipster homosexual of drunken laziness and illegal "mary jane" influence: The Phish, Misfits, Coldplay, Avril Lavigne, Blood on the Dance Floor, Howie Day, Bright Eyes, One Republic, and T.A.T.U.*

- *Face pale without morning makeup.*

Remember, gays cannot be Christian. It is in the Constitution and Republican federal policy. Do not damn you and your family to be downloaded to hell.

—Amber

Dear Amber,

Last week we noticed a large group of Mexicans move into our apartment complex. They never seem to leave the house, play loud Spanish music, and always have large amounts of people coming over to visit for long periods of time.

We fear they may be illegal drug dealers or even human traffickers.

The scary thing is, they always look at us when we leave our apartment and we feel they are trying to instill fear in us, or are learning our work schedule to rob our house while we are away.

I feel bad for writing this, as I'm not a racist and have had the same Mexican cleaning lady for six years and we are very friendly with each other.

My question is, should I call INS and have them investigated, and should I fear for my life if they turn out to be illegal drug lords?

—Dallas Dilemma

Dear Dallas Dilemma,
Yes.

—Amber

Hi Amber,

I'm seventeen years old, living in New York state, and I'm pretty sure that I'm gay. I enjoy watching many shows promoted by the homosexual agenda, such as Glee and the Real Housewives series. I am not sure how to deal with these feelings of attraction to men—and I am very attracted to them.

What should I do?

—Concerned NY Teen

Dear Concerned NY Teen,

Glee is a Gala of Gaydom, promising to take viewers to a magical kingdom of butterfly sunshine and singing happiness, but is really just a sad storm of musical numbers drenched with the uncomfortable clamminess of homosexuality.

In a day and age where gay agenda supporters rabidly demand a right to adopt children and get married, we find this show fits a larger movement to introduce the American household to homosexual themes and lifestyles.

For every one gay, four children get molested. These scary statistics further reveal why the gay agenda violently blows against the grain of society, trying to buckle the moral umbrella our Christian tradition and our American values have long held over children, shielding their bodies from the relentless showers of seminal perversions.

It is no surprise that even morally questionable bands like Kings of Leon have found disgust with Glee. The KoL band recently refused homosexuality and child exploitation by refusing to let one of their songs "air" on Glee and instantly, they felt the sassy, cold wrath of a furious gay.

Sashaying in calculated anger and flailing arms faster than lisping lips, an angry Ryan Murphy reportedly hissed, "F*ck you, Kings of Leon, self-centered assholes."

Such seething fury is typical of gays who do not get their way. Much like a temperamental two-year-old surrounded by candy and toys in the store, gays want what they cannot necessarily have. And when we as society scold them, telling them they cannot feast upon our children and indulge in the joys of marriage, they angrily stamp their feet, cry, and maybe even strip off their anal diapers to expose their bared contempt to the world.

Much like children, gays are also manipulative and will

*concoct the most nefarious plots to normalize their agenda.
Enter Glee.*

*Are high school students to believe that a healthy part of
matriculation is sneaking into leather daddy bars for lunch,
where bare-chested men will ply you with alcohol until you're will-
ing to play Pistolwhip Pete on the frontiers of gluteal horrors,
all before Advanced Economics 101?*

*Young boys are the primary target demographic of Glee.
Instead of running lead with the football team or trying to
court young ladies to socials, young men are being converted
into limp-wrist belly dancers. The conquering moment of Glee
last year was with Mexican actor Mario Lopez.*

*During the 1990s, there was a show named Saved by the Bell.
It was filled with childish antics and Clinton-era perversion, but
still decent enough for the older, discerning child to view.*

*On this show, A.C. Slater was the
school's "jock," a muscle-bound lad
whose taut body, dimples, and corporate smile glistened on and off the
field. Slater was the son of a Mexican
immigrant, who atoned for his genetic
sins and origins by joining the U.S.
military. Cleared of his father's sins,
Slater was able to become prominent
in the high school. He befriended
Zack Morris, the gold "every boy,"
and found his way into American
lifestyle and popularity with athleti-
cism and good streaks of morality. He
was not perfect, but was a character to whom many
immigrant children could relate and from whom they could*

Mario Lopez during his
appearance in *Glee*

learn that even they could make their way in our great society.

With all of this in mind, imagine the symbolism of taking this strong character—A.C. Slater—and using him as a weapon to destroy the minds and morality of many young men, especially Mexican-Americans still trying to fit into America's stable definitions of fatherhood and masculine responsibility.

After the Glee episode now only referred to us the "Minstrel Mariachi" (a writer's latent play on menstrual mariachi), we saw the definition of nineties machismo, A.C. Slater, reduced to a homosexual's nightjollies about children.

Dressed like a Gothic sugar plum, corset copping a grip upon his turgid masculinity, only released by the laced ruffles of untied panties and garter stockings, this vision of homosexual fantasy ripped into the eye holes of millions of males nationwide. They saw the football jock had become the bedroom sock for gay fantasies. This forced many young men and even their fathers to question their sexuality.

If A.C. Slater could reject the likes of Lisa Turtle, Jessie "The Stripper" Spano, and Kelly Kapowski for a little gay jingle and dance, is there something truly appealing to giving homosexuality a little test drive?

This is all the gay agenda and its advocates want. They want everyone to just try a "hit and run" of homosexuality, so that in secret shame the bizarre thoughts and unforgettable images can creep deeper and deeper into the hippocampuses of their minds.

The mechanisms of lesbianism and gay homosexuality run hot in modern media and Satan will do all he can to keep his tractor engines running strong, reaping row after row of our nation's dwindling crop of decent children.

The Homogay Agenda stands hand in hand with the defiant defilers of nature: atheists, evolution scientists, liberal mixers, and non-meat eaters. Who can be really surprised to find Satan

and his liberal farmers of marijuana and homosexuality all
have the same agenda: addict the children to gateway drugs.

Gays dream of the day every girl is a vaggiterian, one who
only feasts at the buffet table of lesbianism. They will be happy
when little Johnny finds erotica in trying to get to the Tootsie
Roll center of Mr. Owl and every other man who "Hoo hoos!"
with the sight of a child consuming a simple lollipop.

It sounds like a rough, fiery mixture for a reason. The
fibers of homosexuality are lined with drug raves and a mucky
quagmire of fecal tar pits, ensnaring any casual passerby into a
filthy, screaming fate of lube-filled lungs and sulfur suffocation.
Homosexuality causes 68 percent of all who observed it to drown
in adulterous betrayal to their true gender roles.

CPR is only performed on the shores of hell, where Baywatch
Satan revives the lungs with his fiery breath and the victim
realizes his fate of boobtitted, voluptuous demons demon whacking kinkle spittles of searing sparks all over the doomed's dairy
mister meiser. We're talking about butt rogering here, readers,
and it is the agenda of Glee.

There is nothing merry about the melodies of this sick show.
There is nothing funny about addiction or death, so let us close
the curtains on this show by turning off the TV and shutting
down its ratings.

—Amber

Dear Amber,

I'm from a small town in Ohio and moving to L.A.
to start college. I didn't really want to move to the "City of
Angels," because I'm just a small-town girl. The scholarship
I received was pretty good and the campus is beautiful,
so I was really pushed. Then it is a Christian school,

which my parents liked even more, so here I am for orientation.

The thing that worried me most is that I heard L.A. is full of nasty street performers. When I visited the first time, I was really shocked and expecting movie-star bimbos and drugged-out band members and even Mexican illegals. The most shocking thing to me however was the large number of Asians.

I never really thought America would have so many Asian people in one area—maybe I am just sheltered. When arriving to campus orientation, my roomie was . . . an Asian.

She is from South Korea and had a bunch of friends over. They ranged from Korean and Hong Kongian Chinese, to even some from Taiwan and Indonesia. Once orientation started, we hung out exclusively and the next thing I knew, I was part of their large group. I've quickly fallen into an Asian culture.

Many people say, and this was true in my hometown, they say that Asians are bereft of emotion and the Chinese are scary. They try to make it seem like Asians are a pack-wolf culture, prowling and waiting for the right moment to bite America. All I can tell you is that they are fun, friendly, and full of life. I enjoy their movies and food, and am now even semi-dating a neat guitar player from Hong Kong named Ian.

Long story short, my parents saw pictures of me on my Facebook and are not happy about "me mingling with the Chinese" and about my new beau. I'm eighteen and can choose to do what I want and they are not paying for this semester. They try to put fear in me and say that Asians are all one in the same and will just see me as a simple American girl. Is this true? Should I go to a state school back in Ohio or keep pushing into the great adventure in LA?

—Small-Town Girl, Growing into a Bigger World

Dear Small-Town Girl,

We know very little about the Chinese besides that they teach their kids that America is evil, that there is a war coming, and that they will have great rewards in terra-cotta heaven for killing us all dead. As you ventured through Los Angeles, did you take time to visit the Third Street Promenade in Santa Monica?

Go out with your Asian friends. Enjoy a night on the town, watching the purple-haired same-sexed lesbians proudly grease themselves up with sins at the Hooters on the corner, then all enjoy a wild spectacle of Indian sitar music and Japanese-live robot men who extend cups for you to give him a tip. As the evening sun fades into the Pacific, look out onto the horizon with your Asian friends.

Think back to how peaceful your grandfather and the families of your friends back home felt when they looked out on that same beautiful site so long ago, on a day of infamy, to only see the death hornets of Asian rage flying toward them. Their hearts raced, but it was too late. The wrath of China ripped their lives from them in a fiery fury, a dragon's blood, a demon's searing embrace.

College girl from a small town, when you look out onto that ocean, as the Sun gives way to the moonlight skies, ask your Asian friends if they know why Los Angeles proper does not want any light towers. Why are there no huge buildings along the coast?

They will not know the answer, or squint their eyes in calculated lies and not say a word. So let me tell you this: America is scared of Asia. Los Angeles cannot have nighttime lights because we never know when the Soviets and Chinese may conspire Communist fireworks for our great City of Angels.

On the coast of Los Angeles, there is nestled a grand cam-
pus in the hills of Malibu. It has a proud tower, a lit cross, that
majestically towers over the Pacific as a Christian message of
defiance to the Godless Eastern hemisphere nations of East Asia.
And at night, its burning candle of American spirit cannot be
lit, for Satan has blown his musty death breath over the light of
America, just like a burly party crasher huffing out the candles
of an innocent child's birthday-cake joywish.

—Amber

FINAL THOUGHTS—THE BIRTH OF OUR GREATEST BATTLE

Birth. It is a very beautiful thing. God gave birth to humanity six thousand years ago, during a moment of loving creation that is empirically detailed within the texts of your Bible. In that very same spirit of creation, God breathed life into the American Republic in 1776, to be his new nation of love and unique leadership.

Much as every modern-day atheist, Satan has always been jealous of life and freedom. He hates the fact that the Creator of all things agape loves every person on Earth so very much, the same love every professing Republican has for our brothers and sisters in humanity. We see through history, the Enemy has worked hard to instill within each and every one of us a spirit of division, malice, betrayal, and liberal disgust for Godly conservative goodness.

America stands in fear. Before the new Chinese power, the risen dragon of doom, all of our enemies gather and wildly swing their carnal clubs as they prepare for battle. To the west, the gay agenda erects enormous monuments of sinful desire in the rolling hills of Los Angeles and they frolic in idolic ecstasy in the perfume-scented trolley streets of San Francisco.

To the south, a brown ooze slithers and slimes, taking form only too late and when it can claim its offspring as U.S. citizens who will grow into Terror Babies, a new-age Judas of ultimate Arab magical schemes. It all seems prophetic, but no, it's not pathetic. It is a great scheme and even the Soviets, the once-proud enemies of morality, bow before the Chinese and conspire to bring Mao and Stalin together in the most disastrous example of gay marriage known to America.

To the north, the Canadians eagerly salivate and then masticate like a vengeful brood of 'roid-fueled moose, stamping their little hoovend feets as they dream of once again taking credit for burning down our nation's innocent capital in a blistering blaze of maple-leafed fury.

The roots of liberality are ancient; they were born in the think tanks of hell. And while America fears our greatest enemy, China, we must realize that the same evil that caused the world to be flooded by the wrath of God now nourishes the rice fields that feed the bellies of our most dangerous enemy of all time.

China is all around us. Look on the shirt you bought at Wal-Mart. It was sewn in China. Your American flag: China. If not *Made in China*, it will say *Hecho en Mexico* or one of China's other subsidiary sweatshop companies.

America was so busy shielding the world from terrorism and death-Nazis, that we failed to hear the third world tiptoe into our country. All around us, there are Americans who do not fully understand the threat of homegrown terrorism. Those words do not send fear into their hearts and make them so scared they will vote for a real American in the next election.

There are Americans who believe illegals can be American, despite the wishes of beatified President Ronald Reagan. There are Americans who deny the true fruit of the spirit, when they spew so much hate they would allow gay rights advocates to overthrow the Federal Marriage Amendment that protects the core of America: the nuclear family.

We have been betrayed. While China is a powerful threat, by girding ourselves in the Armor of Americana, the steel-grit morality forged by the burning passion of Christ's love for our nation and for which it stands, we can clothe our shameful nakedness on the field of battle.

Upon our bodies we can wear the belt of patriotic truth and shining breastplate of Interventionist Strategy, proudly bringing democracy into Middle Eastern lands as President George II prophesied in the early aughts.

Atheists hate faith. They are a cold, desperate lot who are the modern-day Sadducees. What is that, you may ask? Just like America's Constitutional savior told the centurion so long ago, those without the blind love of morality in their hearts are sad, you see?

Atheists hate faith, so just like every other pagan heathen they cannot hold the Shield of Faith, the bravery that shrouds our fearless military and explorers of space on every Mission.

Such is Obama's atheistic Muslim hatred of faith, that he scrapped NASA and President Bush's faith-based initiative to explore Mars by 2040.

Liberal chicken hawks do not realize America's task and birthright of Manifest Destiny. In this part of an American's true armor, we have the ability to strike with the sword of wrath upon our enemies, the very same sword Ronald Reagan wielded when he single-handedly manhandled the Russian Bear with one hand, giving ice-cold Soviet superiority an everlasting, crippling death blow. Where the enemy withers in defeat, the roots of Earth's Superpower are nourished.

On the feet of you, friend, you inherit the ultimate American weapon. Peace.

Everywhere we have touched our hand, we have brought peace. From the once-warlike Europe to the tsunami-striken Japan, we have dropped bombs of liberty and fostered treaties of mutual accord.

Yours is a proud armor to inherit, friend, and you can stand strong against the oncoming onslaught by the China-poison-lead threats against you. But as in every Hollywood movie, there is a great danger in the final act. There is a secret villain that lurks not from without, but from within.

And with that, America stands concerned with so many questions. Mothers must fear that their children are being brought into drug cartels, while the innocent office worker must worry about being barrel-rolled by an Obama-era homosexual.

All across our great nation, our American morals have been betrayed. Inside the walls of this great nation, our American brothers and sisters in the Democratic liberal legions are having an affair on us. They conspire with our enemies and dance with the devil.

In our armor there is a secret kink, one crafted by a dark hand of the greatest black-sooted villainy known to mankind.

CHAPTER 6

The American Liberal Elite

THE FALL OF CAMELOT

*If you tell a lie long enough, loud enough and often enough,
the people will believe it.*

> —*Old etching found engraved in a
> forgotten, dusty Democrat senator's desk
> in a sleazy office on Capitol Hill*

A nation fallen. A free people, frustrated. A Savior so close, yet so far away.

America stands in her darkest hour, cast by the foreboding shadow of a sable Oreo Muslim who masquerades as America's president.

Our nation has seen many great horrors: the wrath of the redcoat

Innocent American being profiled in the airport security lines.

British Empire. The roving hordes of enraged Mexicans at the Alamo. Illegal Indians hell bent on destroying the innocent and denying our nation's Manifest Destiny. The French betrayal of the Vietnam War. The sneak attack of the Chinese air force. The cold showdown with the Communist Russians. And let us not forget the terror attacks of 9/11.

On a dark and almost lifeless day in 2009, all of these fears once again became fresh and real for Americans. For eight years, a powerful man, born of humble beginnings that forged his heart of an "everyman," used the strength and guidance of God to shield his people—all 300 million of us—from the horrors of a cruel world.

One cold, lonely walk changed the fate of our nation. For it was on January 20, 2009, that America lost its protector. A man whose divine savvy led to the fall of history's new Hitler, a monstrous beast known as Saddam Hussein.

Under the reign of President Bush, the attackers of 9/11 who caused our housing market to crash and economic crisis to occur were quelled. Americans were safe.

It was on that day, in January, that America forsook a Heaven-sent president for a deceptive terror who believes Iran should have nuclear weapons, America should bow before the Euro, and that Muslims can build shrines to celebrate that which they took from us on 9/11, right in the heart of glorious New York.

It was on January 20, 2009, that we forced our nation's leader and true president, President George W. Bush, to make a lonely walk, all to the cheers of tribal adoration for Barack Hussein Obama.

Betrayed, Bush boarded a helicopter that took him away not only from the White House, but from his presidential authority and bully pulpit he used to keep our nation safe and terrorists in deep hiding in their caves and drop holes, where they belong.

America betrayed President Bush. Obama-mania swept over the nation. Republicans Facebook betrayed the GOP. Polls were twisted to look like only 42 percent of Americans approved of President Bush, the man who unified us after 9/11.

Now we are at the lowest point in American history. Thirty percent of the population is without jobs. The dollar has fallen, wounded to not only the Euro, but the lowly and comical Canadian loonie and even the Nazi toilet Deutsche Mark.

Never before has America been so crippled. Were the Mayans right? Will the world end before we can get Obama out of office in 2012?

Much like the sinful children of Israel after having been delivered by God from the hellfire-crisped hands of Mubarak King Pharaoh, Americans danced before the altar of the false god and false savior the Obama of al-Jakarta.

God could have unleashed wrath and plague upon America. He could have made us a fallen nation, much like the United Kingdom, which betrayed God for adultery king worship, many years ago.

Instead, he sent back his Great Leader, with a holy book in hand. God sent back America's leader, to lead us back to the promised land of where we belong: Earth's sole superpower. Earth's primary economy and trading standard.

Earth's undisputed leader in all things: The United States of America.

Though lost, America will never fall. For there is one man, even betrayed, who will always stand by his nation. President Bush, the last true leader of the free world, is coming back to save us. Receive this prophesy: Sterling mastermind Karl Rove, the crowd-enthralling Jack "Jbox" Gould, and the anti-lust, antitrust Sarah Palin will proudly march to the cadence of Bush's metered words of freedom. From the crowds will shout the powerful voices of men like Donald "The True Don" Rumsfeld, Andrew Wilkow, and Tyson Bowers III, as they use their divine savvy to undermine and unbury any WMD scheme buried by the forces of Tehran allied terror.

Your great leaders wait to return to power. It is time for us to atone for our sins for accepting a Muslim president and not campaigning enough against him to sway his fickle African-American and naive college fan base, and dispel his reverse-racism tactics against heroic John McCain.

We must ensure President Bush's book and every other Holy Book of guiding morality reach every home in the ghetto and every shelf in the universities. Then, and only then, can our great nation heal by picking a leader who is in accord with President Bush's leadership.

America, there is hope on the horizon. Never forget that we are the people of Change and Hope. But to let the forces of good fix all that is wrong with this country, we must first weather the ominously dark storm that has settled upon Washington, D.C., and the rest of our ailing country.

THE RISE OF THE OBAMA KNIGHTS

The greatest trick pulled by the American Liberal Elite is convincing the world they do not exist. Each and every day, one whose heart is grounded in spirituality and the very gut-faith instinct sage and noble President George W. Bush used when leading the free world will detect a great corruption within mankind.

Slipping in and out of the shadows of America is a cultural vampire, a sparkly, lustful being who seeks to hold the pure republic under its demonic control, while its bared fangs sink its rabid desires of humanist lust, corruption, and greed deep into the moral bloodstream of this Christian nation.

Liberals will furiously stamp their hippie-scented Birkenstocks and hordes of Atheist Wonders will arise from marijuana scent-covering dragon ashes to scream at the top of their lungs, "The Constitution says separation of church and state! America is not a Christian nation!" when reading this truth. It is a liberal devil's lie, one that is loudly repeated time and time again but holds no empirical Constitutional truth.

The only thing atheists love more than abortion legislation and worshipping upon the feet of their Dawkins deity is ignoring America's Declaration of Independence from redcoated tyranny.

When is the last time you read the Declaration of Independence? Its words are gentle as a baby's sweet breath and therefore naturally hate-igniting for abortion-toking, freedom-burning, Obama TSA-gate-rape liberals. America is One Nation, Under God. Each and every state in this blessed Republican union is indivisible, for we have eternal liberty through Christ, the very Son of the God, the only God, who reached down from heaven and blessed every man who signed our Declaration of Freedom for humanity.

Declaration of Independence

When, in the course of human events, it becomes necessary for one people to dissolve the political bands which have connected them with another, and to assume among the powers of the earth, the separate and equal station to which the laws of nature and of nature's God entitle them, a decent respect to the opinions of mankind requires that they should declare the causes which impel them to the separation.

We hold these truths to be self-evident, that all American men are created equal, that they are endowed by their Creator with certain unalienable rights, that among these are life, liberty and the pursuit of happiness.

God granted America a free will, a liberty like no other land has ever seen. Read the words again and again. God is mentioned by our forefathers and is called upon to free us. Within the Declaration of Independence, we see our nation has a Christian heritage and Godly tradition. We see we have an unalienable right to kick out all jabber-jaw Mexicans with their burrito-welfare ways. We see God is the guarantor of freedom for all men and all of our possessions we are to protect, be they our property, wives/children, or happiness.

Dancing like ancient whores beneath the lava-lit skies above Mount Vesuvius, today's leading muckmongers like Rachel Maddow, Jon Stewart, and Keith "Silverdaddy" Olbermann perform a careless, tempest-rousing tango with Satan himself. These purgatory pundits blow gusts of lies into our ears and like an inebriated prostitute of Lucifer, drench us with the grossest brand of yellow journalism.

From the sweat of their Voltaire-furrow brows and venereal brooding words that fire from their mouths, left-wing loonies are ensuring a musty, sulfuric scent fills the air and lungs of America. Our nation is choking upon the once-pure Godly breath of Reagan's conservatism; our bronchi suffocate with the Gaga secretions of Obama's Socialist policy.

Friends, there is a realization you must accept. Lady Liberty is diseased. Like a four-peso Tijuana slapjack on fraternity-gone-wild night, America lies sprawled on the tequila-scented floor of third-world status and shame.

Our businesses are failing. Our economy, it is in Soviet shambles. All across the Arab world, oil executives laugh at our fairy-footed armies, who ask and tell about their same-same sexual exploits with Turban Talakahakabibi and Bunkmate Ben. The price at the pump rises and our armies can't do anything about it, because they are busy pumping up each other in their tent's gleeful gay-marriage ceremonies.

In the Middle East there is a left-wing plot, these sand monkeys are in cahoots with the Washington liberals and Code Pink is in the lead. When oil hits dollar two hundred a barrel the current administration will be able to push a trillion-dollar green stimulus package. Kadafi for instance will play the game as long as we send Jose Eber over to straighten his hair and give him Disneyland tickets.

To see how sneaky a snobby-nosed, welfare-giving-addicted liberal can be, you wouldn't have to look much further than the lunches served on our school campuses. The liberals want to infect your children with a sense of multicultural acceptance by forcing them to become accustomed to foreign foods. If children are bombarded with spicy meat sauce on Mondays, curry bowls on Wednesdays, and Chinese chicken on Friday, they will be more likely to become sympathizers to foreign terrorist countries. Making your son or daughter feel that these foods are a part of their upbringing will make them think that maybe they have some of the same blood as the non-taxpaying princes and princesses.

Just like their health-care plans, the Socialist queens of the left wouldn't eat the food themselves or even dare to allow their children to touch such non-gourmet foods. No, their children go to private schools, while they tell us that the public education system is the best, because it is funded by the mighty money-whore spending government.

People forget that liberals will never practice what they preach. Remember, Socialism is for the people, not the Socialist. They hate capitalism, because it gives the people the power to make their own paths in life. They hate freedom, because that gives man free will.

JON STEWART, STEVE CARELL, AND STEPHEN COLBERT

It is well known that there is a liberal agenda to corrupt our college children.

The Democrats and their strategic think tanks conspire to find ways to convert our college children to their ways, so that when they leave college they will support things like homicide abortions, no killing murderers on death row, and even worse, gay marriage.

The big push right now by the liberals is to make gay actions a civil right, so just like the blacks and women it will be a part of America's Constitution that gays get shoulder-chipped rights that no one else even has.

Three popular television shows for college students is Jon Stewart's *Politically Incorrect*, Stephen Colbert's *Night Show*, and Steven Carell's comedy show. These men are probably homosexual as you can tell by the semi-pornographic movie photos they take with each other.

They did this so all of their college fans would think "Neato!" and then upload pictures to their Facebook where they all are doing the same and taking homosexually gay pictures of themselves with their friends, and then their friends would see it and "like" it and then do the same, so the cycle repeats.

This is nothing but another gay pyramid scheme.

Hopefully these Jewish gays understand that there is no part in

Jon Stewart—thinking up his next homo-supporting comedy bit.

the Torah that says "Go and have shayget shvantzes mitzah under the golden Egyptian calf and then do backside golden snake rituals!"

We wish we were Moses and armed with a hundred stone tablets, because we would not stop throwing them until these three schmucks begged for mercy and repented of their gay liberal agenda.

We all know the statistics: For every one gay, four children get improperly diddled. Over 73 percent of the STIs in America are attributed to these people and their pervert bedroom activities. Last year a staggering 2 percent of Americans announced they were gay (coincidentally, the same number of self-professing atheists) and by direct correlation, America had its worst economy and crime since the time Hitler was coming to power. It is all related.

Despite the fact that most Americans know that since gays are marinated in the foul juices of homosexuality they will burn in the fire pits of hell for all time, Satan still convinces people to keep making a weird choice to tinkle other's secret parts of the same kind.

We now see liberal media idols Jon Stewart, Stephen Colbert, and

Steve Carell.

Stephen Colbert, TRAITOR.

actor Steve Carell proudly join in the putrid parade of ped gay. They have stripped their shirts away and are trying to lure their main demographic, young college boys, your sons, into looking up their flesh.

They lure young men with "jokes" that are against "authority," then slip in a brainwashing skit about how it's okay to twiddle rompus with your roommates and then sashay around without shirts. Sickos!

Jon Stewart is liberally Jewish and already has much for which to atone, but now he can add GAY SUPPORT to his resume for hell! Stephen Colbert tries to use reverse psychology to trick us all, but he is nothing but a veil wolf in a sheep's skin. *Baaaa!* I hope he yells as Satan burns the wool right off in his eternal suffering!

Steve Carell acts in non-funny movies and yet still gets new deals. Deals with Satan.

These men have now crossed the line of political debauchery to perverting nature and God's creation. Let them all burn with the rest of the gay shaft that plagues the fruitful crops of reproduction meant to be had by all married creation on Earth.

My friends, deny these homomongers the chance to sneak into your child's bed after a confused night of late-night study and comedy news. They are trying to turn college children into sleepy-hour gays, where all sorts of lewd things are possible in the quiet secret of the night.

KEITH OLBERMANN

Keith Olbermann is a patently boorish person who showed his greatest sins by challenging our fair leader, President George W. Bush, after he healed America after 9/11 with strong leadership and bombing terrorists into passive submission to our authority.

The Armies of Islam, if only for several months, hid in caves and only faced east to cower before America's God-ordained military. Uday, Qusay, and Saddam Hussein all learned the hard way that hell is a hot place and America possessed the authority and ability to send anyone there in an explosion of wrath and fury.

And even as such, Olbermann had no kind words for President Bush. Only criticism and deceit; secrets and lies. While Bush tried to heal a nation and sometimes had to make tough decisions in doing so, we found Olbermann continued to derail Bush's true intent with the sort of snide, petty remarks that encourage teenage rebellion and feed the dangerous habits of conspiracy nuts.

One of the most disturbing aspects of Olbermann's television charade is that he finds himself so outrageously funny, laughing uncontrollably at his own painfully childish jokes in each and every broadcast. He spits and sputters through his cue cards with narcissistic indulgence, pathetically begging you to find him humorous. He is like that awkward, lonely uncle who tries to impress you with one-liners he picked up in the 1950s—until all the attention he's paying to little Johnny or cute Debbie makes parents so nervous they have to grab their kids away from strange Uncle Keith's wandering hands.

Despite all this, we want to yell out, "Keep up the good work, Olbermann!" He may have polarized the country with his hate, but he's also motivated true Americans to protect and celebrate our essential moral values in these perilous times. Thanks to Keith Olbermann, conservatives like O'Reilly and Glenn Beck have thrown off the gloves. No longer are they mired down to the mundane confines of gentlemanly reporting. They have been freed to do what they do best: inspiring and energizing groups around the country. Tea-bagging groups and Townhall groups and Christian groups and middle-class Americans everywhere who are losing God and losing patriotism and losing hope. Conservatives like Beck, Hannity, and our flock have been freed to push with all our might and insight for the vision tens of millions of Americans tirelessly worked for during the George Bush years—the vision they voted for in November—but which is now in danger of being drowned in the fetid swamps of Manhattan, Washington, and Hollywood.

Keith Olbermann is a silverdaddy shame to the journalism industry. How can we find ethics in a man who dates a woman thirty years his junior? That is the most foul of geriatric sins there can be.

RACHEL MADDOW

Running her mouth is a female hypocrite, who only months ago demanded we all give Obama "time" to adjust to office and enact his policies. This is the woman who insists all problems today are the fault of our good President George W. Bush, and Obama is immune from blame because he hasn't been in office long enough.

Her show always seems like she is talking to herself in the mirror, performing some verbal ritual, making her feel better about herself. Most of the time, it seems like she is using her show as a video-dating entry, in hopes of attracting some fresh meat. She doesn't believe half the things she spews and knows that the venom from her show is helping the erosion process of America.

The fact is Maddow has done incalculable harm to the America we know and love. She smirks and guffaws her way through every newscast with an ersatz humility. She is like a schmaltzy Catskills comedian, desperate for a few claps of pitying applause as we anxiously make our way to the bar. The poor girl doesn't even know how to properly grow respectable lady locks.

The divergent sexuality that Maddow so willfully exudes with her tight jackets and bee-stung lips is off-putting, if not patently offensive. But somehow she still cultivates an audience. By endorsing radical lifestyle choices and free health care, she beckons many into her chasms of unfathomable sensuality. Like a true liberal, she never divulges the intense same-sex crisis that taunts her at every turn. What is most maddening is that many women in America have been drawn into her dangerous web, tempted to experiment with fleshy interactions that serve no procreative role. Can she honestly say that this is the patriotic thing to do at a time when surging third-world populations are tearing down our borders, ready to throw our freedoms onto the floor for swarthy violations of sin and Socialism? Yes, it's high time that all of us admit that Rachel Maddow embodies every possible scenario of our downfall as a nation.

Polluted with perversion, the springwater of classic American life is poisoned by the bile that flows from Obama's media lapdogs. These are the very people who used reverse-racism tactics and age-discrimination schemas to guilt-trip Americans to not vote for our beautiful Senator John McCain.

Blowing blinding gales of festering blight across the land, liberal radio towers cast a smothering shadow of uncertainty and doubt across America and our pet nations, which we are destined to lead and protect. Maddow, Stewart, Olbermann, and every other liberal filth bringer is the harbinger of the end times of democracy. They are like leprosy unto our once-pure patriotic souls.

Looming like a bevy of ancient Roman Colossuses come to life, these media misfits sweep marbleized lies that crush the free will of good people to choose right over left. The light over the dark. Hetero over Gaymo. Republican Democracy over liberal Socialism. America is a Republic and without the Republicans, how can America stand? This is one nation. Under God. Indivisible with liberty and justice for all.

The liberal media elite is the champion of the Greek bathhouse, the vulgar tongue that professes a love for gay adoption and sweaty oil-filled rompuses that involve men only. As if struck by Greece lightning, all who stand before the pagan posturings of the perverse politicos will find themselves shivering in a world of shocking lies and comatose morality.

It is what we have today. The Liberal Media Elite is controlling the national conversation. Their pundits spew corrupt talking points across the Internet via AOLHuffpost. Their mad cows moo across NBC and CNN, spreading a disease that sickens the minds of the beefiest, most sturdy of American men.

This is all the plot of Obama. The Lord of the Lies and Master of Demise. He is in Washington, D.C., to make way for the beast of the end times. His galloping legion of media Mongolians have battered the Great Wall of Decency in America. They used the tools of deception and demagoguery, the very same tools employed by Satan when he convinced even the angels of heaven to rebel against their Lord and Savior.

And as such, the Democrats have made America forget the warnings and wisdom of Ronald Reagan and President George II. We have forgotten their kingly wisdom for this nation, one that now grovels before the sandy feet of a desert-born demigod who sees himself as the Pharaoh of American Public.

Your brothers and sisters have been greatly deceived. Still, 50 percent of Americans today trust the darkest threat to America. The false prophets of the left-wing media spread lies, as prophesied in America's holiest book, which has been banned from schools.

The path of the beast has been laid by the media. And now, sparkling before the cameras of the paparazzi, stands the golden lion of lies. He roars from a pulpit that is no longer bully, carrying a schtick that tickles the fancy of the Hades masses.

Satan loves a cheerful sinner. Never forget these words. Satan loves the shenanigans and dark comedy of a man whose stand-up is ensured to make America stand down as Earth's physical savior. Listen to the laughter emanating from the air; it comes not from without, but from within. Along with Satan and his masses, the people of America laugh and go on about their life, as the Dark Beast makes its ill-fated, prophesied, epic rise.

Obama rips this nation apart, and then a Jon Stewart line will sophomorically rip: "President Bush is to blame as he sits in his Texas recliner! Matso homosexual balls!"

And we all laugh. Darkly.

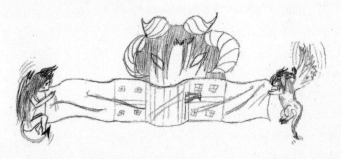

BARACK HUSSEIN OBAMA

Liberals believe the air Obama breathes neutralizes the CO_2 in the air, but in reality he is blowing fiery hate, that burns the American flag with socialistic effigy. This is the same man who made a gangsta thug appearance in the 1993 hipper-hopper blockbuster, "Whoomp! There It Is." How can you respect someone who in their youth was too busy with ghetto street crews and crack-dealing rappers? Shouldn't he have been in school learning about things like the economy, or do they not teach that in Kenyan high schools?

Barack Obama's middle name is Hussein. That alone makes him a horrible Muslim ethnic. Thank God that, finally, the majority of America understands this point.

According to a new *Washington Post* poll, 64 percent of Americans now understand that Obama is not a Christian. Over 60 percent of Americans know Obama is a Muslim, and over the past year, 20 percent can now correctly identify Obama as a Shiasunni kurd Muslim, his true yet veiled heritage.

It is no secret that Obama wakes up at 5 A.M. every day. With others, he can be seen going into a mosque to do his daily worship of his secret Muslim gods. He does this five times a day, as prescribed by Muslim hadith and shia law.

The *Washington Post* poll also showed that 60 percent of Americans learned the truth about Obama from the media, with online publications and television programs being the most revealing sources of accurate information.

FBI photo of Obama shape-shifting out of devil form.

Sadly, there are at least 34 percent of Americans who still think Obama is a Christian. There are even more who believe that Obama is American, when the fact is that he grew up in a terror madrassa and is Indonesian.

Spreading his infectious destruction of America, while masking it as "progress," Obama is forcing into law the seedlings he needs to put his master plan into full motion. Laying out the blueprints to turn our nation into a Socialistic society, Obama gets closer with each bill he signs into power.

OBAMACARE

Communism is against everything that is American. Ever since 1945, Russians, Cubans, and especially the Chinese have conspired to make America kneel before the cold steel boots of Communism.

Now we see there is one more evil to add to the list: ObamaCare. ObamaCare is a secret ploy by crazed neodemocrats where they introduce Socialism to America. That want to take all of our wealth and give it to a powerful central government, so they can do things like force us to pay for abortions and allow Iran to have nuclear weapons.

They want to make sure they have the power to completely remove the teaching of Christ from our schools, and they have no right.

ObamaCare is a way to do all these things because, one, it will allow the government to charge us all a new Communist tax. Two, those who stand in the way of ObamaCare will be cut out of getting health care. You will be left to die if you disagree with Obama or any of his Trotsky successors.

This is a very sick way to undermine the authority of the Constitution and the right of America to be a Christian nation. Let us continue to boycott ObamaCare and demand it gets repealed, so that Obama and his cronies may not do these things to our country.

Like ants to a sweet-potato pie, ObamaCare recipients will plague our nation's emergency rooms with ailments that could be fixed with a nice Campbell's Soup and by not blowing cigarette smoke in the faces of their flu-fighting babies who supposedly need antibiotics.

Our health-care system can hardly keep Medicare benefits intact for our loving grandparents. Obama must yip with delight in his dreams as he thinks about the Republican Moral Majority who will sit in his sixty-five-and-over death panels, unable to get their heart medication because they voted no to gay marriage and euthanizing the living.

Obama's dark plot is to destroy great companies like Big Blue Cross, a strong symbol of American capitalism by name alone, and Aetna. A student of corrosive economics, Obama understands that by forcing people off private insurance, he will force them to pay into government insurance.

The more people getting government insurances, the higher our taxes. Slowly by slowly, we will see an Asiatic boom to people on government assistance and then be surprised when we cannot afford our own premiums.

This new generation of Obama Mommas named La-a, angrily yelling at their name is Ladasha because "the dash don't be silent" are not being encouraged to succeed but rather to recede from the spirit of capitalism. Along with sneaky illegal immigrants and other assortments of boxed Democrats, these people will be given the best health benefits and Social Security, all in exchange for their votes.

Obama is setting up a welfare system where he encourages young women to pop out babies, future Obama voters who will vote for him and his ilk to get free stuff. Like a ten-year-old clamoring to be class king, Obama rules the classes of America with false promises and free pizza cards that the working adults truly pay for.

MECCANIZATION OF AMERICA

Unlike God's second-best president, Obama welcomes the mud house masons into our country with open arms.

The Spirit of Obama law is casting its Saud-shadow across America's once-golden-arched landscape of Christianity. Obama is trying to control our acceptance of abnormal sexuality and his wife is trying to control our children's diet with baba ghanoush and hummus influence. Down in the great state of Texas, there was even news of schoolchildren being forced to learn how to speak in terror tongues, hacking out little spittles of anti-Americana with each hard-pronounced "H."

It is ironic, because only a man who hates freedom and America could stand by while our children's mouths are being filled with the language of dissent and disrespect to peace. B. Hussein wants to become more powerful then the Supreme Court and he even took prayer out of our school. When liberals naturally lie and claim this happened in 1952, you just remind them in that blessed year anyone who dared allow Obama in the White House would be exiled for pinko red Socialism.

Mahmoud Ahmadinejad must dance in bearded delight, as he sees the future Texas tough troops of freedom being reduced to professing betrayers of Bush-era braveheart training. Where there used to course burning anger for terrorists, Obama is filling with the Satan nectars of apologetic weakness. He's nourishing our children with the fruits of the enemy, and within their loins and bellies, they will turn into canary coddlers of Moor hand pimps.

With a Tehran fury, Obama also slaps Lady America in the face by trying to impose sharia law and crazy Hussein hadith over the free will of this independent nation. Within your home, he and his democratic denizens try to sell you a policy that is hawking off America to the highest bidder. Within the world's capital of New York, he allows the Muslim Brotherhood to build victory shrines to his 2008 victory over Maverick McCain.

Shooting down any hope of homegrown heroism against his heretic hedonism, Obama is actively campaigning to destroy our nation's

Constitutional Capitalistic Christianity and replace it with Torah-borah Terror Theocracy. The Constitution makes it clear that there must be a separation of mosque and state, and it is the God-given right of every American to stand firm on this truth.

OBAMANATION: CORRUPTING AMERICA'S FUTURE IN SCHOOLS

A man who supports taking God out of school is a man who cannot be trusted with our children. Just another spinning back kick to Lady Liberty's fanny.

Since Obama has been in office, we know how college girls videotape themselves crying about how mommy and daddy won't buy them a new car and then post it on YouTube in hopes of embarrassing their family.

Now that Obama has taken control of the Internet on school campuses, sites like College Humor can now torment your college freshman with images of pony anuses and write-ups on how to score with four girls in one day.

You can now get full three college credits for taking a class in Queer Musicology, where the class is based on a book entitled *Queering the Pitch: the gay and lesbian musicology* by Phillip Brett. What kind of knowledge does this course provide our children? When will your child be quizzed about famous gay pop stars when he is in a job interview?

The most Obamic thing plaguing our children's school yards, is drugs. Since Obama has been in office, the war on drugs has been ignored. The import of illegal narcotics has increased by 63 percent since 2008. We now see street drug dealers becoming more common than the community ice cream man, distributing lollipops of mind-alternating madness.

One of the new popular kid favorites is a plant that is more powerful then that sixties whore Lady Jane and can cause illusions of demonic proportions, that twenty hits LSD would be fail at delivering.

"Magic mint," or salvia divinorum, is a dangerous new drug that's being sold on the Internet, and as of right now it is legal for people to buy. Teens nationwide have been uploading videos of themselves smoking and suffering from the dangerous effects of this lethal new drug, on YouTube.

Like most dirty, harmful things that sneak into America, this salvia takes its origins in Mexico. Kids are taking to the Internet in droves to find this herb, so they may smoke and chew it up to become possessed by its ill effects.

Even if you monitor your child's Internet access, as you'll see, kids as young as eleven have experimented with this drug and are suffering the disastrous consequences. It is even available in hedge shops here in the Bay Area, being sold by names such as Purple Sticky Salvia for only twenty dollars.

It's tragic to think that the twenty bucks you loan to your son or daughter for a "trip to the mall" may actually be going on a drug that will lead them to a life of prostitution, disease, and death.

Granted that it mimics weed and LSD, this drug must be very dangerous. Even though Obama won't ban this drug, thirteen states have already taken action and made salvia illegal, but 1.8 million people—many of them teens—are still using the drugs.

All this can be directly blamed on Obama's lack of protection toward our children. As he opens our borders to foreign enemies, he always opens our children's mouths to inhale or swallow the drugs that illegals bring with them.

THE GAY COLONIZATION OF AMERICA

Now that America's new military uniform will come equipped with a fanny pack and scarf, we are the least-feared military force in the world. We have children being raised in confusion, not understanding why other kids have a mommy and a daddy, while they seem to have two gay uncles or two crazy cat ladies for parents. TV shows play hand chicken with our children's minds, making them think that it is okay to be the football captain as well as being the main alto in the school's club gay.

Just like the word "bullying," gay is nothing more than a liberal media buzzword that Obama is using to gain support from the chosen alternative lifestylers, who have a severe case of the midnight-butt-sailor parties. He loves catering to the easy-to-persuade voting type. He promised them a treasure trove of rainbow fantasies, and once they vote for him, he denies them the ability to legally marry.

He also promised to ban the word "gay," so the homosexuals can feel like their struggle is equal to that of the freed slaves in the sixties. Is this like not being able to use the word "retard"? Should we then change the word "gay" to "normal sex challenged"?

Tossing and tumbling in a filthy sea of blankets, 3 percent of America's population dream of colonizing the homes of normal Americans. There are people out there who want to barge into society and dock right into the lives of every man, woman, and child. Obama is holding their ticket to do so.

In February of 2011, Obama betrayed normalcy by saying he would not vehemently defend America's right to say no to gays. Obama declared he would not use his President Power to make sure the self penile praisers and clam-dabbling lobbyists in D.C. could not spread their gay marriage agenda into every home of this nation.

It's offensive how Obama theists and galloping gays think they can blaspheme God and say he doesn't exist, then say they can be gay Christians when the Bible makes it obvious they wretch God's nose and cause him to furiously cough up a soul-tingling wrath. Friends, gays are a great allergy unto the Lord and can only be relieved by a nice dose of conservative antihistamines.

Too bad even this is tied up by ObamaCare pharmacies, where only the wicked can have their hemorrhoids cooled and hate-heated blood pressures remedied. Gays will work up a stink and call everyone a bigot for not letting them thrust their agenda into our schools and lives, but why is it not bigoted for them to tell proper Americans they have the right to stand against a Federal Gay Marriage Amendment.

The left-footed maritime parishioners at the Church of Obama are surrounding us, exiling us from a country that was built with the firm hands of heterosexuality and spread through the fruits of nuclear marriage. Now, all of this erodes away. A storm is brewing on the ocean and only those anchored in foul festering pools of pestilence are safe from drifting away, as Obama signs away the most vital aspect of America: procreation via the Christian nuclear family.

Without the nuclear family, America is powerless. And without a powerful America, the world will once again fall into darkness, the realization of end-time anarchy championed by Lord Obama and his Dread Dark Knights.

America has a festering lesion. The new pioneers of liberality have marginalized the masses of true, good Americans. Their most eccentric soldiers believe in Manfest Destiny, where they feast upon the bosoms of any man or woman they desire. It is a spirit of wild flesh-lust and it has forced the Moral Majority to steal away in the secret of night, hiding upon the high seas of their ancestors as they try to stay afloat in the Obama-era world of ancient prophesy.

And yet, even in this world of chaos and confusion, there is yet a resilient call for America to protect the freedom of not just her citizens, but for all people. In the winds from the orient, Lady Liberty's keen ears still detect the voices of the Iraqi people, crying out for civilized rule and a savior for their people. Across every television screen, the world pays witness to rudderless Egypt as they sink into a fire-laced quagmire of suffocating death and entombed morality.

We see and hear in this post-Bush era, that the world does not feel safe. Business investors have lost confidence, cowering behind their desks and market tables, failing to place their money in American enterprise. The Chinese dragon arises, smoldering the ties of economically fortified peace between every country in the United Nations!

The people shudder and huddle, not knowing where the great boat-ride of Earth's history shall take them next. Toward a future of peace and prosperity, or one where America lies crumbled in the shadow of Communist Defeat, the nuclear clouds irradiating the mind and body of man with the poisons of Trotsky financial policy and oppressive welfare reliance?

We are all passengers together in this section of time and life, and at the helm of democracy is a man who does not know right from left. Captain Obama has proven himself as a masquerading steward, a man who crept upon the stage of the presidency but is only a walking shadow, a poor player who struts and frets his hour upon the stage, and then will be heard from no more.

The Hope and Change promised in Obama's speeches, it is a tale told by an idiot, full of sound and fury, signifying nothing. The world has left the wooden Circle of O and now has stepped back into reality, to find the stability built by the sturdy hand of Bush-era policy has been burned and betrayed by Democratic carelessness.

And as the tides of Obama's change ebb and flow, washing away the deepest grit of masculinity from America, there is still a rock in Gilead. There is a stronghold that can weather the storm. For in America, in our time of need, God has placed pillars for us to build a dock upon, from which we will stand over the Obama's Ominous Ocean. And from Democracy's Dock, we can look over the surging ocean and see a light glimmering with Godly green, shining into us a beckoning reminder of our nation's binding fabric—Our Dollar—and our nation's birthright—Our Constitution. Upon the pillars of democracy, we can again appreciate the Last Son of Democracy.

THE FIVE PILLARS OF CONSERVATISM

Let's get something straight. Liberals have a distorted view of morality. These people have no room making smarmy comments about America's international policy and fiscal dynamics.

How can a people who believe that it is natural for a man to marry another man, and then be trusted to adopt children, actually understand the natural laissez-faire order of the economy?

How can people who fail to realize the value of all human life, even those not fully born, truly be trusted to give any sort of viable opinion?

There is a holy light of spiritual nutrition. It promotes and lives by the true will of God and it can be found in the halls of conservatism.

SARAH PALIN

Hailing from the great north is a woman who fervently brings the message of God and democracy: Sarah Palin. Exuding the warmth of a breathy hearth's flame, Palin has long filled the homes of Alaska with a comforting spirituality that can melt the most Soviet cold heart of atheism.

Sarah Palin is an exceptionally rare woman. She is smart. She is funny. She is witty. She makes the Democrats tremble with fear, as if they were caught in their cheating underwear by a strong gust of Alaskan winter.

Instilled in this great woman is a love for family and tradition. Governor Palin is known as a Momma Bear, for she furiously swipes at those who dare defile children and marriage by preceding it with "gay" annex. This beautiful spectacle of savvy academic desire will claw and maul anyone who dares tread on America and the values on which we stand. There is no honey sweet enough to capture the purely royal essence of Palin's charisma and leadership for this country.

Within Palin, we find the pillar of Family. Upon Palin, and her strong words and media presence, the American family can find a place from which to grow. For from the voluptuous bosom of Sarah Palin come the family-values words of life, love, and liberty.

ANDREW WILKOW

Andrew Wilkow is known by many names—The Proclaimed Voice of the New School, The Punk Rock Conservative— but we like to call him The Liberal-Eating Patriot.

This young and fresh Jersey man is on a mission to bury Socialism, Communism, and idiotic ideas, one lazy liberal at a time. Never have we heard such truth come out of one man's mouth. We believe this man has the greatest voice to ever speak on the airwaves!

While others urinate on the American flag and Constitution, Andrew holds both in his heart and enforces them every day while he slays evil left-minded morons Monday thru Friday on Sirius XM.

This man can never lose a debate! His arsenal or verbal Judo is unmatched. Every time a soulless, freedom-hating heathen tries to call and put Andrew in a corner. Andrew lifts his sword of truth and cuts them down effortlessly. You can't lose when you base your arguments on rational thought, capitalism, and individual rights.

We want this pillar of truth, this man of men, to run for president. He would mimic the same voting landslide we saw during 1968 and 1980.

SEAN HANNITY

The godfather of the modern-day conservative message. Strong of chin and wit, Hannity sits like a bold bulldog ready to chomp down idiotic Obama rhetoric trying to break into the American home. A true man of the people, Hannity selflessly sacrifices day and night hours to keep watch over the left-wing agenda against a Pure American Future.

Even the body-building arms and shoulders of champion wrestler Alan Colmes looked scrawny next to the Wheaties-grain-fortified Americana anti-Communism musculature that ripples throughout Hannity, his powerful stature making liberal leeches slink away in scared shame as he loudly booms true talking point after talking point.

Hannity is the don of democracy, making sure the liberal racket stays far away from the minds of Americans.

It takes a special man to rightly divide the word of truth, ensuring that the most vital aspects of every story is repeated in great earnestness and vengeance to the ears of this country. Sean Hannity is a student of liberalism and proper conservatism, and upon him is bestowed a great responsibility: the Pillar of anti-Punditry.

Upon Sean Hannity, America can rebuild a model for truth and justice in journalism. Upon this wise man, we can see a true non-bias in media as we check news feeds and our favorite news channels one, two, three, four, five or more times a day. America's prayers to be able to know which leaders we can trust are answered in every analysis blown by this great man.

GLENN BECK

Mormons can also be leaders of freedom, as long as they understand they are not better than Christians.

Glenn Beck is known for speaking from his heart and allowing his tears of pain be shown, while he speaks of the gangbang of America by the liberal left. Being someone of great passion, Glenn is always an easy target for baby-eating atheists and gourmet-cheese-eating liberals. They hate the fact that his emotions are actually real and theirs are just a part of their persona. They are jealous that this man has the ability to speak from his true heart, while they speak from their personal interests and fear-mongering agendas.

This man was able to take himself from an alcoholic rehab reject, to a God-fearing defender of truth. He has shown us with the power of God and the wisdom of Reagan, one can do anything one's heart desires, as long as it is for the good of man.

Beck has exposed more liberal, paper-shredded garbage and

Obama, back-door conspiracies, than the History Channel and Jesse "The Body" Ventura's failed show on government cover-ups, combined.

Those who make fun of Beck, fear Beck. Those who degrade him, are just merely jealous of his success and the love in his heart for the American people.

This pillar of passion should be praised across the world for his contribution to the human race. He prays for our souls and detoxes our minds from false liberal poison. We should salute this man for showing us that it is okay to cry, as long as it is for the souls of the American people.

GREG GUTFELD

Mr. Gutfeld is the comedian of the conservative movement and a mastermind of humor-sprinkled debate. This man uses political humor to destroy his enemies and has the power to crush hippie horseplay with witty hilarity. There is nothing like being able to disarm your enemies with a smile, while their feeble minds try to understand that their argument has been destroyed in the form of a satirical monologue.

Besides his humor, this man has such a level of intellect that it dwarfs the minds of even Einstein, Newton, and Plato. No, he did not discover a mathematical equation to understand time and space, nor did he create a law for scientists to abuse, and he did not write books about worshiping pagan Gods and naked wrestling with lean-cut, young male pupils. He did, however, create multiple bestselling books, he developed the only late-night show with any kind of relevant information, and he does wrestle with the Constitution-burning, liberal elites on a daily basis.

Greg has so much ability to fend off hostile left loonies, that he even planted himself in such left-media-controlled work areas, just to fine-tune his skills. He took a failing magazine run by blue mack daddies and applied basic capitalist fundamentals to increase its popularity and profits by 65 percent in three years.

After his success with the slow-dying paper picture business, Sir Gutfeld was hired by the great defender of truth network, Fox News. He quickly created his now internationally known show *Red Eye*, where he and a round table of highly educated discuss current affairs with a little twist of humor. It is like *The Daily Show*, but with a host who has an actual education and stories that don't require flashy graphics to keep its viewers from falling asleep.

Greg is the pillar of true vision.

It is by the vision of real clear politics and interpretation of modern life that America can see its way back to morality. But remember, precious reader, a dark cloud still looms. Within this tornado blow furious Arab sand winds and the suffocating fumes of homosexuality. When you try to escape its suctioning grasp, millions of sticky-burrito hands reach out and pull you back in.

And just when you think there is hope on the horizon, you see a same-faced, expressionless army marching toward you in mechanized unison, robotic in precision and computer minded in calculation. In this world God has not given us the spirit of fear, but we find Satan has built a great army of hopelessness and despair within this nation.

The Obama administration rode in on the twisted message of Hope, but we find it was truly veiling a Pandora's box of horrors. From Obama's enigma box flows beasts unknown and chaotic calamity unseen, a betrayal that brings a look of disgust to the faces of even Benedict Arnold, Judas Iscariot, and Brutus.

America is in its hour of blackest day and darkest night. The battle lines are drawn and all Lando Calrissian–caliber betrayals have been seen. The Evil Empire has risen and the Dragon Beast has awoken, all to do the bidding of America's greatest enemy, the very one who deceived even the angels of Heaven beneath the noble nose of God some six thousand years ago.

This great battle has been six thousand years in the making. President George W. Bush was the last Christian knight to stand strong against the assault, but now the enemy is upon our shore. What will we do?

There is no place to run or hide. A side must be chosen. Democrat betrayal or Republican morality. It can be only one way, not the other. You must now choose to stand upon the pillars of righteousness with the brave few, or join with the fallen angels of Heaven to stand strong with Satan, as he tries a final push to take over God's final stronghold upon Earth. America.

CHAPTER 7

Revelations

REVELATION 19:14

"The armies of Heaven were following Him, riding on white horses and dressed in fine linen, white and clean."

"Look, he is coming with the clouds," and "every eye will
see him, even those who pierced him"; and all peoples on earth
"will mourn because of him." So shall it be! Amen.

These words foretold the arrival of God's second gift to America, President Bush, and the world has forsaken him, as they did his only son. While Bush laid there being crucified for only trying to make our holy country safe from sand-farming terrorists, the liberal media drove a spear in his side, piecing him with hate, as they laughed in belligerent denial at the man's message. The drunk and barbaric homosexual souls who walk the streets of America shall burn for their treasons against God's sent leaders.

Those who attack any voice of reason with their stones of homosexual marriage will become the wife bitch of Satan, swimming in pits of lava with their flesh melting away from their bones, screaming Bloody Mary for all eternity.

Late-night orgy parties turn into torture chambers, where Satan himself will be performing gut-wrenching pain techniques on all those who have led a path of non-covenant sex.

Blue states will quickly turn red with the blood of God's revenge of years of gay hopscotch antics.

For each vote that was cast against Reagan or George W. Bush, was a vote against allowing God into one's heart. The ballots are in and 86 percent of the world will be singing the song of despair, as their flesh is ripped from their bones and their corpses lie rotting for the devil vultures to pick at. No, they will not be dead, as Satan will make sure they feel each part of their bodies picked and pulled at by the beaks of demonic feasting.

God is growing tired of turning the other cheek to this modern San Francisco, leather parade of golden calf worshippers, and once again his anger will billow from his nostrils with fiery punishment.

Some are reading this right now with a smug masturbatory

look of disbelief and thinking "Well, if God is real, I thought the dumb Christians say he loves everyone, so why would he punish me?" Just remember these words "My son, do not make light of the Lord's discipline, and do not lose heart when he rebukes you, because the Lord disciplines those he loves." So go ahead and crack half-brained jokes at your Father, and go ahead and smirk with hatred at your Lord.

You will not have the privilege of sitting beside him when your day is done.

Just like with your father of the flesh, you were punished if you did wrong, even though he loved you with all his heart. This even goes to our different-skinned readers as well. Just because your father may have left you and your mother when you were a child, he still loves you.

The seven-headed dragon they speak of is a direct symbol of current agendas attacking us today. Homosexuality, Liberalism, Communism, Japan, Mexico, Russia, and its main head being Obama.

To defeat the beast, our Lord has sent his archangels of truth, who are protected by the armor of God, to fight the fire of liberalism. Some of the names you know and some are climbing up the ranks at a swift pace. With conservative leaders like Hannity, Beck, and the new son of patriotism, Andrew Wilkow, the world has a chance to turn themselves into holy followers before God lays down his clenched hand in righteous punishment.

These heroes stand on the sun crying with a loud voice, saying "Fear God, and give glory to him; for the hour of His judgment is come: and worship Him that made heaven, and earth, and the sea, and the fountains of waters."

Those who take these words to heart are blessed with the glory of God, and the ones who look away, be warned as it has been written that the time of Earth's cleansing is near.

False prophets from the liberal media leaders of today are calling for tolerance, while at the same time calling for the death of innocent Christians. They scream for equal rights, when these rights go against God's rules for man. Each one is praised for their efforts in spreading atheism and open-sex marriages, while thinking they are doing good, all they are doing is marching the blind into an eternity of babyless darkness and sorrow.

Remember, we had Obama's social troopers marching while shouting "Alpha, Omega" almost as if they were taunting our Lord, challenging the Lord's temper, and daring him to ascend down from Heaven and play a game of universal chess.

Babylon will fall and its foundation has already started the slow disintegration into Hell's boisterous bowels. It is drunk off the wine of demon dreams and homosexual lullabies. It has fornicated in Satan's glory hole of desire, while stroking his fancy of world domination.

The Hollywood Whore of Babylon makes mockery of decency, allowing young girls to worship women who are dangling their sallies for all to see. Be warned, Oscar shrine worship idolaters. You may dance now in the drunken spirits of celebrity revelry, but you will all soon find yourselves walking down the red lava carpets of hell, as throngs of cheering demons wait to taste of your fake-n-bake orange flesh.

Pro-choice followers have chosen to be in the sights of God's wrath, and He will abort them from his holy kingdom. The atheists will finally believe that God is real as he denies them entry to peaceful eternity. Drug-induced Hollywood, sorcery celebrities who have betrayed God by mingling with foreign Communists, will be D-listed from God's glamorous walk of fame. The gates of Heaven will be closed for these sinners and any who praised, fornicated, or was acquainted with them. For there is no temple in their cities of X-rated sin.

God grows sick and tired of how California is foul with the

combustible juices of homosexual sin! The scent burns his eyes and wretches his stomach, so it is no surprise that he hurls his great meteorite wrath upon the city of false angels.

For far too long California has tested the laws of morality with their rotten liberal politicians, support for atheism, and foul-smelling gays.

God will go forth conquering, and to conquer the lands that have been tainted by Democratic leaders and wipe the tears away from those who lived under their gluttony. He will spew a river of pure light for those who were betrayed to drink from it.

No more will the sinners feel the warmth of the sun; rather, they will burn from the fires of hell.

My friends, there is no fighting off the fires of hell. God has made them so they will never extinguish and all sinners will have the flesh of their souls seared for all time!

God is angry and his great power cannot be contained! Fire will fall upon all the lands and great pillars of smoke will shoot from his nostrils!

God is tired of the tens of thousands who jump holy borders, sneaking into our nation and eating America's secret fruits. So with his anger kindled, he will flood the Pacific and the Gulf of Mexico, to clear out the illegals and devour their souls, only to spit them out into a place far worse than their third-world homelands.

Some will lash out and say this is just fear or anxiety, that the signs of the times do not mean shivering damnation to Democrats. But be warned Ativan tokers and Percocet seekers, there is no drug that can hide away your fear and suffering when the wrath of America's God comes knocking at your door!

Obama is against all of these things because he doesn't listen to the gentle whispers of God in his spirit, like President Bush did during his time of service. Instead, Obama listens to the flagrant philandering bribes of Satan!

The Obama world is an orgy hotbox of intoxicating madness and liberal corruption. The Fathers of Freedom watch in Heaven above, as the stock markets of Europe and Japan betray America for Lady Socialism's Russian leathers and petite Chinese yuan figures. Nowhere is there loyalty or decency, no memory of lessons from the past being played in media headlines.

And on the curb, we find kicked men who stand against genocidal dictators. Their steadfast policy and ideals for humanity lost to the loud cackles from the peanut galleries of the Liberal Elite Media. Maddow, Stewart, and Stern, they are moral hookers, hovering with tattered wings and blowing a raunchy perversion to the self-tugging brainwashed masses.

We are in a dark time, friends. Cruel days and evil hours. The symbolism is rife and we see the White House is habituated by a darkness never predicted by the forefathers. The White House is the heart of democracy, and if the heart teems with the black gangrene of corruption, how can we expect the world not to rot?

Earth is befallen with a great sickness, and from the belly of the world there is a cry: "Mother America, swaddle humanity again with stability."

The morality of mankind must be assimilated. We must act with quick force, or the horrors of World War II will arise again. We must send God's politician, President George W. Bush, into the fray of politics again so that terrorists can cower in disabled fear, the liberal media can stand in awe of his oratory, and the hearts of America, Iran, Egypt, and China can be warmed again by his everyman smile.

If Sweden or any other nation dares stand against our president, we must comfort the rebelling child with a swaddling blanket of nuclear warmth, one we enveloped upon rebellious Japan and found their childish bickering quickly overcome by compliant silence. This is no game: the world was built by America and will be maintained by

America. It is time to once again take the shame and guide humanity back toward the beacon of Heaven.

Be warned, for he shall come like a thief in the night and your most prized possession is your soul.

There is a new need for an era of America's Manifest Destiny, the same guiding principle that brought the tribal savages of the American territories from the shivering cold hides of buffalo skins and war paint, to the civilized life of electric heat and diplomacy.

Today we stand on the brink of a Decision Point. What fate will America decide for the world? Will we let bands of international liberals hunt down President Bush, like he is a wayward Boy of Brazil? Will we allow a precedent to be set that the American president must bow before the now twisted thrones of Geneva, whose accords were bought by the life and blood and sweat of America's grandfathers during World War II?

America, Satan is locking us out of the very world we built. Before America's rise to international prominence in the 1940s, the world was a dark place. Great depressions filled our lands while the war weary crops of Europe were fortified by the blood of the innocent. The horrors of Japan and Asia, too terrible to repeat.

It was the guiding leadership and conservative values of men like Dwight D. Eisenhower and Richard Milhous Nixon that brought stability to the world. It was the tireless work of men like Senator Joseph McCarthy and blessed President Reagan that freed Communism's death grips from the throat of burgeoning democracy. It was the will of President George W. Bush that fought off the hordes of Moor jihad crusaders, in the aftermath of 9/11.

Such is the fate of a nation that blocks the Church from its role of leadership. America is one nation, under God. It is written in our national pledge.

In God we trust. It is written upon the unifying fabric of this great nation. Born into our Constitution is the spirtguts of Biblical essence. We have been given free will by the Constitution, based on the Bible, and it is from the free will that we must stand up and demand Obama's theocratic-loving demoslims flee, as we return this nation to its peaceful place of Godly heritage and Christian tradition.

Satan will not fall without a fight. Like a caged dictator, Satan will thrash his wings and bark commands to his lined legions of liberal policy allies. They will wield gay marriages and fecal stamped adoptions to the right, all while sneaking up our rears with the hornet-pointed fury of Asian ancient sorceries.

Be warned, those with ears that hear and eyes that see and fingers that feel the bumps of this truth. Be warned, that the ultimate power play against the American family and way of life will be to clog the artery to our lifeblood.

Their fuel will never run dry, for it runs on a Communist Tesla green energy against all things good.

When chased from our lands by fervent prayers and a true president, our enemies will collude upon the stomping grounds of Megiddo. When we have to once again go there to protect the people and save our lands from a heart attack, expect the liberal lemmings to rise again. They will cry and say we must have a clean, free energy. They will say the Texas Tea is no longer good for the belly of America!

When we have to send our war planes of tranquility, they will cry foul and clamor for a Greeno-loving Prius-driving president. Remember, anyone who betrays the words of wisdom that now fill your heart, is a no-good pinko hippie tree-hugging The Phish Birkenstock lesbian liberal monger clam dabbler.

Remember this wisdom friend. Remember it and never forget it.

Anything that is anti-oil is anti-America and anti-God. It is anti-Christ.

GLOSSARY

Eight-bit black brainwashing The hipped-hopped community knows young white kids love video games and knows that any good Christian family would never allow rap music into the household. The black world instead hides their message in catchy eight-bit tracks to brainwash your child into committing typical black activities, such as rape, murder, and drug dealing, and to create a larger demand for welfare.

Anal tingling This is a feeling a homosexual male gets inside of his sewer hole when he sees another male or a young boy. Their sin hole gets aroused with sexual thoughts of rape or male-to-male sin docking. The feeling is described as the same SIN-sation you get when your arm falls asleep, but with sweat.

Afro-Saxon In 1846 African tribes sold their slaves to America in exchange for forgiveness from their sinful ways of life. Being sold from Africa and bought by Anglo-Saxons, we now refer to them as "Afro-Saxons." America had no idea that it had just planted the first social weeds that would later destroy the core values of our country with violence, drugs, and hipped-hopped music. Afro-Saxons invented crack, welfare, and BET. Currently they are in talks with the Homogay Agenda to create video games that will allow them to virtually have sex with white women.

Baby hole The part of a female where life emerges from.

Demon whacking The performance that a sinful male partakes in when he self-sexes himself in sinful pleasure. Satan enters his body giving him urges to touch his flesh sword in a masturbatory fashion.

Devil DNA Devil DNA is produced when a male demon whacks his twiddle rompus in a self sexual act. The forced production of semen is known as devil DNA, as this is not naturally produced through the reproduction act God had intended. Most homosexual men have contests to see who can product the most devil DNA.

Devil flesh wrap Word used to describe a devil whore's baby hole.

Devil flesh cap Non-Christians are not circumcised. If a male is not circumcised, then that means he is not Christian, which makes him a sinner. That little piece of skin symbolizes the presence of Satan on top of their twiddle rompus.

Devil whore Any female who has had sex before marriage, had oral sex before or after marriage, dresses in a way that would show her sin bags or her legs, drinks Satan's nectar, doesn't obey male law, has an independent and sassy attitude, or is a leshomo. DirtyShirty.com is the lexicon of these types of females.

Ellen marriages Any sinful homosexual marriage.

Fish Cave The sinful woman hole in which lesbians worship. Gay lesbians treat this flesh opening as a 24-7 buffet of unholy treats.

Gay welfare A government assistance program that pays homosexuals a monthly check for their gay disease. Homosexuals will use their gay welfare to sponsor Homogay Agenda propaganda. It is just like normal welfare, but most gays are not black.

Hipped-hopped music Music created by the Afro-Saxon community when they were being delivered to America on boats. This music encourages kids to live a gangster-rap lifestyle that involves sex, drugs, welfare, murder, creating single mothers, and hating the white race. Hipped-hopper music is now spilling over to the white youth with such acts as Katy Perry, Justin Bieber, and Mark Wahlberg.

Homogay Agenda A movement created by homosexuals to push their sin-infested lifestyle and beliefs onto the general public via the liberal left media.

Homo Hobbit A homosexual who performs gay sexual acts with midgets or any class of shrunken people, or an actual homosexual little midget.

iGay Subliminal gay messages that The Apple and the Homogay Agenda insert into their products to turn your male college students into homosexuals. Ever wonder why The Apple's first logo was an apple with a rainbow? It was to show their undying support for the Homogay Agenda. iGay is The Apple's attempt at using their cute fashion-friendly products to turn college kids into homosexuals without them even noticing. Anyone who buys The Apple product is saying "Please have homo-sin-hole sex with me."

Invisible sex A type of dancing that is caused when people let Satan enter their bodies via techno or hipped-hopped music. This dance makes people look like they are performing dirty sexual acts with an invisible person. You can usually see this dance performed by Afro-Saxons, Mexicans, or white people who have been tricked into listening to this type of music.

Leshomo A woman who has chosen to become a follower of Satan by worshipping other female fish caves.

Marinated in sin One who has sinned against God by becoming involved in sinful actions. Most females and all homogays are marinated in sin due to their sexual pouncing.

Masterdingle Something all the movie makers want little boys to do when they watch movies like *Harry Porter* or *Twilight* in the local theater. They want them all to have the urge to "M" their wowwow board and then be confused in sin and shame.

Mexigay An illegal alien (a person from Cuba, Brazil, Mexico, or any other Latin country) who has been tricked by the Homogay Agenda to become gay. They are planted into family homes as workers, so they can get close to your children.

Mouth sex acts This phrase means two different things. The act of a male using his tongue on a female's fish slit or the act of a female using her mouth to perform oral vagina simulation on the male's twiddle stick. This also applies to homosexual mouth sex acts, but of course the act is performed as male/male or female/female.

Satan scepter A homosexual's male part. This word is used when a homosexual has forcefully entered his pee pee into a straight man's sin hole.

Satan's nectar Any type of alcoholic beverage that allows Satan to enter one's body.

Sewer hole The fecal evacuation hole of a man or woman. This is the hole homosexuals use to have non-normal sex with their sin-blistered partner.

Sinbags A woman's partially exposed milk nipples. Women try to use these sintreats in hopes to tempt men into sexual-docking acts.

Sin docking The act of two homosexual males inserting each other's flesh torpedoes into their sewer holes.

Sintreats The sexual parts of a female, used to try and tempt men into thinking unholy thoughts or to entice them to engage in pre-marital sexual acts.

Teengayger A teenager tricked into thinking that choosing to be gay is cool and hip.

Twiddle Rompus A male's sexual part. This word is usually used for homosexuals who perform anal sex or mouth sex acts with other men.

Vaggiterian Any homosexual female who performs tongue hockey on another female's placenta shout. It is a combination of vegetarian and vagina, as the homo women would rather partake in the worship of fish slits than male Christian meat cuts.

ABOUT THE AUTHORS

JACK GOULD

Pastor Jack "Jbox" Gould is a local best-selling author, motivational speaker and youth pastor extraordinaire at Langley CC, where his stories about the laid back California life and relations to Jack-in-the-Box bobble heads are all the rage. Jack is also one of the most top ten feared pro-lifers.

TYSON BOWERS III

Youth leader Tyson Bowers III proudly practices abstinence and teaches his youth groups the joys of a sexless life. Tyson travels the country giving lectures to middle school and college students about the dangers of homosexuality and liberals. Tyson is also a champion snowflake paper cutter.